The Princess of

SIBERIA

Christine Sutherland

The Princess of
SIBERIA

The Story of Maria Volkonsky *and*

the Decembrist Exiles

Farrar · Straus · Giroux

NEW YORK

First printing, 1984

Printed in the United States of America

Published simultaneously in Canada by Collins Publishers, Toronto

Designed by Guy Fleming

Library of Congress Cataloging in Publication Data

Sutherland, Christine.

The Princess of Siberia.

Includes index.

1. Volkonskaia, Mariia Nikolaevna, kniaginia, 1805–
1863. 2. Decembrists—Biography. 3. Siberia (R.S.F.S.R.
and Kazakh S.S.R.)—Exiles—Biography. 4. Soviet Union
—History—Conspiracy of December, 1825. I. Title.

DK209.6.V6S87   1984   957′.07   83-16454

To my daughter Denise Hotchkiss

and to my stepdaughter Fiona Sutherland

this story of a brave woman in a faraway country

Acknowledgments

I wish, first of all, to express my gratitude to Mme Elena Cicognani of Rome, née Princess Volkonsky, who has made available to me the memoirs of her great-great-grandmother Princess Maria Volkonsky, together with family records and early daguerreotypes, which are reproduced in these pages, and to Prince George Vassiltchikov of Geneva and London, who introduced me to her. Without that happy coincidence, there would have been no book.

I would like to thank the curator of the Decembrist Museum in Irkutsk and the director of the Pushkin Museum in Moscow for the assistance they extended to me in my research and for locating and allowing me to reproduce the early portrait of Maria Volkonsky which appears on the cover. I also wish to thank Sir Curtis Keeble, Her Majesty's Ambassador in Moscow, and Lady Keeble for their hospitality and help during my two visits to Russia.

My special thanks are due to Mr. Laurence Kelly, who selflessly lent me so many invaluable volumes from his collection of Russian books of the period, and to his wife, Linda, for her encouragement and constructive comments on the manuscript; also to the staff of the London Library and the British Library for allowing me access to the Raevsky Archives. I wish to thank Mr. Howard White, currently of Warwick University, for his help in research and in combing the relevant Russian sources, and to Miss Mary Young for her unfailing patience and interest while typing the manuscript. I am fortunate to have been given the chance to profit from the advice and editorial guidance of Mr. Robert Giroux of Farrar, Straus and Giroux, New York.

I have kept to the more familiar Westernized spelling of Russian names and have followed the Gregorian Calendar, common to Western Europe and the Americas, rather than the Julian Calendar, used by the Russians until the Bolshevik Revolution. Throughout the book, I have relied principally on the manuscript of Maria's memoirs, made available to me by the Volkonsky family, and on the Raevsky Archives, which are in three institutions: the Pushkin Museum in Leningrad, the Pushkin Museum in Moscow, and the British Museum. I have also visited most of the places where Maria and her husband lived, both in European Russia and in Siberia.

Christine Sutherland

Contents

List of Illustrations

The Princess of

SIBERIA

Introduction

Between 1812 and 1825 there appeared a perfect galaxy
of brilliant talent, independent character, and chivalrous
valor—a combination new to Russia. These men had absorbed
everything of Western culture the introduction of which
had been forbidden. They were its latest bloom, and in spite
of the fatal scythe that mowed them down, their influence
can be traced, flowing far into the gloomy Russia of
Nicholas I, like the Volga to the sea.

ALEXANDER HERZEN

THIS IS THE STORY OF PRINCESS MARIA VOLKONSKY, wife of
Prince Sergei Volkonsky, one of the leaders of the so-called
Decembrist uprising. This was the first attempt in modern Russian history to overthrow the absolute power of the tsars, to
bring about a constitutional monarchy, and to abolish serfdom.
They were called the Decembrists, the Dekabristi, because their
ill-fated uprising took place on December 14, 1825, in St. Petersburg's Senate Square, in the shadow of the Winter Palace. It was
in fact the first active political protest—sometimes called the
"first Russian revolution," though there is hardly any resemblance, either in ideology or in scale, between the attempt of the
Dekabristi and the gigantic revolutionary convulsion of 1917.

The Decembrists were "gentlemen revolutionaries," charm-

[3

ing, idealistic, well-educated young men, humane and sensitive enough to be depressed by the appalling conditions inside their country and particularly determined to abolish serfdom—"our national disgrace," as they called it. (In the first quarter of the nineteenth century, Russia was a land of 42 million people, more than half of whom were bound in some form of personal serfdom to individuals or to the state.) The majority of the Decembrists were guards officers, just returned from the Napoleonic Wars, deeply influenced by Western ideas of freedom and by the romantic literature of France, Germany, and England. They had little in common with the type of professional revolutionary that developed in Russia during the latter part of the nineteenth century, or with the entire concept of the revolutionary underground, its isolation from ordinary human life, clandestine cells, its spirit of fanaticism, sabotage, and revolutionary behavior. The Dekabristi were amateurs, novices in the art of sedition, and emotionally divided in their aims, because they all came from families with a centuries' old tradition of service to the monarchy. Their very idealism in its purity made them incapable of carrying out their revolt against the tyranny of the tsar. Their heroic stand and their abortive attempt at a revolution were a sort of Byronic madness, embodying the romantic Slav psychology of the era. The time was not ripe, and the Russian people were not ready for a revolution; the idealists stood alone and fell alone.

As individuals, they were intensely human and attractive personalities. Exiled to Siberia, where they were condemned to spend the better part of their lives (until allowed to return after Alexander II's amnesty in 1856), some of them survived, helping each other, pooling mutual resources, united by their absolute belief in liberty and the dignity of the individual. They left a powerful impact on Siberia that persists to this day in all the different places where they lived. None of their achievements, however, would have been possible without the handful of wives who joined them in exile, watching over them like guardian angels, interceding with the commandants of successive prisons, maintaining contact with the families back home, arranging for the procurement of money, clothing, and medicine. In the later stages of their life in Siberia, after the penal servitude was over and they were allowed to establish themselves as settlers, the wives helped them to build a new existence and to share their education and specialized knowledge with the local population of Siberia.

Of these women, three of whom incidentally were French, the youngest and most outstanding in character and in courage was Princess Maria Volkonsky. She was twenty-one when the ill-fated uprising took place, shattering her tranquil existence. Beautiful, highly cultivated, daughter of a famous general who was a hero of the Napoleonic Wars, she had been married for only a year to the fabulously rich Prince Sergei Volkonsky, scion of a great family, whose mother was Mistress of the Robes to the Dowager Empress. One of Maria's earliest suitors had been Pushkin, Russia's foremost poet, who remained close to her all his life and dedicated several poems to her. Prince and Princess Volkonsky led a glamorous life, moving between St. Petersburg court circles, their estates in the Ukraine and the Crimea, and occasional tours of military duty in the south, where Prince Sergei commanded a division. Maria's first child, a son, was born on the day of her husband's arrest. Prince Sergei was sent to the Peter and Paul Fortress in St. Petersburg and, after a lengthy trial, was sentenced to life in Siberia.

In spite of her family's opposition and the personal inter-vention of Tsar Nicholas I, who admired her, Maria resolved to follow her husband to Siberia, leaving her baby son behind in the care of her family. After a lengthy journey by sledge in the depths of the winter across the width of the Asiatic continent,

Maria was reunited with her husband in Nerchinsk, a village beyond Lake Baikal close to the Chinese border, where her husband and his fellow conspirators were working in the local silver mine. In succeeding years, Maria and Princess Trubetskoy, who arrived about the same time, were followed by nine other women. Altogether, out of eighteen, eleven wives of the condemned prisoners decided to share the fate of their husbands. Six of them were forced to leave behind a total of thirteen children. Through the long years of exile, seven of the mothers lost a total of twenty-two children, due to the harsh conditions and inadequate medical facilities in Siberia.

Not one of the women who volunteered to join a husband or a lover (as in the case of two of the Frenchwomen) had ever been interested in politics; none of them had ever heard of the clandestine societies. What inspired them was marital loyalty, love, and a feeling of moral obligation. Maria Volkonsky had hardly had a chance to know her husband, as he was always away on conspiracy business; she really fell in love with him after his arrest, when her romantic nature identified him with the Byronic heroes of her youth; he became to her the symbol of man's fight for liberty, to be venerated and cherished. She brought to him in exile her light, careless gaiety, her artistic talents and ready laughter; but she also possessed a force of character, a courage, and an integrity which were to sustain them all through the long years. At one point in her later life, another man, also dedicated to the cause of freedom, replaced her husband in her affections; he filled a void left empty by Prince Sergei's personality change and advancing years, and he brought her unexpected happiness and fulfillment.

Princess Volkonsky remained in Siberia for twenty-six years. As time went on, conditions of life for the exiles gradually improved; they were granted marital quarters, children were born, money filtered through from their estates; books, magazines, and foreign periodicals began to arrive. Under a benevolent governor, farming cooperatives were formed to teach Siberian peasants the rotation of crops and soil improvement. The Volkonskys were eventually allowed to settle in Irkutsk, the capital of eastern Siberia, where they lived in a large, well-furnished wooden house with their two children—a son and a daughter, both of them born in the detention camp of Chita in Transbaikalia; they were eventually allowed to have servants.

From the very beginning, Maria had felt great sympathy for the local Siberian tribes, who were proud, gentle people living in scattered hamlets throughout the wild countryside: some were only a short step removed from the Stone Age. She found their sylvan culture enthralling and her diaries abound with visits to local Buriat and Ostiak tribes to learn about their strange pagan ways. In Irkutsk, she was loved and admired by the population because of her dedicated work in local schools, and the benevolent influence she had on Governor Muraviev-Amursky. She became known throughout the province as "our Princess." Among her many projects was the building of a local theater, the first in Siberia; whenever she made an appearance there with her children, the entire audience got up on their feet in spontaneous tribute.

Maria returned to European Russia in 1855, the year prior to the amnesty. She had just turned fifty, still lithe and full of life, "with huge, compelling dark eyes." Sergei followed a year later. At sixty-eight he was already a very old man, exhausted by his long years in prison. They lived at Voronky, the Volkonsky estate near Moscow, surrounded by their children and grandchildren. They also traveled abroad "in search of sun," staying at the Villa Volkonsky in Rome, with Maria's great friend, Zenaida Volkonsky. (The Villa Volkonsky now houses the British Embassy.) Maria died at Voronky, her daughter's estate in the Ukraine, in the summer of 1863.

The principal characters of the Dekabristi uprising and its tragic aftermath have obsessed many great Russian writers: Pushkin, Venevitinov, Tolstoy, Herzen, Gogol, Nekrasov, and others. Pushkin's poetry abounds in allusions and homage to Maria, and one of his most celebrated poems is dedicated to the Decembrist insurgents. Tolstoy was at one time intensely preoccupied with the story of the Dekabristi, and after the publication of *War and Peace* began to write a vast historical novel about them, which he later abandoned.

Part One of this book describes Maria's youth, the Pushkin courtship, her marriage, the growth of the conspiracy, Prince Volkonsky's arrest, the sentencing, Maria's efforts to join him, and her journey across Asia. Part Two concerns their life in exile until their return to European Russia.

PART ONE

1

The Raevskys

THE MANOR HOUSE OF THE RAEVSKY ESTATE stood on a southern bend of the river Dnieper. Called Boltyshka, it was set on a picturesque knoll that overlooked the mighty river. Centuries-old oak trees framed the white walls and colonnaded entrance of the imposing residence; a vast park with terraced flower beds gently sloped to the water's edge. The village of white-washed houses thatched with straw nestled against a glade of silver poplars. The steppe all around had been cultivated— the famous Ukrainian black earth, so rich as to scorn fertilizer or crop rotation. It produced fabulous harvests, making this country the breadbasket of Eastern Europe: wheat, barley, and rye, grown on that ancient seabed from which the waters of the Black Sea had receded, offered yields unknown on the European plains. Tall, golden fields stretched toward the horizon to merge into the distant steppe—a green-gold ocean of gently undulating grasses interspersed with wild flowers. It was peopled with small animals, a paradise for birds and game of all kinds. Like the sea, the steppe belonged to no one; if more land was needed for farming, more acres of the virgin land were plowed up. The black earth never failed to reward the plowman's effort.

"How fortunate are those who farm in the Ukraine, living among their kingdoms of wheat," wrote Honoré de Balzac after traveling from Paris through the Ukraine to visit his friend Madame Hanska on her estate near Kiev. "Nothing ever disturbs the great silence of their fields, while their wealth grows every day; all that's needed is to sow the same crop year in and year out, forever."

The lord of the Boltyshka domain was General Nikolai Nikolaevich Raevsky, a great military hero and popular commander, one of the most romantic figures in the annals of Russian warfare. "The sword of Russia," his soldiers called him. "The stuff from which marshals are made," Napoleon said of him after the Russian disaster at Borodino. Both handsome and brave, the general had brown hair and blue eyes, which could be "stern or cheerful, remote, or kindly compassionate in turn," a fine manly figure. Though not of towering height like the tsar, he looked equally splendid when riding to battle at the head of his troops, or dancing the mazurka in a St. Petersburg ballroom. Most women adored his noble profile, "like a head on a Byzantine coin." More important, according to contemporary accounts, they sensed that "under all that martial hard glitter" Nikolai Nikolaevich Raevsky possessed "an ardent capacity for tenderness."

The Raevskys came from a long line of Scandinavian gentry, and family records identify them as landowners in southern Jutland, part of today's Denmark, as early as the fourteenth century. Following the upheavals of the civil war, which swept Denmark in the wake of the Reformation, the family moved east, acquiring extensive estates in Livonia, the borderland country between Poland and Russia. Family history relates that when in 1529 Tsar Vasily III married the beautiful Polish princess Elena Glinsky, her uncle and guardian, Stepan Raevsky, traveled to Moscow with her. He remained long enough to witness the birth of her son Ivan IV, the future Ivan the Terrible, but returned home hurriedly, "as he did not get on with the boyars." It was a wise precaution, for beautiful Elena, who was as outspoken as she was clever, inevitably made enemies among the dissident boyars, who eventually poisoned her. In the next two hundred years, as Poland, then a great power, pushed its frontiers deep into Russia to encompass Livonia and the city of Smolensk, the Raevsky family became Polish. They took on a middle name, Dunin, and were presented with the family crest of Labedz—a swan—by King Sigismund III, of the Vasa dynasty, who reigned over both Poland and Sweden.

As time went on and Russian frontiers moved west, the Raevskys gradually became more Russified, marrying into Russian aristocracy and transferring allegiance to the tsars, whose subjects they by now had become. General Raevsky's father, Colonel Nikolai Semenovich Raevsky, was a professional soldier and commanded the Izmailovsky Regiment, one of the most distinguished in the army; his mother, related to the ancient powerful clan of the Naryshkins, was a niece of Potemkin, Prince of Tauris, Empress Catherine's legendary proconsul, lover, and secret husband.

The future general was born in St. Petersburg on September 14, 1771, at the very apogee of the reign of Catherine II. As family tradition demanded, he received a military education at the Corps des Pages, the famous St. Petersburg cadet school; at fifteen he accompanied his father to the front in the war against Turkey. Riding to battle at Jassy, he saw his father hit by a Turkish sniper's bullet and was with him when he died at the military hospital at Jassy. But, badly shaken as he was, young Nikolai refused to return home before the campaign ended. A few years later, he distinguished himself in the second Turkish campaign, and at age twenty-one he received his captain's insignia. Off to the Polish wars two years later, more decorations and promotions, then back to a spell of fashionable living in St. Petersburg, where, it was rumored, he had caught the attention of the empress.

It was perfectly natural that Catherine II should have singled out Nikolai for attention; his mother, the beautiful former Katia Raevsky, was one of her ladies-in-waiting and close friends. After Colonel Raevsky's death on the Turkish battlefield at Jassy, the disconsolate young widow, finding herself suddenly alone in the world, turned to Lev Davydov, an older family friend who had always admired her. Lev Denisovich Davydov, an enormously rich Ukrainian landlord, was a charming man and kind husband. He adored his young wife, surrounding her with wealth, luxury, and affection. The marriage, which was extremely happy, was a great blessing not only for Katia but also for young Nikolai, her only child, who welcomed the brood of half-brothers and sisters that followed in rapid succession. As a niece of Potemkin, now allied to the fabulously rich Davydov clan, Nikolai's mother became a woman of great influence.

"Carefree" and "glamorous" describe the life of a guards officer in the days of Empress Catherine, particularly one as well connected as Nikolai. At twenty-four he was a full colonel, commanding the Nizhny Novgorod Dragoons. The duties were none too onerous, alllowing ample time for races, balls, masquerades, drinking with one's cronies at the Nobility Club, visiting assorted relatives in the country, escorting glamorous actresses about town—a life-style that gave one a chance to review the season's crop of eligible daughters brought over to the capital's "marriage market" from the provinces.

Nikolai's marriage was probably arranged by Empress Catherine herself, an indefatigable matchmaker and never indifferent to the charms of a dashing guards officer. If so, her choice was fortuitous. Sophia was the only child of her favorite, Court Librarian Alexander Konstantinov, and granddaughter of the famous Russian scientist Lomonosov, known as Russia's Leonardo da Vinci. It was a family close to the empress's heart; she used to refer to Lomonosov as the "ornament of my reign" and a few years previously had presented him with a vast estate in the province of Oranienbaum, including 6,400 serfs. After her father's death, the estate passed on to Sophia and remained in the Raevsky family until the Revolution.

Unlike many of Catherine's arranged marriages, the Raevsky union turned out well. The fragile, delicately boned Sophia, who "gazed dreamily at the world through her slanting gray eyes, framed by a cloud of black hair," adored her handsome, dashing young husband. After his spell of duty in the capital came to an end in July 1793, Nikolai was transferred to Kiev, headquarters of the II Corps. The young couple, surrounded by a vast retinue of servants, traveled south to the Ukraine, stopping to visit Nikolai's mother and stepfather at Kamenka, their sprawling country estate near Kiev.

Nikolai's assignment to the Caucasus pleased his mother. It was a much-sought-after posting, and a just recognition of his talents; she saw her favorite son following in the footsteps of his great-uncle Potemkin. For although by the time of Nikolai's wedding Prince Potemkin had been dead for over three years, his powerful presence still brooded over the vast expanse of territories, from Kiev to the Crimea, he had ruled so long. It certainly was no detriment to a young officer's career to be connected by blood ties to a legend.

The Raevskys' first child, whom they named Alexander, was born in the Caucasus. A year later, in Dervent, on the shores of the Caspian, in a hastily rigged-up tent, their daughter Ekaterina was born. (No midwife was to be found within a forty-mile radius, and the child was delivered by a fellow soldier, Colonel von Pahlen, the future Governor of St. Petersburg.) Rough living on the wild shores of the Caspian Sea was too much for delicate, city-bred Sophia. She returned to Kiev with her two infant children, while her husband soldiered alone in Baku, then in Persia. Prospects for the glamorous young couple looked a bit gloomy, but two unexpected events changed their lives: in 1796 Empress Catherine the Great died of a heart attack and was succeeded by her son, Emperor Paul, the "tsar whom everyone hated." He was narrow-minded, cruel, obsessed with military discipline, and as lunatic as his father had been. Epic rages, sudden and seemingly unprovoked, led to massive arrests and long sentences in the Fortress, executions, or Siberian exile. Like his father, he surrounded himself with Prussian officers, whom he drilled at all hours of the day or night.

Raevsky had now been in the southern army for three years and dreaded the prospect that one day soon he might be assigned to duty at Emperor Paul's headquarters at Gatchina—a thought which filled most courtiers and military personnel with despair. It certainly was no place for a fastidious, liberal-minded man whose idol had always been France. Since childhood, Raevsky had spoken and read French perfectly and detested the mentality of the Prussians, of whom there were quite a number at Catherine's court and in the army. A family council was held at Kamenka, presided over by his stepfather and his mother; all agreed that Nikolai should apply for "an indefinite leave" from the army and look around for a country estate and a new career in farming.

Nikolai and Sophia were in Kiev, winding up Nikolai's military affairs, when they heard of Lev Davydov's death from a heart attack. This changed everything. To Nikolai's astonishment, his stepfather had left him the lovely huge estate of Boltyshka, with its contingent of more than ten thousand serfs and very considerable revenues. He also became a trustee of the enormous Davydov estate, and financial adviser to his mother and her brood of Davydov children. From a promising military commander to patriarch of the Raevsky and Davydov clans was indeed quite a step, but twenty-eight-year-old Raevsky seems to have welcomed the change. As soon as the transfer of property was concluded, the newly retired colonel and his young wife went to live at Boltyshka, thenceforth their permanent home. During those tranquil years—devoted to farming, reading, and local affairs, and far removed from the intrigues of the court and the senseless military drills of the "mad tsar"—their second son, Nikolai, was born, followed shortly by another daughter, Elena.

In March 1801 a palace revolution took place in St. Petersburg in which the tyrannical Tsar Paul was strangled by officers of the Semenovsky Guard. His twenty-three-year-old, liberal-minded son Alexander was proclaimed tsar amid scenes of universal rejoicing and hopes for an enlightened long reign. One of the first acts of the new tsar was to recall Colonel Raevsky from country retirement and promote him to major general. The two had been friends for a long time. "I need you in my army, Nikolai Nikolaevich," Tsar Alexander had written. There was no arguing with such a summons. In the summer of 1801, Nikolai Raevsky returned to the army and began his march to fame. For the next several years, his life was swallowed up by the ever-increasing demands of an expanding military career, while the family divided their time between Boltyshka, their house on the Blagodarnoe Sobranie in Moscow, and the picturesque dacha near Moscow's Kalugna Gate—another of Lev Davydov's legacies.

On Christmas Day, 1805, as General Raevsky and the Russian armies were heading home after the dispiriting campaign of Austerlitz, in which Emperor Napoleon inflicted defeat on the young tsar and his coalition, Sophia Raevsky gave birth to their third daughter and fifth child. "She is totally unlike anyone in the family," wrote Sophia to her husband. "Her face is all eyes— very dark with long lashes . . . She gazes at me unsmiling and she does not even cry like other babies." When the general returned home, he declared that his daughter must take after Great-uncle Potemkin. No one in his family had such dark looks and such uncannily large eyes. The baby indeed looked unusual. Around the outer ring of the iris was a very dark gray ring, and the iris itself was huge. "They were riveting, uncomfortably serious, grown-up eyes," recalled Maria's eldest sister, Ekaterina. By no stretch of the imagination could the new arrival have been described as a pretty baby—"unusual" was the family's consensus —but as time went on, her looks improved. Tiny arms and legs filled to pleasing plumpness, sparse hair began to thicken and take on a dark, almost bluish tinge. She had the blue-veined transparency of skin common to women of the Ukrainian steppes. For a long time her looks, so different from the light-skinned, blue-eyed prettiness of her sisters and the brown-haired handsomeness of her father, continued to puzzle the family and was the subject of many good-natured jokes. They named her Maria because she had been born on Christmas Day.

Maria's early years coincided with the Napoleonic Wars, in which her father gained glory as an outstanding military commander. In spite of a severe chest wound received while covering the retreat of the tsar's armies from Austerlitz, he succeeded in saving an entire infantry corps from the French, and the tsar gave him two important decorations: the orders of St. Anne and St. Vladimir. Raevsky was well on his way to the top. After a brief stay at his beloved Boltyshka, the general was off again to fight Sweden. On his return, he accompanied Tsar Alexander to Tilsit.

The Raevskys

It was the summer of the year 1807. Europe was in turmoil. One name was on everyone's lips—Napoleon, the victor of Austerlitz, Ulm, and Jena, who had just won a crushing victory over Tsar Alexander at Friedland. From the pinnacle of his power, Napoleon was prepared to make peace: he proposed to the tsar that they meet on a raft in the middle of the river Niemen, the boundary between Russia and Poland. While the two sovereigns, between whom a sudden if short-lived friendship had sprung up, were busy dividing Europe, their staffs entertained one another at sumptuous meals, provided by an impressive array of French cooks. It was part of Napoleon's subtle public-relations campaign aimed to win Alexander's entourage and make them understand the ways and ideas of the French. With his perfect French and openly liberal views, the handsome General Raevsky was an instant success among his new friends. Dining in the French officers' mess, served by cooks in starched white uniforms and powdered wigs, he enjoyed discussing the works of Voltaire and Rousseau, which he had read as a young man in the days of the Empress Catherine, or going over the details of the battle of Friedland with his French opposite corps commander.

While waiting for the tsar to emerge from some lengthy meeting with the emperor, Raevsky would now and then signal to one of the tsar's aides-de-camp, the young Prince Sergei Volkonsky, scion of a great family. The two of them would be seen walking slowly along the bank of the river, lost in deep conversation. The French army fascinated them both. "We often remarked on how different were the ways of the French Revolutionary Army from ours," Raevsky recalled in his memoirs. "Though conscripts like ours, each French soldier had a singular pride and was treated with respect by his officers. Napoleon never ceased to appeal directly to his Grande Armée and always gave them credit for his victories. Many of his now famous marshals had served for years as simple sergeant majors, unable to rise higher until the Revolution opened commissions to all and released such an astonishing flood of military talent."

Raevsky had been particularly impressed by brilliant Marshal Ney, who had led the main attack on the right wing of the tsar's army at Friedland. "To think that this man was a simple Hussar trooper until the Revolution, unable to get officer's training because his father was a barrel cooper in Alsace. Yet it would be hard to imagine a leader of greater courage and skill. It is because of Ney that we suffered such a devastating defeat," he told Volkonsky. And they both wondered how many potential Neys, Davouts, Augereaus, or Bernadottes were being stifled or suppressed under the rigid caste system of the Russian army. These long talks on the poplar-shaded banks of the Niemen made a lasting impression on young Prince Volkonsky. As he later recalled, they helped to set him on a lifelong liberal quest, which ended in Siberian exile. When that time came, he showed little regret.

But he was hurt and surprised to learn, many years after Tilsit, when as a major general with several campaigns and battles behind him he had married Raevsky's daughter Maria, that his illustrious father-in-law had dramatically altered his views. Like the tsar, the "liberator of Europe," who after Napoleon's defeat at Waterloo had reverted to the former autocratic ways in his country, General Raevsky decided that liberal theories were fine, as long as they remained safely outside Russia. He had neither sympathy nor much time for the "foolish, half-baked ideas" of a group of idealistic, "muddle-headed young dreamers." And he never, until the day of his death, forgave his son-in-law Sergei Volkonsky for allowing himself to be caught in that web, dragging his favorite daughter, Maria, with him into exile.

But this was still in the future. After Tilsit, General Raevsky went on to fight Turks in the Crimea, and to receive further accolades and distinctions. It was in the great patriotic war of 1812, when all Russia rose to resist Napoleon's invasion, that Raevsky's name became legend. At Borodino, in the midst of the bloodiest fighting, he personally led the assault on a battery manned by Napoleon's elite grenadiers. He was flanked on each side by his two sons—Alexander, sixteen, and Nikolai, eleven. General Raevsky's advance unit captured the enemy's position and seized the French regimental flag in spite of murderous fire. The eleven-year-old Nikolai saw a bullet pass through his trousers but escaped unhurt, while the sixteen-year-old Alexander, the boy drummer, never left the vanguard of the battle, hardly missing a beat on his drum. He later complained that "the stirring rhythm of his beat could barely have been heard above the din of the battle."

Field Marshal Kutuzov, the "grand old man" of the Russian army, had always admired Raevsky for his bravery and imaginative leadership, and after Borodino he recommended that the tsar award Raevsky the order of Alexander Nevsky, First Class, the second highest military decoration of the time, and a sword set with diamonds. "He was an inspiration to his troops," ran the citation. Today thousands of Russian and foreign tourists who visit the Borodino battlefield are conducted through the local museum and shown portraits of the general and his two sons. The famous Borodino sword is wrapped in the blue-and-yellow order of Alexander Nevsky, its diamond star proudly glittering at the top.

After Napoleon's defeat in the spring of 1814, General Raevsky entered Paris at the side of the Emperor Alexander. Contemporary memoirs note his "flawless French and wise political judgment" during the complex negotiations for Napoleon's abdication and the arrangements for the occupation of Paris by the allies. Leaving the tsar-liberator behind to savor the delights of the French capital, Raevsky returned home to Boltyshka in time for the summer harvest.

A letter in the Raevsky Archives describes the general's delight at being reunited with his wife. He talks of the "statuesque beauty" of his eldest daughter, Ekaterina, then sixteen, and of the "rusalka" (fairy-tale-like) grace of the eight-year-old Maria, who with her raven hair, olive skin, and huge, luminous eyes looks "so startlingly different from us all."

"She moves like a thoroughbred Arabian colt," Raevsky wrote to his half brother Vasya Davydov that summer. "When she sings, her childish voice sounds like the purest crystal . . . She has perfect pitch; we will have to find a really first-rate music teacher for her in Kiev."

Maria's childhood was blissful. Its center was Boltyshka, the lovely house on the Dnieper, where the children spent most of their time. In later years, in the harsh winters of her Siberian exile, the memories of those sun-filled days in the Ukraine provided the emotional sustenance she craved. Comfortable, multistoried, with a white colonnaded portico, the beloved house spread its wings around a spacious courtyard full of trees. In the summer evenings, nightingales sang from the depths of the gardens and orchards. By day, bees buzzed over the rose garden, and from the busy kitchen quarters came sounds of ceaseless activity. At the end of the garden, there was a little summerhouse overlooking the ravine by the river. Here, in the long summer afternoons, around a silver samovar, the ladies of the house gathered to drink tea and entertain other noble families who drove over from neighboring estates to visit. The children were brought over by their governesses or their nannies, made to curtsy, the older ones to declaim some recently learned French or English poem. "We did not stay long," recalled Maria. "We scampered away quickly, back to our rabbits, our pet goats, and our favorite tree house, built in a secret oak grove behind the orchards."

Like most Ukrainian houses, Boltyshka was quite isolated, six miles from the nearest small town and a day's fast carriage drive from Kiev. But the great manor houses of that period were entirely self-supporting; they raised their own cattle, bred their own horses, made their own bread, grew their own vegetables and fruit. Swarms of domestics, carpenters, grooms, gardeners, farmhands, dairy and scullery maids—all of them serfs—tended devotedly to the Raevsky family. It was a patriarchal existence, following the unchanging rhythm of the seasons.

While Alexander and Nicholas attended the Corps des Pages in St. Petersburg, and then studied at Moscow University, the girls were educated at home. The nursery was presided over by the ancient nurse, Evpraxia Ivanovna, who had brought up generations of young Raevskys. In summer, when the red rambler roses reached almost under the nursery windows, the girls liked to lean out of the windows to pick them; they were briskly pulled back by their hair and reprimanded. There were two French tutors, who had earlier taught Alexander and Nicholas, and an English governess, a Miss Martin, whom General Raevsky had met in Paris and engaged as a teacher for his daughters.

Whatever the barriers of geography, politics, or language that isolated Russia from the rest of Europe, vast numbers of French tutors had always found their way there during most of the eighteenth and throughout the nineteenth century. They were followed by an invasion of English governesses. At the time of the French Revolution, hundreds of French émigré aristocrats, fleeing the Terror, took refuge in tsarist Russia, making a living as well as they could—some as music masters, some as soldiers, but most as tutors. They were all welcomed and given jobs, for having a foreign governess or tutor was all the rage. There were some exceptional individuals among them: Tsar Alexander I was schooled by the famous La Harpe, Marat's brother, who fled France after his brother's execution and taught at the exclusive lycée at Tsarskoe Selo; the future Tsar Nicholas I had an adored Scottish governess, the very good-looking Miss Lyons. In the years after Waterloo, having an English governess or nanny became the height of chic in St. Petersburg.

From the days of Peter the Great, when he ordered Russian boyars to abandon their traditional medieval way of life, to cut their beards and exchange padded kaftans for knee breeches, and their wives to shed their veils and emerge from harem-like seclusion, Russian craving for Western styles, Western clothes, Western books, and Western sophistication never ceased. Tutors and governesses had a profound effect on Russian education and culture, adding sophistication and gallicizing or anglicizing their young charges. Even during the Napoleonic invasion, at a time of deeply felt national humiliation and hatred of the French emperor, Russian society went on using the conqueror's language in preference to its own. "Russia," wrote one of the high government officials at the time, "is the only country in which the mother tongue is ignored and the young generation has little knowledge of anything relating to its fatherland."

As a result, for over two hundred years French (and, to a smaller extent, English) replaced Russian as the principal language spoken by the vast majority of Russian aristocracy, landed gentry, government officials, army officers, and wealthy merchants. Their children's Russian was apt to be of the careless and ill-educated kind, culled from the servants, as parents always conversed with their children in French. Years later, when Maria first visited her husband in his prison cell at the Nerchinsk mines in Siberia, she was embarrassed to learn that conversation had to be conducted in Russian, "so the guards would know what was being said." She found that her long-awaited emotional exchange with her husband was restricted to the most basic Russian vocabulary.

Early in 1815, while Tsar Alexander was attending the Congress of Vienna and the defeated Emperor Napoleon was living in exile on the island of Elba, General Raevsky was given the command of the prestigious IV Army Corps with headquarters in Kiev. Now, at least the family would not be separated. Kiev was barely a day's carriage drive from Boltyshka, and an imposing residence in the historic Podol district went with the job. Raevsky's writ ran over a huge area of the country —from the Ukraine south to the Crimea and the Caucasus, where the tsar's southern army was at that time embarking upon the first stage of what was to prove a protracted and bloody war against the indomitable mountain tribesmen of Dagestan in the Caucasus.

There were no roads on the Ukrainian steppe in those days, only tracks. Since it had been a particularly hard winter, traveling by carriage during the spring thaws had to be avoided at all costs. The general and his retinue set off for Kiev on horseback in early March to organize his administrative headquarters and prepare the accommodations for the family, but Sophia and her four daughters decided to postpone their departure until after Easter. Tutors, governesses, maids, cooks, and a huge retinue of various servants were kept busy for weeks with preparations for the move to the big city.

In mid-April, as the waters of the Dnieper subsided and families of black storks returned from their winter quarters in the Crimea and built nests below the gold onion dome of the village church, a long procession of carriages, headed by the Raevsky family coach, a heavy vehicle drawn by a team of six horses, wound its way across the green ocean of grasses toward Kiev.

Facing Ekaterina and her mother, squeezed between Elena and Sophia on the back seat just behind Bogdan the coachman, Maria peered out of the carriage, her enormous dark eyes intent on the flight of a falcon overhead. She was sad to be leaving her childhood paradise of Boltyshka. Though she was to return there again several times, the happiest years of her life were almost over.

2

Kiev, the Crimea,

and Pushkin

KIEV, THE CAPITAL OF THE UKRAINE, was the holy city of Russia, the ancient metropolis, the Rome of the north, of the Tartars and of the Kievan Rus.* At a time when Moscow was nothing but a tribal settlement, when St. Petersburg did not exist, Kiev, the "Mother of Russian Cities," was the capital of the unified eastern Slav state, and the center of trade between the Baltic, the Black Sea, and Byzantium.

As early as the ninth century, there had been numerous contacts between Kiev and Byzantium. Each spring, the pagan Great Prince of Kiev, with an armed retinue known as the *druzhina* and a flotilla of vessels carrying cargoes of fur, honey, and blond slaves, made his way down the Dnieper and across the

---

* Kievan Rus was the name of the unified eastern Slav state, with Kiev as its capital. The name came into use after the death of Prince Rurik in 882. The other Russian state had its capital in Novgorod.

Black Sea to Constantinople. In those days Byzantium, or Constantinople, as the Greeks called it, or Tsarograd, as the Russians named it, was a magnet drawing not only the semi-barbarous Russian princes but people from southern Italy, the Balkans, the Aegean, and Asia Minor. As the capital of the Byzantine Empire and heir to the eastern part of the Roman Empire, poised at the very edge of a Europe just entering the Dark Ages, Constantinople was the most important cultural and political center of its time. A Christian sanctum, it had as its literary and state language Greek. It preserved not only the heritage of Christian thought but also the ancient arts of Greece and Rome that had been largely lost in a torn and ravaged Western Europe.

The Russians returned from these expeditions laden with Byzantine gold, silk, wine, and spices, as well as with Christian ideas totally at odds with their pagan beliefs. As the ninth century wore on, these Christian influences spread throughout Kievan Rus. Then in 957 Princess Olga, widow of Prince Igor, son of Rurik, founder of the dynasty, went on a pilgrimage to Constantinople. Olga, according to the chronicler Nestor, was a woman of "great beauty and considerable wisdom." She returned from the journey a converted Christian. After her death, she was canonized in the Orthodox Church. But it was not until thirty years later, in 988, when Olga's grandson Vladimir married Anna, the sister of the co-Emperor of Constantinople, that Orthodox Christianity was formally adopted in the country and pagan idols were toppled. Some twenty-two years earlier, Kievan Rus's western neighbor, Poland, had also been converted to Christianity. Unlike Russia, however, Poland's conversion was the work of missionaries from the West, sent from Rome. This fact was to prove of immense historical significance and forever affect the destinies of the two countries.

The adoption of the Orthodox Christian faith throughout the

Kievan Rus brought literacy and the Cyrillic alphabet, devised for the Russians by two Orthodox monks, Cyril and his brother Methodius. To celebrate his victory over the Pechenegs, a wild pagan tribe, Prince Yaroslav built the Cathedral of St. Sophia, which to this day remains one of the great masterpieces of eleventh-century ecclesiastical architecture. The prince himself lies in it, buried in a magnificently carved marble sarcophagus. Not far from it is the famous Monastery of the Caves, built about the same time; by the end of our century, it will have occupied the same site for a full thousand years.

In the first half of the eleventh century, Kiev, "the radiant and many-colored," standing high on the banks of the Dnieper, was one of the most beautiful, animated, and prosperous cities of Europe. It was larger than Paris, which at the time had only about seventy-five thousand inhabitants, and twice as large as London, which was then a modest town. Dynastic connections linked Kiev with a number of European ruling houses. Yaroslav's wife was the daughter of King Olaf of Sweden; his three daughters all married kings: Elizabeth became Queen of Norway; Anastasia, Queen of Hungary; and Anne, of France, when she married Henry I in 1051. (She is thus an ancestor of Queen Elizabeth II.) The city was visited by scholars from both Rome and Byzantium, and due to its geographical position at the crossing of the great river routes, it controlled all trade between the Black Sea in the south and the Baltic in the north, and from the Volga to the frontiers of Poland in the west.

Kiev's decline in both prosperity and influence was brought about by its destruction at the hands of the Mongols, followed by constant and costly dissension among the local princes. With the decline of Byzantium, the political center of Russia shifted north to Suzdal and then to Moscow. The Ukraine (the name means borderland, *ukraina*) became a battleground between Poles, Cossacks, and Tartar hordes from the East. By the end of the seventeenth century, however, after the Turkish and Tartar invasions had receded and the Ukraine had been won back from the Poles, Kiev came into its own again. It was recorded that the city by now included "no less than seven small towns, 189 villages, 56,000 serfs, thirteen monasteries, glassworks, and numerous merchant houses, as well as several thousand craftsmen." Many new churches and monasteries were built in a mixture of Oriental and baroque styles, trade started to flourish again, and wealthy Ukrainian landlords built themselves magnificent mansions on the Dnieper. In the middle of the eighteenth century, Bartolomeo Rastrelli, the famous Italian architect who created the Hermitage, temporarily deserted St. Petersburg to add two splendid buildings to the city's rich architectural heritage. One is the Church of St. Andrew, which still stands overlooking the Dnieper from the heights above Podol, a fine example of Russian baroque; and the two-storied Marynsky Palace, a replica of the Anichkov Palace in St. Petersburg. (Destroyed in the last war, it was completely restored in the nineteen-fifties.)

At the time of the Raevskys' arrival in Kiev, the city was no longer a group of scattered monasteries and townships; it had already become compact, animated, picturesque, with wide avenues bordered by pink acacias and red and white chestnut trees, which flourish so very well in the Ukrainian black soil. There were several theaters, an excellent university, and the Kiev Academy, of which Lomonosov, Maria's great-grandfather, had been the most illustrious graduate. Several fashionable regiments were stationed in and around Kiev, and as the war in the Caucasus intensified, large numbers of dashing guards officers, some of them motivated by a lack of cash, others by a desire for adventure, decided to abandon the salons of St. Petersburg to take up fighting on the frontiers of empire. Kiev, of course, was the central stopping place on the way to the front or for recuperating from battle. Rich, carefree, and anxious for pleasure after their rough and celibate life in the field, those young blades created an atmosphere of excitement and gaiety around them. According to contemporary memoirs, the Kiev season was "almost as brilliant as that of St. Petersburg or Moscow."

As befitted his elevated station, a large house in the center of town had been commandeered and made ready for the general and his family. Set behind a high fence, where lilacs and sunflowers sprawled, it included a huge private garden, stables, and separate quarters for the innumerable domestics and serfs. Miss Martin, the English governess, lived with the family, but the two French tutors occupied small houses down the street. Music and deportment teachers were engaged, and a singing coach for Maria, as well as a dancing master, a Monsieur Grünn, whose task was to teach the young ladies how to waltz.

The famous military hero, around whom so many legends had been woven (after Borodino, the official lithography and poetry had practically canonized Raevsky), was enthusiastically welcomed in the town. Their house soon became the gathering point for local society, army officers, government officials, landowners from the neighboring estates, poets, and visiting writers. Anybody who was anybody could be found in the Raevsky salon, paying court to the general and his wife, discussing the latest news from the Caucasus, or admiring the classic beauty of the eldest daughter, Ekaterina, for whose hand suitors were already lining up.

Young Count Gustav Olizar, a wealthy Ukrainian landowner, has left a description of the Raevsky family at the time: "I often used to visit the Raevskys in their splendid house on Khorevaya Ulitsa, near the spot where Peter the Great had once lived during his long stay in Kiev at the time of the Swedish wars. The general, an upright, generous, fine-looking man, is much beloved for his hospitality and his highly cultivated mind . . . His wife

Sophia, a dreamy, slightly faded former beauty, floats from one visitor to another, welcoming, but not quite of this world. She simply worships her husband and her oldest son, Alexander, but appears to be rather indifferent to her other children ... There is another son, Nikolai, and four girls ... The eldest, Ekaterina, has a lovely mouth, a Grecian profile, dark blue eyes, and a mass of light chestnut hair. She is extremely willful ... Elena is more ethereal ... Blond, blue-eyed, she seems timid, chaste and delicate. She will flower briefly, like a cactus, then wilt away. [Elena had TB and spent most of her adult life as an invalid.] The little girls, Maria and her younger sister, Sophia, are still very young, but I find Maria, the graceful, mischievous little brunette, who looks like a diminutive Indian princess, full of promise." Count Olizar was to reappear in Maria's life a few years later, when he unsuccessfully bid for her hand in marriage.

According to contemporary descriptions, the general's two sons, Alexander and Nikolai, though each a personality in his own right, differed considerably from each other and bore little resemblance to their illustrious father. Like the rest of the family, they adored him, but they had ambivalent feelings about the fame and the esteem with which he was universally regarded, which made it hard for them to grow up in his image. At the time of the family's move to Kiev, Alexander was just twenty-one—an officer in the guards light-cavalry regiment, able, arrogant, somewhat sneering. He had a long, bony, emaciated body, ending in a "little bird's head," as his colleagues in the regiment described it. His mouth was hard, like a "ragged gash," his brown eyes flickered, his cheeks and forehead constantly formed grimacing wrinkles. "His whole being exudes condescending mockery," writes Olizar, who knew him well and in spite of Alexander's negative personality admired him for his "critical intelligence and cruel but oh so funny sense of humor." Much of

Alexander's behavior and his so-called disparaging attitude to life was a pose. He knowingly affected the stance of a cynic and skeptic in the mode of Voltaire, and he liked to pretend that there was nothing for him in this world worthy of admiration or affection. He loudly rejected conventions and most of the accepted ethical and aesthetic principles; he refused to admit the existence of genuine human emotions—except when he was with his mother, to whom he was truly devoted. Even so, such was his pleasure in shocking people that he was once heard to exclaim to a fellow officer in the regimental mess: "Such a silly idea, to talk about honoring your mother. Why should one—just because she carried one for nine months in a pocket full of water? What nonsense!"

Needless to say, such pronouncements did not endear Alexander to his father, who worried about his being "so cold." "He does not reason, he always argues, and the more he is in the wrong, the more irritating and coarse his language becomes. He and I have agreed never to discuss any important subject again and to avoid conversation on the rare occasion we find ourselves alone with each other. It is sad." Alexander never really achieved an intimate relationship with his father in his father's lifetime, but as the years went on and the family's misfortunes mounted, Alexander did mellow. The youthful rebellion subsided, and he stopped making outrageous pronouncements as he strove less forcibly to stake out his own personality away from the powerful shadow of his father.

Nikolai, six years younger, was a non-intellectual, an athlete with a muscular neck and a swelling chest. His physical strength was enormous. Already in his late teens he could bend an iron poker in his hand. He was lazy and a bit uncouth and liked dubious practical jokes. "Do take yourself in hand, my dear Nikolai," his father wrote him in February 1820. "The tone of your various jests in your father's presence and your habit of sprawling on the sofa in front of me and the young ladies and pulling your trousers up over your fat legs are most objectionable. You are intelligent, but so far you have done less than any idiot." But Nicholas was not an idiot. After graduating from the Corps des Pages, he got himself assigned to a regiment of Hussars at Tsarskoe Selo, where his jolly, carefree manner and athletic prowess made him extremely popular. Closer in age to Maria than Alexander, he had always been her favorite friend and confidant.

General Raevsky's duties involved extensive traveling, not only all over the Ukraine, but also south to Russia's two newest provinces, the Caucasus and the Crimea. Thirty-five years before, his great-uncle Potemkin, conscious of the strategic importance for Russia of an outlet to the Black Sea, annexed the whole of the Crimea and laid the entire romantic and beautiful province at the feet of his empress. To a people used to the infinite flat expanse of northern bleakness, the Crimea with its glorious blue skies, its warm sea, lemon groves, mass of flowers, and the vine-wreathed shores of the Black Sea was a Garden of Eden. And so it must have appeared to the Raevskys when they came there for the first time in the summer of 1816 after an arduous carriage drive from Kiev. Their destination was Gurzuf, a Tartar village on the beautiful southern shore of the Black Sea where, according to Maria's description, "romantic rocks and turfy terraces, dark cypresses and pale minarets, picturesque hovels and pine-covered steeps are surmounted by the jagged brow of the high plateau."

About half a mile from the village stood a replica of an eighteenth-century French château, built in wood by the celebrated Duc de Richelieu. A peer of France, the duke fled his country at the time of the Revolution, and as a brilliant administrator, he was soon appointed not only Governor of Odessa but also Viceroy of the "New Russia," the Crimea. This rather incongruously located classical structure, more suited to the banks of the Loire than to a Tartar village, with a mosque and minarets for a neighbor, was solidly built to withstand Black Sea storms and attacks by the corsairs. It stood three stories high, had long French windows, balconies, and outside galleries running the length of the house—all overlooking the sea. There was a huge garden filled with orange trees, myrtle bushes, pink and mauve oleanders, and various tropical shrubs. Black umbrella pines and elegant cypresses cast their dark silhouettes against the bright azure sky. By the time General Raevsky first visited Gurzuf, the Duc de Richelieu was back in France, where after the fall of Napoleon he twice served as prime minister under Louis XVIII. The house had occasionally been used by the Governor of Odessa, who gladly let the great national hero have it as a holiday retreat for his family. The Raevskys adored it, and from then on Sophia and the children used to spend at least two or three months each year at Gurzuf, and were joined there by the general, his military duties allowing.

Preserved in the Raevsky Archives in St. Petersburg is a very early letter from Maria, aged ten, dated March 29, 1816, to her brother Alexander, then twenty-one, serving with a guards regiment in St. Petersburg:

We will be going to Kamenka on the first Tuesday after Easter [she writes in her childish hand] and from there on to the Crimea, oh blissful prospect . . . We are sending you the volume of Walter Scott you have asked for, also the one by Mme de Guignon. Tell me if you want any more books . . . I will try and compose a drawing for you and will send it to Belaya Tserkov [her aunt's home].

Take care of yourself, my dear brother,

Your devoted sister,
Maria

In the spring of 1820, General Raevsky, who was suffering from arthritis, was ordered by his doctors to take the waters at the mineral springs of Goryachevodsk in the Caucasus, which were supposed to be miraculous. He set off from Kiev, accompanied by his younger son, Nikolai; the two youngest girls, Maria and Sophia; his personal physician; the girls' English governess; two French tutors; and an assorted retinue of domestics. After six weeks in the Caucasus, they planned to continue on to the Crimea and rejoin Madame Raevsky at Gurzuf, where she was waiting for them with the two oldest girls, Ekaterina and Elena.

It was to be a memorable trip for Maria. During those four summer months, between the Caucasus and the Crimea, the little dark-haired girl emerged from her childhood chrysalis and timidly, tentatively began to spread her wings as a woman. Only a man could have brought about such a transformation; and she had met him on that journey. His name was Alexander Sergeevich Pushkin; he was twenty-one years old—a liberal thinker and famous as one of Russia's great poets.

They met in Ekaterinoslav, a drab garrison town of unpaved streets, wooden shanties, and an empty, dilapidated old palace in which Potemkin had once lived. Pushkin, the darling of the St. Petersburg salons, had just incurred Tsar Alexander's displeasure for his "underground revolutionary writings," in which he openly mocked the tsar for his inconsistency, for imagining himself a liberal and being in fact a notorious tyrant ("In face and gesture both he was a Harlequin"). Pushkin's three revolutionary poems published between 1817 and 1819, and particularly his famous *Ode to Liberty* ("I will sing of liberty, and scourge the evil that sits on thrones"), reached people throughout Russia and were being quoted in Moscow's and St. Petersburg's literary circles and as well among the more liberal-minded army officers, students, shopkeepers, even ordinary soldiers.

They sparked particular excitement and enthusiasm among the vast numbers of a peculiarly Russian group of people called the "intellectual serfs," gifted young men and women whom their masters would send up to town to educate as architects, painters, doctors, musicians, or actors and who, upon completing their studies, were expected to return to the families who owned them, without any legal change in their serf status. Pushkin became their hero, their poet. Even before he was twenty-one, the lively, curly-haired, dark-skinned, thick-lipped youth, descendant of an Abyssinian slave, found himself the literary idol of all Russia. It was not surprising, however, given the political climate of the times, that as Pushkin's fame and notoriety increased, so did the number of his enemies. Once Emperor Alexander's attention had been drawn to the *Ode to Liberty*, he found it particularly offensive because of the allusions to his father's assassination in the Mikhailovsky Palace. Later the emperor became exasperated by the poet's attacks on Arakcheev, the dreaded governor of the military settlements, one of the most unpleasant figures of the period but a close friend of the tsar. There was talk of sending the irrepressible young man to Siberia, but Alexander liked to think of himself as a man of enlightened generosity.

"With Pushkin, the emperor *played* the tsar," noted Turgenev when writing about their relationship some years later. So, instead of being sent to Siberia or to the Peter and Paul Fortress, young Pushkin was dispatched to Ekaterinoslav in southern Russia, to the offices of General Insov, administrator of the southern colonies. He left St. Petersburg on May 6, 1820, with a thousand assignats (scrip) to cover traveling expenses and a letter to General Insov from the tsar, written in French, suggesting he be given employment in his office. Disaster had been averted.

Not unexpectedly, Pushkin found Ekaterinoslav deadly. "Soon after my arrival," he recalled in one of his letters, "I became so bored that I went rowing on the Dnieper, bathed, and caught fever." His lodgings in "a wretched little Jewish cottage in Mandrikovka Street" were dismally uncomfortable and gloomy. It was while he lay there, racked by fever, that General Raevsky and his suite arrived on their way to the Caucasus and the entire town turned out to welcome the hero of Borodino.

Like most Russians, Pushkin was an admirer of the general, but he had not previously met him. Young Nikolai, however, was his friend. Two years older than Pushkin, he was serving in a guards regiment, while Pushkin was still at school in Tsarskoe Selo. The young Hussar and the precocious schoolboy poet met at the house of Peter Chaadaev, a brilliantly intelligent, well-read, elegant guards officer of the Semenovsky Regiment, the future author of the intensely pro-Western *Philosophical Letters*, the man who in his later years was to become one of Russia's leading intellectuals. Young Chaadaev belonged to a group of highly cultivated young men who had served in the French campaign, were in Paris after the fall of Napoleon, and had become imbued with a passion for politics and a desire to reform the Russian system. Five years older than Pushkin, he took a liking to the boy, whom he called "the peripatetic philosopher." Pushkin hero-worshipped Chaadaev from a distance and spent as much time as he could in his salon, whenever he could get away from his school's "locks and keys" (which he seemed to manage with great ease). It was in Chaadaev's house that he met Nikolai Raevsky, and within a few weeks the two became intimate friends.

When Nikolai heard that Pushkin was in Ekaterinoslav, he rushed off in spite of the very late hour to search for him. He found the unfortunate poet delirious, with no doctor, no medicine "except a jug of lemonade." Getting his father's physician out of bed, Nikolai forced him to see his friend. "We came to a sordid little thatched hut," the doctor recalled in his memoirs. "I found in it a young man sitting on a wooden bunk. He was deathly pale, thin, and unshaven. Sheets of paper lay on the table and all around him . . . He was writing poetry in spite of a very high fever."

Nikolai begged his father not to leave Pushkin behind, and the good-natured general gave way, though the young man appeared to him "anything but a restful companion, whether in ill health or not." He also magnanimously agreed to obtain permission from General Insov for Pushkin to take a prolonged leave of absence in order to accompany the Raevskys to the Caucasus and on to the Crimea.

The general's family was traveling in an open barouche and two broughams. Weak and feverish, Pushkin was not at first fit to travel in the open air, so Raevsky ordered him to be put into his own carriage with Nikolai, leaving himself, Maria, Sophia, the English governess, French tutors, and the rest to squeeze into the two other overladen vehicles. As the journey continued, Pushkin's health took a dramatic turn for the better and he regained his fierce vitality, singing and making up poems for every occasion, which he declaimed every time they stopped on the way. Though her father often found him tiresome, the young poet fascinated Maria. Her huge eyes followed every movement of the "strangely exotic-looking youth," curly-haired and dark-skinned, as he jumped in and out of the carriage, fought mock battles with Nikolai on the grass, and sang at the top of his lungs.

The farther south they progressed, the more attractive became the landscape and the higher rose everyone's spirits. One morning, as they were rounding a corner of the road near Taganrog, the sea suddenly came into view, bright blue, shimmering in the sunshine. "I will always remember that moment," wrote Maria in her memoirs years later. "I was sitting in the barouche, rather uncomfortably squeezed between Sophia and our English teacher. Our Russian *nyanya* and Mother's traveling companion, who was to rejoin her at Gurzuf, were with us, occupying the back seat. At the sight of the sea, we ordered the carriage to stop . . . Sophia and I jumped out and ran to the shore. The surface of the water was covered with waves, gentle, caressing waves, lapping at my feet, pursuing me back and forth as I ran."

Maria began to play in the surf, chasing the waves, running away with happy shrieks as they returned. Unknown to her, Pushkin, whose carriage she thought was some way behind, had caught up with her and was watching with delight. "The dark-haired little girl was so graceful, so young, and fleet as a cat," he recalled. "I longed, like the waves, to lap your feet with my lips," he wrote that evening. Two years later he preserved this moment in *Eugene Onegin* (chapter I, stanza xxxiii):

> How I envied the waves
> Coming in rapid succession
> Lovingly lapping your feet!
> And I longed, like the waves,
> To kiss your charming feet.

The party spent two months at the Goryachevodsk mineral springs in the Caucasus. They were joined there by Maria's older brother, Alexander, whom Pushkin now met. The poet was fascinated by the somber-faced Alexander. He called him "the Demon" and insisted on talking to him in the dark, by the light of a candle, "because his eyes were phosphorescent, like the devil's." He made Alexander the hero of his famous poem "The Demon":

> Our meetings were melancholy,
> His smile, his wonderful eyes
> And sarcastic speech
> Filled me with icy poison.

As they idly discussed life on the banks of a Caucasian stream, in the shadow of the towering mountains, Pushkin's romantic enthusiasm and still somewhat adolescent naïveté were affected by the cynical worldliness of Alexander, who taught him about the darker sides of life that he felt a poet ought to become acquainted with. They rode together in the evenings and drank far into the night, talking.

This was the world of adults, one which excluded the fourteen-and-a-half-year-old Maria and her sister. Her father, her two brothers, and Pushkin spent much of the day at the mineral baths, which were installed in improvised shacks. Most of the springs were then in their natural state, gushing, steaming, and pouring over the mountainside in all directions, leaving white or reddish trails as they ran. One got up to them by riding the local ponies over steep, stony paths bordered by wild bushes and skirted by precipices.

In 1820, before the spa of Pyatigorsk came into fashion and "taking the waters" became a popular high-society pastime for both sexes, the mineral springs of Goryachevodsk were considered to be the most invigorating of all Caucasian waters. Indeed, the air around them was so impregnated with sulphur that any metal carried around, including officers' epaulettes, became tarnished. Unlike Pyatigorsk in Lermontov's day, there were no elegant ladies dipping their wicker-covered glasses attached to white strings, escorted by mustachioed guards officers twitching their aristocratic nostrils at the nauseous smell of the "miracle water." The embryo spa at Goryachevodsk was simply an overgrown Tartar village, and following the local custom, all ladies, and particularly young girls, were kept apart from the bathers.

Like the rest of the summer visitors, the Raevskys and their entourage lived in tents on the banks of the picturesque mountain streams, but because of the general's rank and importance, there was a military escort to protect the family from night raids by the unpredictable mountain tribes. Kidnapping for ransom was an ever-present danger, but still there was plenty of fun for the girls—picnics, and riding, and lovely walks on the trails. Even the lessons became so much more agreeable when taken out of doors in the invigorating air with the magnificent backdrop of the giant mountains. From their tent, Maria and her sisters could see the famous twin breasts of Mt. Elbrus, through which Noah's Ark was reputed to have passed on its way to Mt. Ararat.

There was also the startling change that had come over their nice English governess, the ultraconventional, rather remote Miss Martin—Matty, as the girls called her. Was it the air of the Caucasus? Or was it perhaps the presence of the several exceedingly handsome guards officers, on leave from fighting the rebels, who—from a respectful distance, it was true—paid homage to the female entourage of the commander of the IV Army Corps? Or was it the sight of the dashing Circassian tribesmen, those free men of the mountains, so different from the serfs of the plains? Whatever the reason, it was obvious to all that Matty had become a new person since the family's arrival at Goryachevodovsk. She laughed, sang, and quoted long passages from Byron with renewed vigor. The girls' lessons were suddenly filled with excitement, changing from simple routine into voyages of discovery. Maria thought it all wonderful.

The usual length of stay for a cure was two months—about sixty baths. So, having spent June and July "taking the waters," General Raevsky and his family, accompanied by Pushkin, left for Gurzuf in the Crimea on August 5, 1820. In those days, southern Russia was still a newly conquered territory only partially subdued. The Caucasian mineral springs were practically on the frontier, and the demarcation line shifted daily, following the course of border warfare. Rebel tribesmen presented a constant danger, particularly to women; a lady of quality was worth her weight in gold on the Turkish slave market. No wonder Raevsky had an armed escort of Cossacks. Pushkin recalls that they even dragged "a loaded cannon behind them, with a lighted fuse."

Crossing from Asia back into Europe by boat, from Taman on the Asiatic shore to the Kerch peninsula on the mainland, they stopped in Kerch to visit the tomb of Mithridates, the first-century warrior-king, Rome's greatest enemy in Asia Minor. All there was left of the tomb was a watchtower that used to guard the entrance to the sanctuary, but as Maria noted, "the site was so strangely evocative of Greek dramas, and nature so beautiful around it," that they spent most of the afternoon there. Recalling that Mithridates had supposedly murdered his mother, as well as most of his harem, Nikolai insisted that Maria must declaim Racine's *Athalie* in French. She knew it well, and, noted her father, "gently prompted by me," she complied. Eyes shining, musical voice resonant in the clear, dry air, her young, still childish face framed by dark curls and flushed with excitement, she made a lovely silhouette against the distant backdrop of rocks and the glistening waters of the Crimean shore. There was a momentary hush when she finished. Pushkin bowed, picked a wild rose, and handed it to her. "I suspect she secretly put it under her pillow that night," wrote the general, probably pleased at the recollection.

The remainder of the journey was by sea, in a small brig. The ship anchored in sight of Gurzuf before dawn the next day, and the party awoke to the sight of fishing boats with mottled sails, flat thatched roofs of Tartar huts, upright poplars and black umbrella pines, all against the background of dazzling mountains, blue sky, and the radiance of the southern air. Madame Raevsky with Ekaterina and Elena—all three wearing long, flowering robes of white cotton with colored sashes, hair loosely bound in the back to denote the informal holiday atmosphere of the house—awaited them on the spacious terrace. The parents' quarters were on the first floor. The girls, together with the rest of the female staff, lived on the second floor; Alexander, Nikolai, and Pushkin were relegated to the attic.

"At Gurzuf I lived like a recluse," wrote Pushkin. "I bathed in the warm sea, and gorged myself on grapes; I felt immediately at home in the southern climate and luxuriated in it with all the insouciance of a Neapolitan lazzarone. There was a young cypress close to the house; every morning I went to visit it and in the end felt something akin to friendship for it . . . I lived carefree and idle days in the midst of a charming family . . . It is my dearest hope to see the southern shores and the Raevsky family again" (Pushkin's letter to his brother, September 24, 1820).

The Duc de Richelieu had left a well-stocked library in which Pushkin discovered Chénier and reread Voltaire with enthusiasm. The girls had brought Byron's *The Prisoner of Chillon*, *The Corsair*, and the first cantos of *Childe Harold*, which had arrived from England just before their departure from Kiev, probably ordered by Miss Martin. Sitting among the rocks on the shore, they jointly tried their hand at translation. When a new word puzzled them, it was usually Ekaterina, whose English was almost perfect, who scored highest. In the first part of the nineteenth century, the great works of English, German, and Italian writers, and for that matter the masterpieces of the ancients, were not yet available to Russian readers in the original texts. They were read almost exclusively in French translations of varying degrees of competence. As Nabokov remarks in his commentary to *Eugene Onegin*: "The gentleman author, the St. Petersburg fashionable, the ennuied Hussar, the civilized squire, the provincial miss in her linden-shaded château of painted wood—*all* read Shakespeare and Sterne, Richardson and Walter Scott, Moore and Byron, and even Italian romancers like

Ariosto and Tasso, in French versions and French versions only."

In 1820 in Russia, Byron was all the rage, and as everywhere in Europe, anything he did or wrote was of utmost interest. Pushkin, who was fascinated by Byron and liked to "immerse himself in the surf of his poetry," must have first read *The Corsair, Manfred,* and the beginning of *Childe Harold* in Pichot's French translation while he was still in St. Petersburg, but it is quite probable that he first heard the original version in English at Gurzuf, as read by one of the Raevsky girls.

It has often been said by Pushkin's biographers that at Gurzuf the amorous young poet fell in love with all four Raevsky girls. After all, the girls were all charming, ranging in age from Ekaterina's twenty-four down to Sophia's thirteen. Pushkin certainly admired the beautiful and haughty Ekaterina (he later modeled his character of Marina Mniszek in *Boris Godunov* on her), but she received his attentions with a detached, amiable, polite smile. He was much too young and too insignificant for her to notice. The delicate, ethereal Elena, whose parents feared for her life, spoke excellent English and French and loved to translate Byron and Walter Scott into French. But she was too shy to admit it and often tore up the pages of her work to keep it secret. Pushkin once found several pieces of paper under her window, put them together, read the verses, and congratulated Elena on her skill. But it was obvious to all that the poet's favorite was Maria, the dark, mischievous little Indian princess, or "daughter of the Ganges," as Alexander had nicknamed her, who was slowly unfolding and becoming a woman. Pushkin's real feelings for Maria, which ebbed and flowed over the next several years, have been the subject of much biographical speculation. He immortalized her childish playing with the waves in *Eugene Onegin*; he was to give her name to the heroine of *The*

Fountain of Bakhchisarai and her features to the Prisoner of the Caucasus. It is thought that *Poltava* is dedicated to Maria. All these refer to a much later period in her life. In the Arcadian days of the early Crimean autumn of 1820, Maria was not even fifteen, still in the care of her English governess and her *nyanya*. What did she think of the ardent, unorthodox youth, so different in both looks and behavior from the men she had been used to in her world? She loved his poems and she must have instinctively sensed the genius in him. Few letters from her have survived from that early period, but according to a number of references by her father in the Raevsky Archives, one can guess that even if she did not fully understand Pushkin's romantic allusions, she must have been thrilled and excited by the attention he paid her. The Crimea's magnificent scenery and blissful climate intensified all emotions; no wonder that the attentions of young Pushkin, the first man who did not treat her as a child, triggered in her an awareness of herself as a woman. That summer became a watershed for Maria. She had left Kiev as a schoolgirl, whose thoughts did not much extend beyond lessons and childish pursuits. She came back from her holiday in the Tauris prepared for her emotional life to begin.

In the meantime, however, the holidays were drawing to a close. In the last days of September, Pushkin and Nikolai left Gurzuf together, traveling along the Tauric coast to Bakhchisarai, to visit the Fountain of Tears, a monument built by the lovelorn Khan of Crimea for Countess Potocka. This visit gave rise to one of Pushkin's most lovely poems. Maria and her parents remained at Gurzuf until early October, then traveled by easy stages back to Kiev.

3

The Liberals Gather

at Kamenka

NOVEMBER 24, 1820, was the seventieth birthday of Dowager
Madame Davydov, Maria's rich grandmother. For days,
from far and wide, friends and family had been converging
on Kamenka, the impressive Davydov estate on the river Tasmin. Kamenka was a typical prosperous and hospitable
Ukrainian country manor of the period. Perched on a knoll
overlooking the river, it was surrounded by a huge park, at the
end of which was a village dominated by its onion-domed
church. Though it lay in the heart of the monotonous Ukrainian
steppe, the surrounding countryside was exceptionally varied,
cut up by hillocks, coppices, and forest glades. The house itself
was large, spacious, and renowned for its comfort. There was a
large library, a billiards room, and a ballroom; there was also a
serf orchestra with excellent singers trained in Moscow, and
good food and vintage wines chosen with loving care by the

gourmet of the family, Alexander Davydov, the older of the two Davydov brothers. Maria's grandmother, now a widow, presided over a house full of children, nephews, nieces, family friends, old relations who remembered the days of Potemkin, and assorted "distinguished parasites" who, as often happened in Russia, came to visit for a few days and remained for months or even years.

Mme Davydov was tall and regal, with almond-shaped dark eyes and steel-gray hair drawn in a chignon under a lace cap. As a former lady-in-waiting to Empress Catherine, she wore a brooch with the empress's initials set in diamonds, pinned on the bosom of her voluminous, richly flowing robes. On feast days, the noble dame had a salute fired from her private cannon. Maria loved her grandmother, who always called her Mashenka and talked to her in faultless, idiomatic French learned from aristocratic French émigrés at the court of Empress Catherine. Babushka ("Granny") was warm and jolly, with her deep-throated laughter and large, comfortable bosom, to which she pressed her grandchildren. It made up for Maria's own mother's vagueness, for Sophia, as her daughters had always been well aware, had eyes only for her husband and her older son, Alexander. Often, when the family was alone, Sophia would rise from a chair, cross the room to where Alexander or her husband was sitting, take either of them by the hand, and squeeze it with affection, while ignoring the girls' and Nikolai's presence in the room. Sophia was not a bad mother, they all loved her, but there never was any doubt as to where her priorities lay. But Grandmother Davydov, though to strangers she might appear formidable, was all love, softness, and laughter to her family.

Kamenka was like a second home to Maria ever since she was a small child. She loved the huge, sprawling house, with its long, outside verandas, on which the children were put out to sleep in the summer heat; the immense park filled with grottoes, rookeries, Chinese pagodas, and mysterious little stone temples, collected by successive generations of Davydovs. She loved the bustle and excitement of the large patriarchal establishment, and the smiling family retainers who greeted the children with such warmth.

Of the two Davydov uncles, the younger, twenty-eight-year-old Basil, nicknamed Vasya, was a war hero; good-looking and cheerful, he was active in politics and had many connections in the liberal circles of Moscow and St. Petersburg. His older brother, Alexander, forty-three, was a very different person. A truly Falstaffian figure, he was famous throughout the Ukraine for his gourmet tastes and marital misfortunes. In 1815, in the final stages of the Napoleonic Wars, while serving with the army in France, he asked to be garrisoned in a town of high gastronomic repute. He was sent to Dijon, in Burgundy, and there met and married Aglée de Gramont, a plump, fresh-complexioned young widow of aristocratic family, who had grown up in the worldly Parisian atmosphere of the Boulevard Saint-Germain. Brought home and installed at Kamenka, in the sleepy Ukrainian countryside, and forced to live under the wing of her charming but overpowering mother-in-law, poor Aglée, like a character from Chekhov, suffered from intense boredom. She craved fun and masculine attention and was only happy when surrounded by admirers. Her pert nose and "pouting, velvety mouth" turned the head of every male visitor to Kamenka, from generals down to cornets. Aglaya was quite generous with her favors, and her husband, whom everyone liked, became affectionately known through the district as that "magnificent cuckold." "She is as good as a harem," remarked Pushkin, who was ten years her junior, after a prolonged flirtation during one of his visits to Kamenka. With all her frivolity, Aglée was a warm and generous person; and there was something childlike about her which young people found particularly attractive. Maria was very fond of her French aunt; they played duets together on the piano and sang with the music master, Monsieur Serre, and Aglée also taught her how to do her hair prettily with a velvet ribbon, according to the latest Paris way.

This autumn's festivities at Kamenka promised to be particularly splendid, for besides Mme Davydov's seventieth birthday, there was an additional reason for celebration. The dowager's eldest granddaughter, the beautiful Ekaterina Raevsky, was about to announce her engagement to Mikhail Orlov, the tsar's favorite aide, one of the richest and most attractive men in all Russia. An illegitimate son of the youngest of the six famous Orlov brothers at the court of the Empress Catherine, Mikhail Orlov was a well-known and admired romantic figure. It was he who had negotiated the surrender of Paris to the allied armies in the spring of 1814. It had been a difficult assignment for a relatively inexperienced young man, for the Russian emperor was intent on sparing the feelings of the vanquished Parisians. But Orlov's handsome face, distinguished bearing, great tact, and impeccable French made him a popular messenger. As he rode back to the Russian lines with the act of capitulation signed and sealed, the Emperor Alexander rushed out to embrace him, exclaiming: "Your name will forever be associated with this event." The greatest honors and distinctions seemed to be his for the asking; his career stretched before him like a luminous upland path. But there was one obstacle to his progress: Mikhail Orlov was an ardent liberal.

In 1816, at twenty-six, shortly after his return from the campaign and still basking in imperial favor, he submitted a memorandum to Tsar Alexander, urging emancipation of the serfs. It remained unanswered. He then proceeded to form a secret association, the Society of Russian Knights, which was to "assist the tsar in carrying out constitutional reforms in the country." In those early days, Orlov's intentions were not revolutionary, far from it. He even contemplated sending the projected charter of his society to the tsar for comment. (He never got around to it, however.) That same year he joined the influential literary club, the Arzamas, and soon became known for outspoken speeches and what were then called "subversive remarks." All of this, secret police agents duly reported to the tsar. Alexander, however, was fond of Orlov and tended to dismiss such reports as exaggerated. But Orlov was pushing his luck. In late 1818, he had drafted a secret memorandum criticizing Alexander's policy toward Poland. Summoned to the presence of the tsar, he refused to show the text because he did not want to compromise other sponsors. Understandably, the emperor became angry: he never forgave this act of defiance, which confirmed his suspicions that Orlov was an "incorrigible liberal." Orlov was relegated to a provincial command in Kiev, where he became immensely popular with his troops. Upon taking command of a division in General Wittgenstein's Second Army, he issued an order of the day which according to contemporary notices caused a "real sensation": "I will regard as a scoundrel any officer who, following the dictates of blind fury, takes advantage of the authority vested upon him in order to torture his men." It was a sad commentary on prevailing conditions in the Russian army that this simple, humane pronouncement should have caused such a stir; but from then on, Orlov was a god to his men.

It was in Kiev, during the 1819 carnival season, the first winter of his so-called exile, that Orlov and Ekaterina met and fell in love. On the surface, it seemed like a splendid match for Ekaterina; here was a romantic hero, straight from Byron, dashing, handsome, universally admired and respected, brilliant and fabulously rich and, though much younger, a companion-in-arms of her father. But the old general remained worried. Somewhere along the path to military glory, the ideas he had cherished in his youth got left behind. He did not trust the new liberal ideas and the much discussed associations his future son-in-law was said to belong to. Was it true that Orlov had been known to mix with people dedicated to the overthrow of the tsar? That was too much. A Raevsky could never tolerate sedition in his family.

When Orlov formally presented himself with a request for Ekaterina's hand, the general demanded that he give up his hare-brained schemes and ideas "forthwith." It was a precondition without which he would not agree to the marriage. Orlov asked for time to reflect, but according to contemporary correspondence, he does not seem to have been unduly worried by his prospective father-in-law's arbitrary stance. As a man of the world, he disliked making drastic decisions under pressure. He was in love and wanted to press on with his suit, but he also had to keep faith with fellow conspirators in St. Petersburg and Moscow. He believed that if he avoided firm commitments the matter could somehow be settled to everyone's satisfaction, without his being called upon to make a choice. They agreed to defer the formal announcement of the engagement until February. Only the family were to be told at Kamenka; and in the meantime, preparations for the wedding were to go on.

Handsome Orlov was not alone in indulging in what Maria's father called "those silly, delicious dreams, which are bound to end in Siberia." There were hundreds of men of similar social background and upbringing who shared his views, all intent on reforming the way of life in their country by introducing constitutional changes that would curb the autocratic power of the tsar. Their first objective was the abolition of serfdom, "our national disgrace," as they called it.

In the generation before them, a handful of outstanding men, fired by the ideas of the French Revolution, had called for the abolition of slavery and a reform of corrupt bureaucracy.

Alexander Radishchev was a young, idealistic landowner who, while at the University of Leipzig, had come under the influence of Rousseau. He gave a horrifying description of serfdom as "a condition that creates a gulf equal to that between men and animals." His book *Journey from St. Petersburg to Moscow* so infuriated Empress Catherine that she ordered him to be exiled to Siberia. The publicist Novikov, who pioneered primary schools and famine relief in Russia, was declared a Jacobin and thrown into the Schlusselburg Fortress for the "subversive nature of his writings." They were the first in a procession of talented Russian intellectuals who dared to say what they thought and were severely punished for it.

Orlov's generation came of age in the Napoleonic campaign. When they returned with their troops, "having liberated Europe from the tyrant," their desire for radical reforms was reinforced by everything they had seen while abroad. In the words of a contemporary, "There was only one subject of conversation in the army from generals down to the humblest private—how wonderful life was abroad." Since the days of Peter the Great, Western Europe had always held special appeal for the Russians, but this time it was not only the variety of landscapes, or the amazing prosperity of the French or German countryside, or the joys of Paris; it was the atmosphere of freedom and relaxation, the uninhibited, uncensored writing and discussion, that made a lasting impression on them. That freedom was of course relative; both in Napoleonic France and in Metternich's Austria, serious restrictions were in force, but compared with the rigidity of the Russian system, living there was like living in an intellectual paradise.

Listen to Ivan Yakushkin, a young sub-lieutenant in the elite Semenovsky Foot Guards: "I was attached to the First Division garrisoned in Oranienbaum [one of the tsar's suburban residences on the Gulf of Finland] when it arrived home from

France. During the solemn *Te Deum*, the police brutally man-handled the crowds, who tried to get nearer to the homecoming troops. A few hours later, I was standing with a fellow officer close to the ornate arch of triumph, topped with six alabaster horses, which had been newly erected to celebrate the victory. The Dowager Empress Maria was there in her gilt carriage, watching the approaching regiments. We were just about to re-mark on how splendid and dashing our Emperor looked as he lowered his sword to salute his mother, when a luckless peasant happened to run across the road before the oncoming column. Wrenching his horse forward and brandishing his sword, the Tsar started off in hot pursuit, while the police showered the poor, cringing fellow with blows. We simply couldn't believe our eyes. We felt so ashamed for our beloved Tsar that we turned away . . . I couldn't help recalling the story of the cat which was turned into a fair maiden and lived happily ever after, except that she could never see a mouse without chasing it."

To those who had never been outside Russia, such incidents, without, of course, involving the tsar, were a matter of daily occurrence. Most people were inured to them; yet, to those who had just returned from abroad, they were shameful. What particularly upset Yakushkin and his friends was that the man who had acted in such a cruel, inhuman way was their monarch, the same Tsar Alexander who only a few months before had magnanimously restored freedom to defeated France, saving her from Austrian reprisals and Bourbon spite. They recalled him riding his pale gray horse into conquered Paris on that sunny summer day, how he had been acclaimed by all as the modern Agamemnon, the living symbol of the noble cause that had just been fought. That day marked the zenith of Russia's fame and Alexander's personal popularity. They had been proud of their tsar-liberator; they had really believed that a happy future lay in store for the vast Russian empire, its splendid ruler, and all the idealistic young men who had ridden to war at his side. In those halcyon days—only such a short time ago, it seemed—everything had been patriotic fervor and pride, but now disappointment had set in.

Just before returning to Russia, Tsar Alexander, at Metternich's instigation, was persuaded to join the Holy Alliance, an association of states dedicated to perpetuating monarchy's absolute rule. As a result, most of the liberal reforms which had been initiated and introduced before the 1812 war were now abruptly dropped. Instead of emancipating the serfs in recognition of the people's heroism and sacrifices during the great patriotic war, the government was now rushing the establishment of military settlements, which were to enslave the wretched conscripts still further. And while Alexander traveled from one diplomatic congress to another as a self-appointed leader of European reaction, the real ruler of Russia was his grim confidant, Count Arakcheev.

As it happened, the early nineteenth century was the era of patriotic associations everywhere. There was the Tugendbund in Germany, dedicated to the revival of Prussia; the Carbonari in Italy, scheming to expel the Austrians from their land; and masonic lodges were mushrooming all over Europe. In the wake of the recent upheavals caused by the Napoleonic Wars, there seemed to be a widely shared desire for working in associations for the good of one's fellows. In Russia, men like Orlov, Yakushkin, and their friends, who stood out among the generally frivolous society of the day, joined with Alexander Muraviev, a gifted young colonel on the general staff; Pavel Pestel, a fiery idealist; and several others in a secret society. It was first called the Union of Salvation, later transformed into the Union of Common Weal, or Welfare. At first, their meetings took place in Moscow and St. Petersburg, but when in the autumn of 1820 the Semenovsky Regiment mutinied and the tsar, suspecting a plot, ordered its officer corps dispersed, many of the most active members of the conspiracy found themselves in the south, attached to General Wittgenstein's headquarters in Kishinev. It was important for the two branches of the conspiracy to remain in touch, and as a Moscow reunion was planned for the beginning of next year, Yakushkin was dispatched to Kishinev to invite Orlov and a few other kindred spirits to attend it.

On November 20, 1820, a morning of sparkling frost and light mists, General Mikhail Orlov was on his way to Kamenka to attend Mme Davydov's birthday party. As he later recalled: "Reclining in my comfortable dormeuse, I was dreaming of duck shooting and of Ekaterina." At a roadside post station he unexpectedly ran into Yakushkin, who a few days previously had set out from Moscow to contact him. Though the two men were aware of each other's activities, they were not well acquainted. Ivan Yakushkin, who owned vast agricultural estates in Smolensk, was intent on abolishing all serfdom. His own peasants were forbidden to prostrate themselves before him, as was the custom elsewhere; instead, he encouraged them to approach him informally whenever they needed help or advice. Much to the surprise of other landlords, Yakushkin refused to sell any of his own serfs, no matter how tempting the price. He caused a sensation in the county by refusing an offer of four thousand rubles, a small fortune, from a neighboring landowner for a talented serf musician; he gave him his freedom instead. Having failed to obtain the government's consent to release all his peasants from bondage under the so-called Free Plowman's Act, he continued to grant freedom to individual serfs whenever the occasion arose. Tall, vivacious, with unruly brown hair and a charming, musical voice, Yakushkin was less polished than Orlov and not as well educated, but he made up for it by an extraordinarily creative, quicksilver mind, of which he was very proud. According to Yakushkin's memoirs, the two men got along famously. Yakushkin was charmed by Orlov's winning manner, his erudition and splendid appearance, though—as might have been expected—he found the general's reputation for intelligence "somewhat overrated."

Orlov invited his new friend to accompany him to Kamenka, where they could further discuss their secret plans. Though averse to social gatherings, "I let myself be persuaded for the cause," wrote Yakushkin, and they drove on to Kamenka in Orlov's comfortable equipage, over the barely defined tracks in the steppe, amid the swaying red and golden grasses, now in the full glory of their autumnal hues. After crossing the Dnieper, they followed the river Tasmin for a while, and suddenly on the other side of the river the estate of Kamenka rose before them, the onion dome of its church glinting in the late November sunshine.

Maria, with her mother and three sisters, had arrived at Kamenka two days before. As their carriage drove up to the colonnaded entrance, young Uncle Vasya came onto the terrace beaming, arms outstretched. Behind him, in rapid succession, came Alexander, the "magnificent cuckold," fat and cheerful; and Aglée, dressed according to the latest Paris fashion and excited at the prospect of a large, predominantly male house party. A surprise was in store for Maria: as she walked through the familiar rooms to see whether any changes had taken place since her last visit—a ritual she performed each time she came to Kamenka—she found in the old billiards room, lying on his stomach on the huge table, her friend Pushkin; he was writing furiously, in a state of creative intensity. Sheets of paper were scattered all around him and he seemed totally oblivious to his surroundings; *The Prisoner of the Caucasus*, inspired by his recent visit, was taking shape. He had hitched a ride with Nikolai, Maria's brother, a few days earlier, having managed to obtain another "short leave" from the long-suffering General Insov in Kishinev. And all the way—as he recalled in his memoirs—"I was excited at the prospect of seeing Mashenka, my wonderful muse," and the rest of the Raevsky family again.

Though Maria was thrilled to see Pushkin, and was in raptures over the free-flowing verses of *The Prisoner*, not everyone in the house party shared her pleasure. The poet's lack of discretion was well known, and as every liberal for miles around was due to arrive at Kamenka, ostensibly to extend birthday wishes to the chatelaine but really to formulate ideas and discuss plans, the presence of "that irresponsibly babbling youth" was unwelcome. Orlov's joy at his long-awaited reunion with Ekaterina was somewhat marred by the sudden appearance of "the brat." Yakushkin was frankly alarmed, and Uncle Vasya, himself an influential member of the southern Union, roundly berated Nikolai for bringing his talkative friend to the house at such an inopportune time. Such an attitude might not have been quite fair to the young poet. He was soon to outdistance them all with the gigantic strides of his genius, but his violent changes of mood, his irascibility, his tendency to associate with unreliable characters—all this frightened even his closest friends. "Each time I thought of telling him about the society," wrote Jeannot Pushchin, one of his most devoted friends from the days of the Imperial Lyceum at Tsarskoe Selo, "I found myself loath to entrust him with a secret which was no longer mine alone, since the most trifling imprudence on his part might have jeopardized the whole venture."

Pushkin sensed that something was stirring, and it enraged him not to know. The friendship of what was known in St. Petersburg as the "intelligent society," many of whom formed the backbone of the Union of Welfare, meant even more to him than the goodwill of court circles. And yet, no matter how many revolutionary poems he wrote, no matter how often he was sent into exile, still they wouldn't trust him. They drank with him, they declaimed and rejoiced in his subversive poems, they gave him comradely pats on the shoulder, but that was all. He was denied entry into crucial negotiations; in the very thick of conspiracy, he was rejected by the conspirators and it drove him wild.

And so it was at Kamenka. Here again, as earlier in St. Petersburg, Pushkin came to suspect the existence of a secret society. Why were so many military men, both active and retired, gathered there at the same time? Surely men like Orlov, Yakushkin, and Okhotnikov, a known liberal, were not there together by accident?

Yakushkin describes in his memoirs how a little comedy was staged to put Pushkin off the scent. Meeting in Vasya Davydov's room one night, they pretended to argue whether it might not be a good thing to organize a secret society in Russia. To make it seem more convincing, they elected old General Raevsky to preside over the debate. He took it all very seriously, armed himself with a bell, and conducted the discussions according to the rules of the game. Orlov, wary of his prospective father-in-law, produced arguments both in favor of and against the society. Pushkin passionately advocated its usefulness. Yakushkin objected. General Raevsky spoke mildly in favor, arguing that such a society "could be" of service to the country. "Let us assume," said Yakushkin, "that such a society already exists. Would you join it? Surely not you, General!" "On the contrary," said Raevsky, "I would probably join it." "Well then, shake hands," said Yakushkin. But when Raevsky extended his hand, Yakushkin and others burst out laughing. "I was of course just speaking in fun," he said. The others joined in the merriment. Pushkin alone remained tense. Then he stood up, crimson in the face. "For a moment I thought my life would assume a high purpose, but now I see it was all a cruel joke," he exclaimed. "I have never been more unhappy." "In that instant," Yakushkin recalled rue-fully, "he was truly magnificent and we felt guilty."*

Maria was totally unaware of the historical importance of what went on around her. The seeds of the conspiracy, so casu-ally sown into the fertile intellectual atmosphere of Kamenka, spawned events which were to destroy her life five years later. Though several of the protagonists in the drama were gathered under her grandmother's roof, blissfully unaware of the fate that awaited them, the man who was to be responsible for her own personal tragedy had not yet made his appearance.

In the meantime, there was much to enjoy at Kamenka. There were the early-morning duck shoots in the marshes on the shores of the Tasmin, mushroom-picking expeditions in the glades on the edge of the immense park, horseback rides along the Dnieper and into the surrounding steppe, outdoor camping in the frosty November air, music and dancing at night. And over all this fun, serious and secret talks, and Aglée's flirta-tions, spread the gentle glow of Orlov and Ekaterina's love. They had grown very close during that week, and what an ex-ceptionally handsome couple they made. Maria noticed how her grandmother's eyes followed her beautiful older sister with deep satisfaction. With everybody, including her parents, her grand-mother, even her English governess, Miss Martin, and the old *nyanya*, concentrating on Ekaterina's coming wedding, Maria was left to her own devices. Few had time to notice that the skinny, freckle-faced child had grown into a lovely young girl. She herself was secretly aware of it, and since her return from

---

* A letter from M. S. Volkonsky to L. N. Maikov has recently been found in the Pushkin Archives in Leningrad, stating that Prince Volkonsky was at one time asked by the society to enlist Pushkin into the conspiracy, but he deliberately refrained from carrying out the instruction in order to protect him from danger. (Memoirs of Volkonsky's grandson)

the Crimea she had been looking into the mirror from time to time, taking pleasure in the shape of her face, the sheen on her blue-black curling hair, which now reached almost to her knees. Hers was a nature in which imagination played an important, even a key role, and Pushkin's courtship the previous summer, his half-serious, half-affectionate banter, had heightened the romantic streak in her. Nurtured on Byron since the age of nine, she fell into the habit of composing poems and ballads and fairy tales in which she was the beautiful and sometimes misunderstood heroine. Like most girls of her age, she dreamed of an all-sweeping passion for a young man, whom she would follow to the ends of the earth. Since the Crimea, that young man had been Pushkin, but at Kamenka his image became somewhat marred. Was it because of his ostentatious flirtations with Aglée, or because he seemed to be constantly distracted by every pretty face, including Aglée's twelve-year-old daughter Adele? "I realized that as a poet he likes and loves all women," she wisely wrote in her memoirs, an unusually shrewd observation for a girl who was not yet fifteen. Strangely enough, it was Pushkin's love which outlasted Maria's.

After a late-evening reception and a concert on the night of Mme Davydov's birthday, which Maria was allowed to attend for the first time in her life, the guests gradually dispersed. The Raevskys went back to Kiev for Christmas. Only Pushkin remained at Kamenka, ensconced in the billiards room, writing. *The Prisoner of the Caucasus*, the story of a Russian soldier helped to freedom by a beautiful Circassian girl, was completed by the end of February 1821. Pushkin's leave was now more than three months overdue; he had to return to the dreary existence of the provincial garrison town and face his angry superiors once again.

Ekaterina's marriage to Orlov took place on April 20, 1821, in Kiev's splendid Church of St. Andrew, built by Rastrelli.

Banks of early spring flowers and huge tubs of Crimean lilies sent from Gurzuf filled the church with fragrance. Following the custom of the day, a great ball was given by the Raevskys at the Nobility Club in Kiev. Maria, in a white muslin dress with blue flowers, a flowing red scarf around her shoulders, attracted much attention at the ball with her exquisite dancing and the "luminous sparkle of her dark eyes." The ball marked the appearance of the first suitor for Maria's hand. His name was Count Gustav Olizar, a twenty-four-year-old Polish nobleman, owner of vast estates near Zhitomir, the grain capital of the Ukraine. He was known to the family, having been a frequent visitor to the Raevsky house in Khorevaya Ulitsa. "I remembered her as a dark, skinny child, exhausted by her teachers and governesses," Olizar wrote in his memoirs, "and then there she was on the dance floor, her wonderful fiery eyes framed by heavy dark lashes, which seemed to have suddenly 'sprouted out,' each movement graceful and flowing . . . a lovely, exotic child woman."

Gustav Olizar was a typical product of the Ukraine—that odd, forever shifting borderland between the West, as represented by Poland, and the entirely different culture of the Russian East. His roots were firmly implanted in the fertile soil of the Ukraine; all of his considerable wealth came from it. As marshal of the local nobility, predominantly composed of Russian landlords, he owed allegiance to the Russian tsar; his command of the Russian language was faultless. Yet he thought of himself as a Pole and was an undiluted product of Western culture. Educated first by private tutors and later at the prestigious Lycée of Lvov in eastern Poland, he also spoke perfect French and Italian, as well as German; he translated from Latin into Polish and wrote French poetry, inspired by the fables of La Fontaine. Shortly after his eighteenth birthday, he set off on a protracted tour of Italy and returned, much to everybody's surprise, with a

French bride, who herself was barely out of her teens. Caroline Mollo, whose family had been ardent Bonapartists and as such had to leave France after the fall of the empire, was employed as a *lectrice*, or reader, in the Roman household of Pauline Borghese, the beautiful youngest sister of the defeated emperor. Times were hard for members of Napoleon's family and their sympathizers. Only the prudent Madame Mère had managed to save enough for a rainy day; everyone else was in dire straits. The arrival of a handsome young Polish count, reputed to be very rich, caused a high degree of interest among the small contingent of French mothers, clustered around Pauline and Madame Mère, who despaired of ever finding suitable husbands for their eminently nubile daughters. It wasn't long before young Olizar was hooked. After some judicious scheming on the part of Caroline's mother, and with the active encouragement of Princess Pauline, the two young people met, fell in love, and were married. Cardinal Fesch, Napoleon's famous uncle, officiated at the wedding ceremony in the presence of Madame Laetizia and members of Napoleon's family. The couple left for the Ukraine two weeks later, accompanied by Caroline's mother, who expected her young son-in-law to provide her with a separate establishment on his estates. They seemed to have been genuinely fond of each other, but no amount of love could bridge the gap between the beauties of old Rome and the muddy, monotonous countryside of Zhitomir. Disappointment set in almost at once, quarrels and recriminations began, and after two years of the "most intense boredom in the accursed, limitless countryside," Caroline left for Rome, taking their two baby daughters with her. An amiable divorce was obtained, with ample provision for the children. At twenty-three, Olizar found himself alone and surprisingly keen to try matrimony again.

As an old family friend, now with the aura of the great world and an unhappy romance about him, young Olizar became a popular visitor at the Raevskys', always ready to escort the girls to the theater, dance attendance on them at the balls, or partner Maria on the skating rink during the clear, sunny days of the winter. In December 1822, a few days after Maria's seventeenth birthday, a letter on heavy vellum, sealed with the Olizar family crest, was delivered to General Raevsky's residence by the count's personal servant. It contained a request for Maria's hand in marriage. The Raevsky Archives do not tell us whether the general discussed the matter with his daughter. Of all the children, Maria was the one closest to him, and he must have suspected that she was not in love with Olizar, however much she enjoyed his attention. But the letter he wrote to the young suitor, which is quoted in Olizar's memoirs, gives a fascinating illustration of the complex Russian–Polish relations of the period. It is also a tribute to Raevsky's wisdom and kindness of heart.

My dear Count,

In the course of my long life I have rarely been faced with a task as difficult as writing this reply to your letter—the arrival of which, I must confess, I have been dreading for some time. It distresses me to have to give a negative answer to your request, for you must be well aware of how much I like and esteem you. There are grave and to me insurmountable obstacles to this union, the most important of which is the difference between your two religions and your very different attitude to what constitutes duty in this life. But the most insurmountable barrier is the one between our two nationalities. As time goes on, you would find it irreconcilable . . .

I shall remain, dear Count, your most devoted friend

Nikolai Nikolaevich Raevsky

Poor, disappointed Count Olizar. He gathered up his sadness and his broken heart and, following the fashion of the day, went off to the Crimea to meditate and write sonnets. In time, he became a substantial Crimean landowner, built a large house by the sea, which he named Kardya (Greek for "heart") for Maria. They met again only once, thirty-four years later in Dresden, shortly after Maria's return from Siberia.

In the meantime, Prince Volkonsky had appeared on the scene.

4

Sergei

PRINCE SERGEI VOLKONSKY bore one of the noblest names in Russia; his family's origins stemmed from the ninth-century Prince Rurik and a long line of feudal overlords. The title was among the top ten in the hierarchy of princes of the Russian empire. They were a family whose roots were entwined with those of their native country; their immense wealth came from land tilled by thousands of serfs. Behind them, stretching back through many reigns, lay a great tradition of service; they were Russian magnates who let nothing, not even the tsar, interfere with what they believed was their duty toward their country and their high estate.

Volkonsky men had been distinguished generals, army commanders, governors of far-flung provinces, holders of high crown offices. The Volkonsky women had worn the scarlet ribbon and star—the Order of St. Catherine—the mark of esteem and friendship on the part of successive empresses. Sergei's father, Prince Grigory, an eccentric, was Governor of Orenburg Province, while his mother, Princess Alexandra, was Mistress of the Robes to the Dowager Empress (the widow of the murdered Tsar Paul), and her closest friend. Prince Sergei's brother-in-law, General Prince Peter Volkonsky (from a different branch, married to Sergei's sister Sophia), was Emperor Alexander's trusted adviser and constant traveling companion.

"Monsieur Sergei," as Volkonsky was known to his friends, was born in St. Petersburg in the family palace on the Moika on December 8, 1788, the third of three Volkonsky brothers. The eldest brother, Nikolai Grigorievich, took the family name of Prince Repnin after the death of their maternal grandfather, Alexander Repnin, who had no sons of his own and arranged for the title and estates to be passed on to his grandson. The second brother, Nikita, was the husband of Princess Zenaida Volkonsky, a famous hostess, patron of the arts, and owner of the Villa Volkonsky in Rome. Young Sergei was educated at home by private tutors, but from the age of twelve attended Abbot Dominik Nikola's Institute on the Fontanka, a fashionable school started by French émigrés after the Revolution, and patronized by the sons of St. Petersburg's society. One of Sergei's companions at games was Alexander Benckendorff, the future head of police, who twenty-five years later signed the decree exiling Sergei to Siberia. The abbot provided an excellent education within traditionally narrow classical lines. "He taught me self-discipline and a great respect for memory," wrote Sergei some years later. "I emerged steeped in French culture, speaking French like a native, but almost a foreigner in my own country."

After a short spell in the Corps des Pages and then in the First Cadet Corps—there never was any question that he should follow any other career but the army—he joined a cavalry regiment and received his baptism of fire during the first Russian campaign against Napoleon's forces in Poland in the early days of 1807. The battle of Eylau, fought among the deep birchwood forests of east Prussia on a day of smothering blizzard, is remembered as one of the most terrifying of the Napoleonic campaign; the casualties on both sides were calamitous. It was the first time that the victorious progress of the Grande Armée had been halted. The eighteen-year-old cornet Volkonsky was wounded from a bullet in his side. He had fought bravely and well and was awarded a gold medal for courage. Soon after, as a result of some gentle lobbying at court on the part of his mother, young Volkonsky was transferred to the imperial headquarters to join the elite group of aristocratic young men selected as aides-de-camp to the tsar.

At Tilsit, where the French and Russian emperors met in the middle of the river Niemen, Volkonsky first came into contact with the famous General Nikolai Nikolaevich Raevsky, the military hero, revered by the troops and now close adviser to the tsar in the complex negotiations with Napoleon. "He became my friend and my confidant," wrote Volkonsky in his memoirs. "I met him at a crucial time in my life, when I very much needed to consult with someone older and wiser than myself with whom I could discuss the avalanche of new impressions that all of a sudden had overwhelmed me. Little could I have guessed at the time that the great warrior of the days of Catherine the Great, who so kindly found time to listen to my youthful outpourings, would one day become my father-in-law . . ."

That "avalanche of new impressions" resulted from his association with the French officers at Tilsit; it transformed Volkonsky's outlook on the world. How free and outspoken they were, those sons of the French Revolution; what splendid soldiers they were, and how admirable was a military system that made it possible for non-commissioned officers to become marshals of France. And how protective they were of rank and file, more like brothers than stern military superiors. The gigantic sacrifices of Russian soldiers, their huge death toll, remained forever unrewarded. But the Grande Armée was Napoleon's pride; its welfare was a constant concern of his generals. There was fervor and excitement about those young Napoleonic eagles; they were the heroes of the century, and they knew it. Time and again, when riding alone in the country, Sergei would find himself whistling the *Marseillaise* under his breath—that joyful tune which had led thousands of young soldiers to glory and death.

While at Tilsit, Sergei came into contact with two older French officers who had served with Lafayette in the American War of Independence and had fought at the battle of Yorktown. Their stories of the new country across the seas, the perfect democracy where all citizens had equal rights, fascinated Volkonsky; he determined to go to France the moment peace was declared and from there to embark for the New World. All of a sudden, Russia appeared suffocating to him. But such plans had to wait, for there were several more years of soldiering before him: the Swedish campaign; fighting the Turks under Bagration's command in Moldavia; being wounded at the siege of Silistra, and spending a year recovering in Bucharest; finally, being sent home to St. Petersburg, where he was once again appointed aide to the tsar, this time with the rank of major general. (There was always a proliferation of major generals in the Russian army in tsarist times.)

At twenty-four, Prince Sergei was a pleasant-looking young man with the distinguished features and aristocratic bearing of his family. Of medium height, very fair, with blue eyes and small hands and feet, he had a charming voice and a most agreeable social manner. He was not a commanding personality like his older brother, Repnin, the apotheosis of the Volkonsky family. There was a certain weakness in the Byronic features, a dreaminess about the eyes, an occasional hesitancy and lack of decision in matters of everyday life. "The boy hasn't got enough steel in him," thundered his father, the old prince, after Sergei had paid him a long visit. "He *thinks* too much—you must stop him from reading all that romantic drivel from abroad!" he wrote angrily to his wife. But the young Prince Volkonsky was unwilling to abandon his new world of ideas, even to please his father. He continued to read avidly, both in French and in English, much at the expense of his social life—"that empty day-to-day court routine," he called it.

Napoleon's invasion of Russia was a painful shock to Volkonsky, as it was to the majority of Frenchified Russian nobles. But it also evoked an immediate surge of patriotic feeling for "Holy Russia" and the tsar. Sergei asked to rejoin the army in the field, fought with Bagration at Mogilev, and after the fall of Moscow waged a relentless partisan campaign at the head of the Astrakhan Cossacks against the retreating French army. The "heroes of the century" of Tilsit days had now become a hungry, half-frozen rabble, fleeing westward. One thing only mattered to Prince Sergei—to drive them beyond the borders of Russia.

After Napoleon's abdication at Fontainebleau, it seemed that peace had been restored for years to come; it was a good moment to apply for an extended leave from the army and start traveling. With twenty thousand gold rubles from Princess Alexandra (an enormous sum in those days), who insisted that her son should travel in style—accompanied by two manservants and a driver—Prince Sergei set off for Vienna, where the Congress was then in full swing. And so was the mad social round, more hectic than even St. Petersburg at the height of the season. He stayed with the beautiful Princess Bagration, thirty-two-year-old widow of the heroic general, a great favorite of the tsar, and one of the leading hostesses at the Congress. Sergei enjoyed a ringside view of the political drama, fraught with intrigues, shifting alliances, and endless amorous escapades—the air and substance of the Congress. He remained only ten days, long enough to collect letters of introduction from Talleyrand to a wide assortment of intellectuals and politicians in Paris. While there, he spent most of his time in the company of Chateaubriand and Benjamin Constant. In the salon of the Duchesse de St.-Leu, frequented by a crowd of Bonapartists, he renewed many friendships of Tilsit days. It was as if the invasion of Russia had never happened, for in those days friendships and social relations between certain classes of society in different countries were maintained in spite of wars, conquests, or change of frontiers.

Next it was London, at the Riga Hotel in St. James's Square, and visits to Parliament, where he listened to some amazingly frank debates on the state of madness of the reigning monarch, an extraordinary experience for a Russian. For this was Regency London, when George III's madness was freely talked about everywhere and scurrilous broadsheets were handed out on street corners. It produced an indelible impression on Volkonsky. Through his contacts he met several members of His Majesty's loyal Opposition, weekended in the lovely countryside, and for at least a few weeks led the carefree existence of a young Regency buck. At the house of Princess Lieven, the wife of the Russian ambassador, Sergei ran into an old friend, Sir Robert Wilson, the English military observer sent to Russia during the 1812 war. Together they made plans to visit the United States, an idea that had been constantly on his mind since he met Lafayette's companions-at-arms in Tilsit eight years before. "I was determined to spend some time in a country where the idea of a free, responsible citizen had fully been put into practice," he reminisced in his memoirs. "I was young, rich, and uncommitted —it seemed the perfect time for a voyage of discovery." But the voyage was not in the cards. On a day of spring sunshine in late March, while crossing St. James's Square on his way to lunch in

Piccadilly, he was hailed by an excited Sir Robert Wilson with the news of Napoleon's return from Elba. The war was to be resumed, and his place was with the Russian troops.

Volkonsky joined Tsar Alexander in Frankfurt, but did not go to Paris with him. He returned to Russia, instead, after Waterloo, and spent a year with a guards regiment in St. Petersburg and then was given a senior command near Zhitomir in the Ukraine. The next few years were to be crucial in Sergei's life. It was inevitable that a man of his temperament, imbued with liberal ideas, a patriot with a family's tradition of service to his country, should find kindred souls among the members of the Union of Welfare. He had known Mikhail Orlov for years. They were approximately the same age and, like many of St. Petersburg's young bloods, had been members of the same masonic lodge before Sergei went abroad. Now he found him again in Kiev, still under discreet police supervision, older, wiser, but ideologically unchanged. (Orlov decided to leave the conspiracy before the fatal events of December 1825, partly because of his marriage to Ekaterina Raevsky and partly because he became disillusioned with the confusion of aims and the rivalry between the main factions. He thus saved himself and his family from exile.)

Mikhail Orlov was the first link, but the man who captured Sergei's imagination and turned him into a full-fledged conspirator was Lieutenant Colonel Pavel Ivanovich Pestel, an intellectual, and a natural leader bursting with vitality and a passion for politics. Born into a country where only one leader could be recognized and where democratic politics were forbidden, he inevitably resorted to conspiracy to implement his own radical ideas. Five years younger than Volkonsky, he was born in 1793 (the year of Thermidor), joined the Union at twenty-three, and a year later took complete control of the organization in the south. The son of a notoriously corrupt and brutal Governor

General of western Siberia (who had been nicknamed "the Monster" and nearly ended up in Siberia himself for his misdemeanors), he had been educated in Germany before winning outstanding honors at the St. Petersburg Military Academy, where he received a personal citation from the tsar. After distinguishing himself at Borodino, he was appointed aide to General Wittgenstein, commander of the Second Army Corps in the Ukraine. Pushkin, who met Pestel in 1821, probably at Kamenka or at army headquarters in Kishinev, when he had just been promoted to command the Vyatka Regiment, called him "one of the most original minds I have encountered."

The story of the development of the Decembrist conspiracy, from 1817 to 1825, is largely the story of Pestel and his efforts to promote radical solutions and encourage those who, while accepting in principle the necessity for breaking the autocracy (including, if necessary, the murder of the tsar), were reluctant to discard historical traditions. In the context of the times, Pestel's views were genuinely revolutionary: they provided not only for the deposition of the tsar, the abolition of the monarchy, and its replacement by a republican form of government, but also for a free-enterprise, decentralized, free-trade economy. It was visionary and impractical, given Russia's economic setup, but it was faultlessly argued and exciting. It appealed to the imagination of the mild-mannered, idealistic Major General Prince Volkonsky, the officer with a brilliant future and invaluable connections at court. Pestel liked to surround himself with people who were willing to yield him the spotlight, and Volkonsky was a typical hero worshipper who was bound to become blindly devoted to one he considered his moral and intellectual superior. According to his memoirs, Sergei entered the sacred circle of Pestel's friends, the so-called nine-men cell, which in the autumn of 1819 included such gifted men as General Yushnevsky, who headed the Second Army's commissariat, and

Dr. Wolff, the surgeon general. His military duties left him plenty of time to travel on the organization's business, carrying messages and discreetly recruiting new members.

"I have never been so happy as I was in those years," Volkonsky recalled. "I had a purpose in life, as well as the companionship of the most stimulating men of the decade. I felt strong and fulfilled and hopeful for the future of my country." He even put aside his dream of seeing the New World; there was too much to do in Russia. Was he aware of how dangerous the path he had chosen might be? Several of Sergei's superiors suspected the existence of some sort of a secret society, but those who did failed to attach much importance to it. As far as they were concerned, it was just idle chatter, a bandying around of chimerical dreams. As for Sergei, the Volkonskys were known for their loyalty and deep personal devotion to the imperial family—so why worry about idle headquarters gossip? But eventually even the army's chief of staff, General Kiselev, a fine, liberal-minded man who himself believed that much in Russia needed changing and that serfdom could no longer be tolerated, became alarmed at his friend's reported activities. "Listen to me, friend Sergei," he pleaded with Volkonsky one night. "You and some of your closest friends have God knows what in mind. Forget those dreams . . . I tell you . . . All this smells of Siberia!" There is no record of how seriously this warning was taken by Volkonsky, but by then it would have been difficult for him to turn back.

It was at this crucial stage in his life that Prince Sergei met Maria Raevsky. He was spending a few months in Odessa, where, attracted by the multinational character of this fast-developing seaport, gateway to the Crimea and to Europe, he had recently bought a house. Living in Odessa at the time was Prince Sergei's sister-in-law, Princess Zenaida Volkonsky, a gifted, artistic young woman, fluent in five languages, whose house in the picturesque Turkish quarter was a center of Odessa's social life. One day, as he walked into Zenaida's drawing room, Sergei noticed standing by the ornate wooden stove a lithe, graceful young girl with the most enormous dark eyes. She was Maria Raevsky, he was told, the daughter of his old Tilsit friend, who had come to Odessa for a visit, to stay with her sister Ekaterina and Mikhail Orlov.

Opposites are said to attract. It would have been hard to imagine two human beings more different both physically and temperamentally: the soft-spoken, reflective Volkonsky, fair-skinned, blond, blue-eyed, epitome of the aristocratic northern Slav; and fiery, impetuous Maria with the skin, Oriental eyes, and quicksilver movements of a gypsy, "the daughter of the Ganges," as the family called her. For Prince Sergei it was love at first sight. It is surprising that they had never previously met. A close friend of Mikhail Orlov, Volkonsky was a frequent guest in his and Ekaterina's house, though he did not attend their wedding in Kiev (he had been on duty in St. Petersburg). But he *had* seen Maria before, for he now vaguely recalled one frosty afternoon two or three winters before, when on a short visit to Kiev he had got out of his carriage in the hills surrounding the skating ground on the frozen Dnieper and, hearing the jolly tune of the skaters' waltz, had walked down to watch the picturesque scene. He remembered how the old chestnut trees around the rink, their branches laden with snow, looked as if they had been freshly decked with festive vestments. Well-dressed people, their faces glittering, crowded the entrance. All Kiev seemed to be there, he noticed, for at that hour people who belonged to the same set and knew each other well would meet there to parade their skills on the ice. While idly looking around, Sergei noticed a dark teenage girl dressed in a long crimson skating skirt bordered with white fur, with a little muff hanging on a cord around her neck, and a fur hat. She was gliding on the smooth surface of the rink, skating effortlessly, oblivious of everything around her. The customary "shaggy footman" (*kosmoty lakei*, so called because of the fur coat he wore over his livery), without whom no young lady of noble birth ever ventured forth, was in attendance nearby, a gilt cockade in his hat. Sergei recalled asking who she was, and on being told that she was Nikolai Nikolaevich Raevsky's daughter, filing it in his memory as something "to be looked into in the future." And then he forgot her.

Prince Sergei was now just a few weeks short of his thirty-fifth birthday. He had of course known many women in his life; being an attractive man, scion of a great family, he was considered "the great catch" by mothers of nubile daughters throughout the length and breadth of the Russian empire. When he was only twenty, he had fallen in love with young Princess Lobanov-Rostovsky, an enchanting girl, who had been taken away from him by a regimental colleague. This hurt him deeply. During his stay in Paris he became engaged to the niece of the Duchesse de St.-Leu, but the difference of religion proved to be insurmountable and her family refused to let her leave France. Then came the secret meetings of the Union of Welfare, Pestel, and the all-absorbing work for the conspiracy; there seemed to be no time for anything but passing, inconsequential affairs, mostly with young actresses in St. Petersburg or Moscow. But, as time went on, he became conscious of his family's pressure for him to marry. "I was the only one of my three brothers still a bachelor," he wrote. "Whenever I looked around, I saw my friends married, with expanding families . . . It was just that as I was so busy I had to meet someone who would appeal to me instantly."

In Maria he found what subconsciously he had been looking for all his life: gaiety, liveliness, and the drive and steely determination he sensed under her carefree laughter—the qualities he himself lacked. She was the woman he needed, and this time he was not going to let her escape him. That evening he told Princess Zenaida that the "little Raevsky" was going to be his wife. And from then on, he called on the Orlovs every day. They drove together in his carriage along the bustling waterside of Odessa, and the more he saw of Maria, the more convinced he became that she was the ideal life companion for him. "The only trouble," he recalled, "I would have so very little time to woo her."

Mikhail Orlov strongly advised his old friend to distance himself from the conspiracy, as he had done, so as not to upset Maria's father. He himself had resigned from the Union of Welfare the preceding year, because he disagreed with Pestel's revolutionary objectives and wanted to devote more time to Ekaterina and their two sons. But Volkonsky was too deeply involved in and convinced about the affairs of the Union even to pretend that he planned to resign. Besides, one could not lie to a national institution like Raevsky, the mentor of one's youth. So Sergei drove to Kiev to call on the old warrior.

Prince Volkonsky's request for the hand of his favorite daughter was a bolt from the blue for Raevsky. At first, he was deeply gratified. Though a military man above all, he was not free of social snobbism; he knew there could be no more splendid match for Maria in all Russia. Next to it, Ekaterina's alliance with Orlov paled into insignificance. Prince Sergei was like one of the Grand Dukes, quite as rich and as closely linked with the court. And besides, since Tilsit days, the general had had an affection for Volkonsky. But Tilsit was long in the past, and Raevsky was now a different man from the youthful division commander who had so eagerly discussed new ideas with his French military friends while walking along the banks of the Niemen some seventeen years before. He had aged and become disillusioned, like the tsar. The *Marseillaise* did not stir him any longer; he had left all "that liberal nonsense" far behind. What perturbed him was that Prince Sergei seemed so close to Pestel, and it was common gossip in military circles that the effervescent Pestel, brilliant officer though he was, indulged in "dangerous activities" in his spare time. The general had worried enough about his first son-in-law, Orlov; now, thank God, Mikhail had distanced himself from "the dreamers." What was Prince Sergei up to? Did he know that even a Volkonsky was not safe if he incurred the tsar's displeasure? Talking to his prospective son-in-law did not reassure the general. Yes, Volkonsky admitted he was a member of a secret society, but he could not give any details, since the secret was not his to be shared. No, he would not follow Orlov's example and resign. But he was deeply in love with Maria and he thought that she in time would love him. The last was fine, but not all the old man had been hoping for.

Why did Raevsky give in so easily? Surely the obvious answer, as later correspondence indicated, was the irresistible attraction of a brilliant alliance, with its glittering prospects for Maria. In his mind's eye, the general could perceive his favorite daughter as Lady of the Bedchamber to the future empress, taking precedence at court functions—or perhaps even at the coronation—over all the ladies of the land, opening court balls on the arm of the emperor, living in splendor in one of the courtiers' palaces in Tsarskoe Selo. What an honor for all the Raevskys! How could one throw obstacles in its path? The general's wife, Sophia, supported Sergei; vague though she was, it flattered her vanity to have one of her daughters marry a prince whose mother was an intimate friend of the tsarina.

And Maria? She was quite dazzled by Volkonsky. Like most girls who are very close to their father, she had always liked older men. Sergei's romantic looks appealed to her, and he fitted her concept of a Byronic hero. His worldliness, his splendid army career, and the glamour surrounding his family undoubtedly made a strong impression on her. She had not yet had time to fall in love, nor was it considered an essential condition for marriage in her day. When called in by her father in Sergei's presence, she happily accepted his proposal to be his wife.

They were married in Kiev on January 12, 1825, in the same lovely Church of St. Andrew where Ekaterina and Orlov had taken their vows. Prince Sergei's present to his bride was a ruby-and-diamond necklace with matching earrings and tiara—the Russian *Kokoshnik*. There were pearls and an inlaid lacquer cabinet from the tsarina, a turquoise parure from Prince Repnin, Sergei's brother. So many gifts arrived that a neighboring house had to be taken to display them. "The array was magnificent—straight out of the Arabian nights," recorded one wedding guest. They went to Gurzuf in the Crimea for their honeymoon. Upon their return, Sergei resumed his army career and took up his secret life once again.

"I was sad to leave home," wrote Maria some years later. "My parents were convinced that they had assured me the most brilliant future, but I felt strangely uneasy, as if through my wedding veil I had been able to discern the dark fate that awaited us."

5

The Doomed Conspiracy

MARIA RECALLED IN HER MEMOIRS that she hardly knew her husband before she married and that during their first year of marriage they spent only three months together. It was not enough to forge a close relationship, particularly with someone almost twenty years older than herself. Those first months could not have been easy for the fun-loving, exuberant girl who exchanged the cheerful bustle of an affectionate family and the companionship of a father she worshipped for a life in which she was left to her own devices most of the time. "Mashenka looks beautiful, but she has lost much of her sparkle," wrote her sister Ekaterina Orlov to their father after staying with the Volkonskys in the family palace in St. Petersburg. In spite of the brilliance of her marriage—much envied by her contemporaries—and the wealth and splendor of the Volkonsky connections, Maria was far from happy, for she felt that her husband remained a stranger to her.

It was not lack of attention on his part; Sergei was truly in love with his young wife and physically attracted to her. In his absence, hardly a day passed that she did not receive a note, a small present, or a reminder of some kind. Her jewelry box was overflowing; she had furs, dresses, expensive trinkets, "like an imperial favorite," joked her brothers. But during their infrequent moments together, Sergei seemed absent-minded and remote. Even in moments of passion, "which seemed to flare up suddenly," when she craved his proximity and affection, he would soon disengage himself from her embrace and stare moodily into space or nervously pace the floor, lost in thought. It was puzzling and disconcerting behavior for a young bride to contend with. Maria, of course, was totally unaware of the secret burden her husband was carrying on his shoulders. "I had no idea of the existence of any secret society, or Sergei's involvement in it," she recalled. "Sergei was so much older than I. In his eyes I was still a child. How could he confide in me in matters of such gravity? And yet it would have brought us together, had I known. I would have helped him to share the burden." Instead, she was left feeling inadequate and bewildered.

Nor was the Volkonsky family of much help. In the damp, ornate palace overlooking the Moika Canal in St. Petersburg where generations of Volkonskys had lived since the days of Peter the Great, long rows of family portraits stared at her, coldly handsome, arrogant, and superb. There was not a smiling, warm face among them, and perhaps the coldest of all was Sergei's mother, Alexandra Nikolaevna, born Princess Repnin. Whatever residue of human affection remained in her bejeweled, voluminous bosom was reserved for the imperial family. Both the Repnins and the Volkonskys had been powerful boyars long before the Romanovs ascended the throne. They had always been rich and strongly attached to the crown. Indeed, it was from the crown that they had derived their importance. As the First Lady of the Bedchamber and friend and confidante of the Dowager Empress, Sergei's mother, the old princess, had been privy to many secrets. The imperial family—their joys, their sorrows, and their dark tragedies—was the foundation stone of her life, to the exclusion of her own family. Through the years, very little attention had been devoted to the existence of her husband and her four children.

Sergei's father had a different view of life, but he was usually away. Grigory Semenovich Volkonsky, the old prince, a lusty, lovable eccentric, had long ago distanced himself from his wife. As governor of the province of Orenburg (today's Chkalov), the wild country at the foothills of the Ural Mountains, he seldom visited St. Petersburg, spending most of his time in his exotic palace on the river Ural, surrounded by Tartar and Kirghiz khans and Bashkir tribesmen, whom he referred to as "my natives." A well-known and popular figure, he was often seen walking in the narrow streets of Orenburg, among the bazaars and the caravans, dressed in a red brocade dressing gown lined with fur, benignly chatting with local merchants, tribesmen, or camel drivers. He would sometimes hitch a ride back to the palace in a local cart, much to the horror and despair of his entourage. The prince liked Italian music, particularly opera, which he tried to import to the Urals, with mixed success; he was also fond of English toilet water and peppermints. His other hobbies included Kirghiz horses, ceremonial uniforms, and bear hunting. He was devoted to his children, whom he treated with unusual gentleness and affection. He deplored the fact that he saw them all too infrequently. Now and then, he complained about his "Asiatic solitude," for his wife visited him only twice in eighteen years. The great ambition of his youth was to be Russian ambassador to Constantinople, for he had come to love that particular part of the world when he first visited it with the army, but nothing ever came of that.

Maria met him once only, shortly after her engagement to Sergei, during one of the prince's rare visits to St. Petersburg, and an immediate sympathy sprang up between the eccentric old man and the graceful, striking young girl who was to become his son's wife. He presented her with an antique Chinese jade pendant and a cloak lined with sable, in which she later traveled to Siberia. The old man died a month before her marriage to Sergei, and she felt a sense of real personal loss.

Sergei's oldest brother, Prince Repnin, former Governor of the Ukraine, a handsome but remote figure, even to his own family, could not be looked on as a friend. Neither could Sergei's sister Sophia, the youngest of the Volkonsky brood, too much under her mother's influence to have any personality of her own. Married to Prince Peter Volkonsky, a distant cousin and a member of the state council, intimate friend of the tsar and his constant traveling companion, she spent her time administering her husband's estates; her hobby was the acquisition of money, at which she turned out to be very skillful, as her brother, to his loss, was one day to discover. The one member of the family who was to prove a close and faithful friend to Maria was her sister-in-law, Princess Zenaida, wife of Sergei's second brother, Nikita. It was in her house in Odessa that Maria and Sergei met and fell in love. But, after leaving Odessa, Zenaida traveled in Italy for a year before finally settling in Moscow, and did not reenter Maria's life until later.

In mid-May, as they were about to move to Uman in the Ukraine, the headquarters of the 9th division, which Sergei was to command, Maria discovered that she was pregnant. Delighted as she was at the prospect, she was suffering from a bronchitis infection contracted among the icy splendors of the Volkonsky Palace in St. Petersburg. Sergei's mother seemed to be immune to the cold; she walked about her house wrapped in a long caftan superimposed on layers of silk and goose down, contemptuous of all those "delicate creatures who could not stand up to the climate." An exception among St. Petersburg ladies, she despised open wood fires and the cozy, attractive tile stoves built into walls which were a feature of most houses. It was agony for Maria to stay there.

When General Raevsky came to visit the young couple in Uman late in May, he declared that Mashenka looked like a shadow of her old self. Though eagerly expecting her baby, she confessed to feeling exhausted, with frequent chest pains. As it became evident that Sergei would have to be away frequently in the months to come, they decided that Maria should go to Odessa with her mother and her English governess, Miss Martin. It was hoped that the mild maritime climate of that southernmost, fastest-growing Russian city, regular saltwater baths, a complete change of atmosphere, and comfort would have a beneficial effect on her health. She would stay with the Raevskys' glamorous cousin, Elizabeth Vorontsov, a great-niece of Potemkin, whose husband, Count Michael, had recently been appointed Governor of New Russia and Bessarabia and had established himself in magnificent state at Odessa. Sergei accompanied his wife to Belaya Tserkov, her aunt's house, then turned around and drove back to attend a meeting in Kiev chaired by Pestel.

Events were inexorably moving toward a climax. There were now two main centers of conspiracy, each with a separate constitution and plan of action. They were both growing in membership and gathering momentum: the northern branch in St. Petersburg, led by Nikita Muraviev, whose members maintained close contact with Moscow; and the southern branch, with headquarters at Kiev and Tulchin and cells scattered throughout the Ukraine. The southern branch, of which Pestel and Muraviev-Apostol (a cousin) were the leaders, was by far the more numerous and important; it claimed to command the allegiance of more than seventy thousand troops. It had recently reinforced its ranks by joining up with the Society of United Slavs, an association of liberal-minded middle-class officers and impoverished noblemen determined to bring about a change in the country. There was much disagreement between the two groups, mainly on ideological grounds. The constitution of the northern group had been drawn by Nikita Muraviev, a young officer on the general staff, who at seventeen had been among the troops that entered Paris after Napoleon's defeat. Through his family connections, he met there many prominent intellectuals and liberal-minded politicians, participants in the great events that had stirred the Continent. He became an ardent liberal and on his return to Russia joined the underground movement, founding the Union of Welfare with Mikhail Orlov. The political program drawn by Nikita Muraviev for the Northern Society was essentially reformist and far more conservative than Pestel's. According to him, Russia was to become a federation presided over by a constitutional monarch vested with presidential powers. The legislative power was to be with a national assembly, and the executive in the hands of a hereditary emperor, his power subject to a supreme council. Freedom of speech and of the press, religious tolerance, and trial by jury were to be guaranteed. Serfdom, of course, was to be abolished.

Pestel, a convinced Jacobin, wanted a republic and was prepared to resort to regicide to achieve it. His credo, "Russian Truth" (*Russkaya Pravda*), provided for the deposition of the tsar, abolition of the monarchy, and "in order to maintain peace and discipline while the republic was being established," the introduction of a "temporary dictatorship." In fact, Pestel's model state was to be so highly centralized that he envisaged himself as another Napoleon. Vehemently opposed to any form of federation, Pestel was an exponent of total Russification (as Stalin was years later). Great Russians, Byelorussians, Ukrainians, Tartars, the troublesome newly conquered tribes and others of the empire's multinational people were to be thrown into a melting pot, made to renounce their own past and national inheritance. The Jews were to be assimilated, or, "preferably," summarily deported to Asia Minor, where they would be allowed to establish their own state. All Russian citizens would be equal under the law, but order was to be kept by a secret police far more powerful and better organized than any previous entity of its kind. The only exception in Pestel's scheme of things was Poland, which had a long history of independence going back eight hundred years before the Partitions. Poland was to regain its independence, but would have to adopt a new republican constitution and enter into a "formal, eternal alliance with Russia."

Though himself a Protestant, Pestel gave a dominant position to the Orthodox Church, but acknowledged freedom of worship for all other creeds. *Russkaya Pravda*, as a treatise on state control, was in some respects brilliant, but not surprisingly, it aroused violent antagonism, not only among the members of the northern branch, but also among Pestel's own people in the south. It was much talked about outside the confines of the Union. Pushkin, who at first had admired Pestel, said of him that he had "Napoleon's profile and Satan's soul." Many in the southern group were swayed by Pestel's rhetoric, but others, like Sergei Muraviev-Apostol, strongly disagreed. Muraviev-Apostol's view was important, because his influence in the group almost equaled Pestel's.

Sergei Muraviev-Apostol was probably the most attractive of all the Decembrists. He came from an old, highly cultured, and talented family with a strong liberal tradition. (At one time, as many as eight men bearing that name belonged to Russian secret societies.) Even as a young boy, Sergei was acutely sensitive to human misery and keen to rebel against injustice. Brought up in

France (his father was a diplomat), he never forgot the revulsion he had felt when, upon his return to Russia, he first came into contact with slavery. Like his cousin Nikita, he joined the conspiracy at an early age and, when posted to his regiment in the south, fought tirelessly against corporal punishment, which he finally managed to have abolished in his unit. Fair-haired and fair-skinned, with lively, expressive green eyes and a winning smile, he was an excellent conversationalist, dazzling with charm and original wit. He was beloved by his friends and adored by subordinates. While Pestel inspired awe and admiration, Sergei Muraviev-Apostol aroused enthusiastic devotion. His men were prepared to follow him to the ends of the earth if need be, an essential attribute in an uprising. Muraviev-Apostol, though dedicated to the overthrow of the autocracy, disagreed fundamentally with Pestel's plan to murder the entire Romanov family. He believed that the road to freedom should not involve the slaughter of innocent women and children whose only crime was that they happened to be born into the imperial family. This attitude irritated Pestel. *"Il est trop pur,"* he would say. "It is not the way to bring a revolution about."

Though there was little unity between the groups, it was universally felt that some decisive action would have to take place very soon. Otherwise, precious momentum would be lost. The summer of 1826 was tentatively fixed as a target date, and meantime it was vital to go on expanding and gaining allies. The year before, thanks to Muraviev-Apostol's initiative, the Southern Society had joined forces with the United Slavs. It now occurred to Pestel that they should approach the Poles, who had experience in conspiracy and whose cooperation in an uprising would be essential. The Polish Secret Society, dedicated to freeing Poland from the Russian yoke, was larger and better organized than its Russian counterpart. It maintained links with

France, Sweden, and even England and hoped to obtain from them financial and moral aid. It also had the advantage of unanimous support from the Polish people. Early in 1825, Pestel, accompanied by Volkonsky, met with the Polish emissaries, Prince Jablonowski and Count Grodecki, at the opulent Nobility Club in Kiev. Gustav Olizar, on one of his visits from the Crimea, was in Kiev at the time and, as marshal of the local nobility, was privy to some of the talks. He left us a vivid description.

"All four of them," he wrote, "shared the same high-society background, which in itself greatly facilitated the rapprochement . . . What with the clicking of spurs, the bubbling of champagne in long-stemmed crystal glasses, the charming smiles, the exchanges of compliments in impeccable French, both parties had for one brief moment the exhilarating illusion that they were engaged in the most important military negotiation, that they were genuine statesmen, settling the fate of nations for centuries to come."

In exchange for the restoration of Poland to its pre-Partition frontiers, Pestel demanded that, upon the outbreak of an insurrection in Russia, the Poles should imprison or assassinate the Grand Duke Constantine, the tsar's younger brother, who was Viceroy of Poland and commander in chief of its forces. They should also prevent the Polish and Lithuanian army corps from coming to the assistance of the Russian authorities. This having been vaguely agreed on, Pestel lost all further interest in the talks. Years later, many Decembrists realized that if they had had the close cooperation of Polish conspiratorial cells, the outcome of the revolution might have been different. The Russian plotters were amateurs, but the Poles had thirty years' experience behind them and were true professionals. For all their dedication to the spirit of liberty, the dashing Russian guards officers and conscience-stricken aristocrats were mere apprentices in sedition. Pushkin left a picture of many of them in this verse:

> 'Twas all mere idle chatter
> 'Twixt Château Lafite and Veuve Cliquot.
> Friendly disputes, epigrams
> Penetrating none too deep.
> This science of sedition
> Was just the fruit of boredom, of idleness,
> The pranks of grownup naughty boys.

This is perhaps unfair to men like Pestel who thought of themselves as dedicated revolutionaries, or to idealistic dreamers like Muraviev-Apostol and Sergei Volkonsky. It nevertheless gives a fairly accurate picture of the majority of the plotters; it helps to explain why their high-minded attempt to improve the lot of their countrymen failed.

At the time when Maria left for Odessa and her husband drove off to attend the meeting in Kiev, the atmosphere in both the Southern and Northern Societies was one of explosive confusion. It was all very well, it was said, to draft constitutions and win adherents for the cause, but something had to be done to satisfy the hotheads, who called for action "for action's sake." Most of their plans, however, foundered on the one insoluble problem—what to do with the tsar. The Russian people's devotion and the unswerving loyalty of the simple soldier to their tsar was the greatest obstacle to revolution. Pestel was convinced that, in order to make any headway, the revolutionaries had to do away with the tsar and the institution of the monarchy. But the idea of regicide was hard to accept for men to whom traditional loyalty to the dynasty was second-nature. Gradually, however, most of them bowed to Pestel's logic and agreed to the tsar's assassination, though the line was drawn at the rest of the imperial family. In the latter part of 1825, two halfhearted attempts were made on Tsar Alexander's life at the time of the southern maneuvers; both failed when the tsar did not turn up at the places where he had been expected.

Meantime, new life had been injected into the hitherto flabby northern conspiracy by the arrival of a man of magnetic personality and drive, the poet Kondrati Ryleev. He had been an assessor on the criminal courts, where he earned for himself, among the simple people, the reputation of a tireless fighter for justice. He was also one of the foremost poets of his generation, almost as greatly admired as Pushkin, and an outspoken critic of the regime. He talked in "bursts of colorful images and moved in a state of perpetual agitation." Ryleev brought recklessness and rhetoric to the northern branch. He saw eye to eye with Pestel on the need to eliminate the tsar, even if the attempt failed. Mistakenly, he imagined that this would "awaken the country." Through his St. Petersburg apartment drifted a succession of fanatics, some of them partly unbalanced (like Kakhovsky), begging for the "privilege and supreme honor of killing Emperor Alexander." Ryleev was delighted to have so many volunteers for the job, but he warned them that in case of failure they would be instantly disowned by the society.

One of Ryleev's close friends was Adam Mickiewicz, Poland's foremost poet, a gifted and distinguished young man who composed poetry in Polish, French, German, and Russian. He was to become a well-known figure in St. Petersburg literary circles and a close friend of Pushkin's, the two mutually influencing each other's writings. Mickiewicz arrived in St. Petersburg in November 1824, just before the great flood, when the Neva burst its banks and thousands of people were drowned. He saw Ryleev, who gave him letters of introduction to Pestel and Muraviev-Apostol in the south. After traveling to Kiev to meet them, he went on to the Crimea (where he visited Count

Olizar), then Moscow, and returned to St. Petersburg in the autumn of 1825. His first call was on his friend Ryleev at the apartment he then shared with two other Decembrists, Alexander Bestuzhev and the twenty-two-year-old Prince Odoevsky, another poet.

"I had the great privilege of knowing and enjoying the friendship of the purest and of the noblest Russian youth of the time," wrote Mickiewicz in his account of the visit. The poet's intimacy with the Decembrists was surprising. These men had never taken Pushkin into their confidence, yet they admitted a foreigner, a young Pole, to their most secret assemblies. The reasons, of course, were that he *was* Polish, and a close friend of Ryleev; as such, his discretion was beyond doubt. Here is a description of a meeting in Ryleev's apartment "one foggy day in October," from Mickiewicz's memoirs:

I got out of my droshky by the Anichkov Bridge, where the cobblestones give way to hexagonal blocks of wood and the clatter of horses' hooves becomes muffled. I walked toward the Admiralty, turning right by the great red mass of the Winter Palace, and followed the granite quays along the Neva . . . It was late, even the *budochniks* [policemen] had retired inside their little huts at street corners; quiet reigned over the city, a damp, penetrating chill rose from the river.

An old servant opened the door. "They are all in there," he whispered, pointing to a room at the end of a very long passage. Ryleev's pretty young wife, Natasha, was nowhere to be seen; she must have been sent to bed with the children.

There must have been more than a dozen people in the room, but at first I could not distinguish anything because of the dense blue haze of pipe and cigar smoke. They were sprawling on sofas and on the deep windowsills; young Alexander Odoevsky and Bestuzhev sat cross-legged, Turkish fashion, on a Persian carpet on the floor. The officers had undone their tunic buttons and stiff collars, the civilians wore voluminous cravats à la Byron; some were dressed like Directoire dandies. Through the wide-open windows swirled great white puffs of St. Petersburg fog.

An intense youth, pale-complexioned, with a prominent forehead, a face like Shelley, lifts a glass—"Death to the tsar." The toast is received with emotion. Ryleev's jet-black eyes light up with an inner flame . . . Everyone drinks except me, a Pole and a guest . . . They sing of death to the tsar:

> One, two knives,
> One, two, three,
> Long and sharp . . .
> Comes the blacksmith,
> Wields a hammer . . .
> Big and heavy . . .

The rhythmic chant flows through the open windows for all to hear. A glow of a lantern out on the quay suddenly lights up the room. The chant stops abruptly, as fear sobers them up. The shadow of Radishchev in the Fortress crosses my mind . . . I can almost hear the sinister cry of a raven, a raven circling the gallows.

Mickiewicz's foreboding was correct. Just around that time, the conspirators were being betrayed to the tsar by a man from Pestel's own regiment, a captain by the name of Maiboroda, whom Pestel had implicitly trusted and had showered with favors, but who in fact was a government spy. This was not the first time that Emperor Alexander was being told about a conspiracy. A few years before, an Englishman named Sherwood, whose father was an engineer working in Russia, infiltrated the meetings at Kamenka and reported them to the secret police. A year later, there was a report of an agent provocateur called Gribovsky, which was duly sent to the tsar. But Alexander never acted on the reports. That young aristocrats should be flirting with revolutionary societies did not worry him; he could not believe they were serious, particularly since he had known most of these men since childhood. After all, he himself in his young days had been carried away by the same theories; in a sense, he too had been one of the Carbonari, taught by La Harpe; he was almost like an older brother or a mentor to them all. His dreams had not withstood the test of time; he had changed; but this was no reason to arrest these men. In due time they would change, as he did, and realize that idealism does not pay.

But Maiboroda's report was different. He was an army man; he had been closely associated with the society, knew most of its secrets, and could supply detailed information on Pestel's and Ryleev's plans, including the projected assassination of the tsar. Police sources confirmed his reports. This time the emperor had no choice but to order an investigation. As the noose was about to tighten around their necks, the two groups pressed on with their plans, blissfully unaware of the danger. Suddenly, in the third week of November, came the news that Tsar Alexander was dead. He had gone to Taganrog, a remote provincial town on the Sea of Azov, to be at the bedside of his ailing wife, and was struck with malaria while inspecting the troops. His death that month caught the conspirators by surprise, unleashing a cataclysmic chain of events.

At the end of September, Maria returned from Odessa and rejoined Sergei at their house near the 9th division headquarters in Uman. Her health and her spirits had recovered; she was feeling immeasurably better, buoyed up by the gaiety and the comfort of her stay in the Vorontsov Palace on the shores of the

Black Sea at Odessa. Countess Eliza, who was very fond of her niece, encouraged her to take piano and singing lessons with the visiting Italian singers and teachers, had her recite poetry, ordered the latest French and English books for her pleasure. An exception in the family, Countess Eliza had never approved of Prince Sergei; she thought he was too moody and temperamentally unsuited for her naturally extrovert niece.

The beneficial climate of Odessa reestablished Maria's health. As her pregnancy advanced, her face became gently rounded and her skin acquired the translucent quality "of an alabaster vase with a light shining through it," as her aunt used to say. The prospect of the baby's arrival in early January filled her with joy. The only worry, as usual, was her husband. He visited her at the Vorontsovs' several times, looking "preoccupied and, if anything, more anxious than before." When they returned to Uman in early autumn, though ostensibly delighted at their reunion, he appeared even more worried and unsettled. Soon after, he departed for Tulchin, headquarters of the Second Army.

Maria describes in her memoirs how one night in early December her husband returned home unexpectedly just after midnight and burst into her room, calling "Get up at once!" "I woke up trembling," she recalled. "I was far along in my pregnancy and his sudden noisy return scared me. I saw him build a huge fire in the fireplace in our bedroom and carry bundles of papers, which he proceeded to burn one by one. I tried to help him as best I could, and kept asking him what it all meant. 'Pestel has been arrested,' he cried out. 'But why? What is happening?' No answer. His face and his deep silence were frightening, and I started to tremble uncontrollably, trying to get hold of myself so I could be of comfort to him. He seemed so infinitely sad and terribly distressed. But he said little, except to tell me that he had promised my father to take me to Boltyshka for my confinement and that we would be leaving the next morning. We arrived at my home in the afternoon. Sergei deposited me with my parents, bade me a brief farewell, and departed almost immediately, before I had time to elicit any more information. The next time I saw him was as a prisoner in the Peter and Paul Fortress."

What Maria quite understandably omitted from her memoirs, which were written for the benefit of their children, was the bitter exchange which took place between Prince Sergei and her father. The old general was incensed. Through his network of military contacts, he had learned that shortly before the tsar's death a full-scale police inquiry had been launched, which had just resulted in the arrest of Pestel, Sergei's closest companion. He knew the mortal danger his son-in-law was in. Seized by a towering rage, he accused him of "sheer stupidity and selfishness," of ruining the future of his wife and their unborn child, of jeopardizing the safety of the Davydov family and that of Alexander and Nikolai, his own sons, and bringing shame on the entire Raevsky clan. He should have severed those dangerous connections the moment he married Maria, as his brother-in-law Mikhail Orlov had done.

It must have been a heartbreaking confrontation. Prince Sergei does not tell us how he defended himself. He probably did not remind his father-in-law that, at the time of his marriage, he had refused Raevsky's request to withdraw from the secret society, and the general agreed to the marriage in spite of this. He could hardly point out to the old man that the prospect of a brilliant match had overcome his misgivings. He was not Mikhail Orlov; he was too deeply committed, and now he would have to remain with his friends, rather than flee abroad, as had been suggested.

"I left early the next morning," wrote Volkonsky. "There was only time for a brief farewell to my wife. I could hear my horses whinnying at the door." He wrapped himself in his lynx-lined military overcoat and, accompanied by his servant, stepped into the waiting sleigh, driving off through the snow toward Kiev. He was never to see lovely Boltyshka again.

6

The Fortress

As Prince Sergei was speeding toward Kiev, momentous events were taking place a thousand miles north. Gathered on St. Petersburg's Senate Square, off the Neva embankment, between the Admiralty with its soaring gold spire and St. Isaac's Cathedral, were some three thousand men of the elite units of the tsarist army, incited to mutiny by their officers. This was the long-awaited insurrection; after weeks of inconclusive discussions, the northern branch of the conspiracy had finally decided to move on the day of the installation of the new tsar. The square had been chosen as the focus for the revolution because troops could more easily cut off the Senate from the Winter Palace. Falconet's colossal statue of the Bronze Horseman—Peter the Great seated on a rearing horse, a memorial ordered by Catherine II for her ancestor—dominated the square.

It was Monday, December 14, a late gray winter morning. The troops stood in the shadow of the giant statue, shivering in the icy winds that swept across the Neva from the Arctic, waiting for orders. But there was no one to tell them what to do. Their leaders were unprepared and divided, the attempt doomed to failure from the start.

When the news of Tsar Alexander's death reached St. Petersburg on Friday, November 27 (he had died in Taganrog eight days before), it caught the conspirators by surprise. No one had expected his death; he was not yet forty-eight. It was bad news for the plotters, because his heir presumptive, Constantine, the next brother (Alexander had no children of his own), was popular with the troops, particularly with the important guards regiments, whom he had led into battle on many occasions. It would be difficult to persuade them to rise against him. They then heard that Constantine had renounced the crown in favor of the third brother, Nicholas, who was reluctant to ascend the throne, however. The result was an interregnum, which should have given the conspirators a breathing space in which to recruit new adherents in the regiments and to coordinate plans with the southern branch. But they failed to take advantage of it.

The next two weeks were unique. All Europe watched, fascinated, as the Russian crown was offered around "like a cup of tea which nobody wanted," according to a contemporary. As *The Times* of London put it: "Russia is in a strange predicament of having two self-denying Emperors and no active ruler." The reason for this state of affairs lay in the quixotic personality of the recently deceased emperor. When in 1823 Constantine formally renounced his right of succession to the throne in favor of Nicholas, Alexander kept the information a secret. Only the Dowager Empress, their mother, and a handful of his closest advisers knew, as if this were purely a family matter and not of vital concern to the state. It is doubtful, in fact, whether Nicholas was told. Constantine's Manifesto of Renunciation was deposited at the Uspensky Cathedral in Moscow and in the state council in St. Petersburg, with orders that "it should be opened in the event of my death, prior to any other business." For reasons that have never been clearly understood, Alexander did not refer to the question again. Naturally, when the news of his death reached the capital, the guards, ministers, and officers of state institutions took the oath of allegiance to Constantine. And so did his brother Nicholas. All over St. Petersburg that weekend, and a few days later in Moscow, prominent window displays blossomed with the squat, coarse features of the new sovereign, "Constantine I, Emperor and Autocrat of All the Russians." But Constantine was quick to reiterate his renunciation of the throne and declared his allegiance to Nicholas. Installed in Warsaw, in the lovely eighteenth-century Belvedere Palace, he relished his nearly absolute power as Viceroy of Poland and commander in chief of its forces and enjoyed all the pleasures of a Western way of life without the burden of responsibility to his own people. He reorganized the Polish army and became deeply committed to Poland, especially after his morganatic marriage to Johanna Grudzinska, a talented Polish pianist, to whom he was devoted.* This was one of the reasons why he had renounced his right to the throne. Another factor must undoubtedly have been the impact made on him by the assassination of his father, Tsar Paul. That memory had haunted his older brother, Alexander, all his life. Constantine, conscious of the way things happened in Russia and deeply distrustful of the guards, had no desire to end up strangled on some dark, stormy night, like his father. So he categorically

---

* At the age of seventeen, on the orders of his grandmother Catherine II, Constantine married the fifteen-year-old Princess Julia of Saxe-Coburg-Gotha, an aunt of Prince Albert. He made her intensely miserable and they were soon divorced; there were no children. There are numerous references to "poor Aunt Julia" in Queen Victoria's letters.

refused to budge from Warsaw and flew into a violent rage when he heard that Nicholas and the rest of St. Petersburg had sworn allegiance to him a week before and that the rest of Russia was following suit. He dispatched still another courier to reconfirm his reunuciation in the most emphatic terms, and advised Nicholas to get himself crowned, "the sooner the better." If only the telegraph had been invented! It took almost a week for a courier to cover the distance between Warsaw and St. Petersburg and another week to get back a reply. The farce went on for nearly three weeks, and the members of the northern conspiracy prepared to strike.

It took until December 12 for it to become clear that Constantine would not move, though his brother had sent him an urgent message in Warsaw: "For the love of God, come, if only to confirm your renunciation!" Finally, spurred on by police reports of growing unrest in the army, Nicholas decided to proceed with the installation.

The interregnum had favored the conspirators by creating suspicion in army ranks that the tsarevich (as Constantine indeed was) had become the victim of some "dark family plot." In spite of his pug-nose features, strongly reminiscent of his much disliked father, Constantine had a large following in the army. He had had a scintillating military career, had a reputation for great courage and for looking after his soldiers' welfare. The pay of the Polish army under his command was much better than in Russia, and the length of service had been reduced to ten years, instead of thirty as in Russia. Nicholas, on the other hand, was a twenty-nine-year-old lieutenant general, cold and distant, not well known, and disliked by the guards regiments, who were used to having their own way in matters pertaining to the succession to the Russian throne. When the plotters learned through high-level contacts that Constantine would not come, they decided to foster the rumor that he was a victim of family intrigue and to appeal to the troops on his behalf. Conscious of the Russian soldier's almost mystical belief in the supremacy of the rightful tsar, they set aside the prepared leaflets and high-flown appeals to "freedom and human dignity" and instead called on the garrison troops to back the "rightful heir Constantine" against "Nicholas the usurper"—a language that the soldiers understood. Gathered on the Senate Square that gray morning in December, they called for "Constantine and Constituzia [Constitution]," which they thought meant Constantine's wife. The day's action was made more urgent by the news that one of their own group had betrayed them to the newly sworn emperor the night before. There was not a moment to lose. In spite of the chaos in their ranks and the lack of communication between the leaders, Ryleev, Muraviev, and Trubetskoy decided to march on the Senate Square. Before noon on the first day of his reign, Tsar Nicholas I had an insurrection on his hands.

The dramatic scene on the Senate Square has been described many times. Edward Crankshaw in his masterly *Shadow of the Winter Palace* talks of the "dreamlike quality of inconsequence and unreason . . . of an attempt that appeared less like a revolution in the making than a premature and tentative rehearsal of the first act of a play, still uncompleted, enacted under open skies, with great crowd scenes against an architectural setting." Some of the principals had not turned up at all, having decided overnight that they did not like their parts, though omitting to inform the others; some had not even begun to learn their lines and fluffed about the arena, while the patient ranks of supers stood stolidly waiting for their cue, which never came.

And indeed no revolutionary headquarters ever came to be set up anywhere. Prince Sergei Trubetskoy, the appointed so-called dictator, changed his mind at the last minute, slipped away to swear allegiance to the new emperor, and then hid in the Austrian Embassy, from which he was later taken to the Fortress. Two others supposedly in command rushed back to pledge their allegiance to the tsar, then went home and shot themselves. Many simply did not turn up at all; those who did issued contradictory orders to the troops, who fired haphazardly, mainly to keep their spirits up. In the nearby Winter Palace, the new tsar was still hesitating, reluctant to shed blood on the first day of his reign; his son, "little Sasha," the future Alexander II, was quietly sitting in his playroom, copying a picture of Alexander of Macedonia crossing the Granicus.

Orders were finally issued by the emperor for guns to fire into the serried mass of mutineers. By 3 p.m., when the early winter dusk enveloped the tragic city, it was all over. Dead and wounded lay scattered over the square, the ice on the Neva was spattered with blood, marking holes where men had fallen in and drowned. Nobody knew how many had died.

And that night the police toured the city, hunting out and arresting the leaders of the conspiracy. The tsar himself never went to bed, but sat up to interrogate them, one by one, to see who they were and why they acted as they did. It was the beginning of a personal inquisition that was to continue for many weeks—a personal vendetta, or a *raison d'état*, as he saw it, that he exercised against the prisoners for the rest of his reign.

Charlotte Disbrowe, wife of the British minister, recorded in her journal a firsthand account of the confusion and horror of the events at the Senate Square: "One of the regiments refused to take the oath to Nicholas, bayoneted two of their officers and a general . . . They are now this very minute drawn up in the square, have loaded with ball, and Heaven knows what will follow! . . . Troops are marching up from all sides to surround the rebels. They hardly deserve that name, poor misguided people . . .

"*Half-past nine*. It was dreadful to hear the firing. Every round went to my heart . . . Some say the mutineers have retreated across the river and dispersed . . .

"*16/18 December*. The poor soldiers seem to have been entirely misled by their officers, and soon returned to duty. They have received a general pardon; but of course a similar clemency could not be extended to those who excited them to revolt, and a great many officers are arrested; I am told upwards of thirty . . .

"I went out in a *traineau* for the first time today. The town presented a curious spectacle. The traces of the sad event on Monday were horrid: pools of blood on the snow, and spattered up against the houses."

After he left his wife at Boltyshka, Prince Volkonsky had only one thought in his mind—to see Pestel. He needed to get instructions from him, but, above all, he needed his encouragement and moral support. Prince Sergei was not a natural leader of men, nor was he a good organizer. Pestel's arrest, he recalled in his memoirs, "drained him of his very life blood." Pestel was being held in the town major's office at Tulchin, a rather inglorious ending for the brilliant rebel who had dreamed of toppling an empire. As a division commander, Prince Sergei had no difficulty talking his way into Pestel's place of detention; he found Pestel's jailer, the town major, sipping tea with his prisoner. Volkonsky burst into the room, and the two friends embraced and started conversing in rapid French, something the town major apparently found quite normal, as most educated Russians talked French among themselves. "*Ayez du courage,*" urged Volkonsky. *"Je n'en manque pas,"* answered Pestel, and added: "Above all, don't admit anything, even if they torture you." They continued in this vein for some time. Prince Sergei's memoirs don't tell us whether the town major left the room or how they knew he did not understand their presumably secret exchanges. Finally Pestel asked Volkonsky to make sure that his treatise *Russkaya Pravda* was hidden somewhere safe, for "we are lost if they find it." But before Volkonsky had time to locate the document, others among Pestel's followers buried it clumsily in a field, where it was soon discovered by the police. It was a devastating document at their trial.

In spite of the failure of the insurrection in the north, the conspirators might still have had a chance of success in the south, where the main revolutionary forces were massed. The southern revolt was much more serious and on a much wider scale than that in the north and involved several crack regiments. But, like Prince Sergei, many of the commanding officers were so shocked by the arrest of Pestel that they did not go into action until five days later, on December 19, losing valuable time. Led by Muraviev-Apostol and his Chernigov Regiment, the revolt could have become a major military operation, but it failed two weeks later because of general lack of coordination and the dreamy idealism of Muraviev-Apostol, who saw himself as leader of a holy crusade and insisted on addressing his soldiers in mystical, almost religious terms, way above their heads, talking about "divine liberty and sacred justice," instead of urging them to fight for Constantine, a tsar who would provide better pay and reduce their length of service. Since the "pure and idealistic" Muraviev-Apostol refused to deceive his troops, and his soldiers failed to understand his lofty language, they soon went over to the government side. Historians agree that he should have marched on Kiev, taken it, moved close to the Polish border, and quickly established a connection with the

Poles. The fall of Kiev might have sparked a civil war involving Poland—with unforeseeable results, possibly beyond the control of St. Petersburg. This heroic romantic was doomed to failure; he later insisted on taking the entire blame for the southern uprising on himself and died bravely for it. On the night before his arrest, while government troops were converging on his quarters from all sides, Sergei Muraviev-Apostol and his twenty-year-old brother Ippolit sat together drinking claret, reading Byron, and reciting Lamartine's melancholy *Meditations*:

> I will pass fleetingly upon this earth,
> Always lonely and always a dreamer,
> With few people ever recalling my name . . .

Upon leaving Pestel, Volkonsky tried to rally his own regiments and establish communication with his friends. It wasn't easy, for by then disorganization had set in and mutineers were roaming the countryside in what had become a no-man's-land. Sergei now realized for the first time how difficult—indeed, how hopeless—was the venture on which they had so rashly embarked. Yet he felt that it was his duty to stay and see the action through to the bitter end. On the way back to Uman, he ran into Alexander Poggio, a vivacious, attractive Italian whose parents had brought him to Russia in his childhood and who had become Pestel's enthusiastic adherent. Poggio and Vasya Davydov were fleeing from Kamenka minutes ahead of the police, who had descended on the estate with orders to search the house and the grounds, in spite of Mme Davydov's indignant protests. "I experienced a feeling of impending doom," Sergei recalled. "More than anything else in the world, I wanted to be with my wife and my child."

On the fifth of January, he set off for Boltyshka, determined to spend at least a few moments with Maria, "and to hell with the old man her father." While changing horses at a roadside station before dawn, he learned of Muraviev-Apostol's arrest. He turned back toward Uman, where he heard that his own unit had gone over to the government. As he came into the courtyard of his own house, he saw a sleigh with two police officers, accompanied by a government emissary, who had driven all the way from St. Petersburg with orders, personally signed by the tsar, "for the arrest of the peer of the realm Major General Prince Sergei Grigorievich Volkonsky." A five-man military-police detachment escorted the prince to St. Petersburg, where he was thrown into a damp, gloomy cell in the Peter and Paul Fortress, just across the Neva River from the Winter Palace, where at that very moment his mother was smiling in attendance on the Dowager Empress.

Maria, in the meantime, was undergoing the agonies of childbirth. "My son was born on January 2, 1826," she recalled. "I suffered greatly, as there was no midwife to attend me . . . Because of a raging snowstorm, she did not arrive until the next day. My father insisted I give birth while sitting upright in an armchair, though my mother, with her long experience, said I would be warmer and more comfortable in my bed. And there they were, quarreling over me, while I suffered. As always, the man prevailed, and they settled me in a huge armchair, where I was to undergo a long martyrdom, without any medical aid. Our doctor was away at the time tending to a patient fifteen versts from our house—a difficult journey in that dreadful weather; the village midwife who came turned out to be a simple peasant. She was much too awed to approach me and remained on her knees in a corner of the room reciting prayers. Our doctor finally arrived the next morning with an experienced midwife, and I brought into the world my little Nicholas, from whom I was later to part—forever. I had just enough strength left in me to walk barefoot to my bed and crawl in; the sheets felt icy cold."

She came down with a violent fever—probably a post-puerperal infection—which kept her in bed for two months, unconscious much of the time. In her rare lucid moments, she kept asking for Sergei, her husband, but was told that he was in Moldavia with his troops. Maria's youngest sister, Sophia, in a letter of February 3, 1826, to her brother, described her condition and the concern felt by the family: "It is more than four weeks since Maria gave birth, but she is still confined to her bed with fluctuating post-natal fever . . . Her nerves are utterly shattered. She does not know of the arrest of her husband, or the departure of Nikolai and yourself for St. Petersburg . . . She has not heard of the arrest of Mikhail Orlov, Poggio, and Vasya Davydov . . . It is Sergei's absence that particularly troubles her. When the longing becomes too great, she insists that someone be sent for him. You can judge for yourself how difficult is our position."

The fever gradually abated, and Maria started to regain her strength. "One day—it was early March," she recalled, "I sat up in bed, looked around, and decided that this absence of Sergei's was not normal. I realized that I had not even had a letter from him since December. A terrible fear seized me—was he dead?" General Raevsky was in St. Petersburg, trying to assess the extent of the damage done to the family's good name by the conspirators and to help clear his two sons of any involvement. So Maria turned to her mother, "demanding to know the truth." There was no point now in keeping the news from her, so she was told about her husband's arrest, and her Uncle Davydov, their good friend Poggio, and all others, whom she had known for many years. Her first reaction was one of overwhelming relief: Sergei at least was alive. The picture that unfolded was undeniably grim, but it helped to explain many things that had been beyond comprehension until now.

So this was the reason for Sergei's preoccupation with "other things," for his moodiness, for his speaking sharply to her and then feeling guilty about it, for keeping her at a distance, as if he could not trust himself to get closer, for fear of betraying a secret. "A tremendous wave of affection swept over me," she noted. "From then on, I had only one thought in my mind—to go to him."

She wrote to him on March 5: "My beloved Sergei: Two days ago, I learned of your arrest. I will not allow my soul to be shattered by it. I put my hope in the mercy of our great-hearted Emperor. One thing I can assure you of: whatever your fate, I will share it."

As Maria had never bothered to conceal from her sisters that her marriage was not altogether happy, that she often found Sergei's behavior "intolerable," this reversal of her feelings surprised them. Obviously, a deep psychological process was at work: her pregnancy, the birth of a son, her long illness combined to create a need for her husband. And there was more. In spite of her complaints about Sergei's moods during the first year of their marriage, Maria was in love with her husband. The physical tie between them was very strong. (She alludes to it several times in her letters to her sister Ekaterina.) In spite of her youth and inexperience, Maria was a hot-blooded Ukrainian with a great capacity for passion—she had Potemkin's blood in her veins—and Sergei had been her first lover. How many times had she worried that his occasional coolness might be due to an involvement with another woman! Her self-esteem was restored now; she knew who her real rival was. At last she could give free rein to her feelings.

But this did not mean that she approved of Sergei's involvement in the plot. Maria was very much her father's daughter, and Raevsky had ceased to be a liberal while she was still in her teens. Her brothers, Alexander and Nikolai, had always kept their distance from the conspiracy; among her family and their circle of intelligent, well-educated friends, the tradition of service to the dynasty was uppermost. How could she feel much sympathy for a cause that threatened to wreck her own and her child's life? She wrote to her brother Alexander a few days after hearing of Sergei's arrest: "It absolutely broke my heart. The state of my health makes it worse; some different time I might have borne it more easily. It is not so much his arrest that pains me or the punishment that awaits us, but that he allowed himself to be lured—and by whom? by people for whom neither his father-in-law nor his brothers had any sympathy. As for myself, I never did hide my opinions from him . . . But none of this has any importance right now. I want to go to him as soon as is humanly possible."

The moment she was able to travel, Maria and her baby son left for St. Petersburg by way of Alexandria, the palatial Ukrainian estate of the old Countess Branitsky, mother of the famous Eliza Vorontsov. She deposited baby Nicholas with her aunt, who lived in immense luxury surrounded by hundreds of servants and the best medical care of the day. "I knew my son would be safe with her, for she was devoted to all of us," she noted later.

It was April—an exceptionally cold and rainy spring. After a grueling journey of more than a thousand miles over roads made impassable by spring floods, Maria arrived at the Volkonsky residence on the Moika, to be greeted by her mother-in-law, who was preparing to leave with the Dowager Empress for Moscow. Her daughter-in-law's appearance was an embarrassment to the old princess. Hadn't she suffered enough with her son's foolishness? On being told of Sergei's arrest on charges of treason and sedition, the old lady left court and remained home for three days, not knowing what to do. Relief came in the form of a personal note from the emperor informing her that "nothing in her status had changed." She instantly returned to her duties. Court attendance was her life blood, more important than either husband or children.

By now it was evident how seriously Prince Sergei was implicated. Mikhail Orlov and Maria's two brothers had been arrested in January, but the charges against the two Raevskys were soon dropped. Mikhail Orlov had a powerful ally at court in the person of his brother Alexander, commander of the guards regiment, who, by remaining loyal to the tsar, had kept the all-important guards from mutiny. The handsome Mikhail was temporarily suspended from military service and ordered to be put under detention for a fortnight. The Raevsky brothers were freed. "I want you to know, Nikolai Nikolaevich," the tsar wrote to General Raevsky in his own hand (in French), "that the Commission of Inquiry, having studied in the greatest detail the case relating to the conduct of your two sons, has pronounced them totally innocent of any links or connections with the conspiracy. This finding has given me great pleasure, and I want to be the first to inform you of it and rejoice with you. It is only fitting that the sons of such a distinguished father should be freed of suspicion. I shall always remain, dear Nikolai Nikolaevich, your très bienveillant Nicholas."

The letter delighted the old general; soon after, Alexander was offered the post of court chamberlain. There was much talk in the Raevsky household of the sovereign's "infinite goodness and humane heart," qualities that unfortunately Nicholas I sadly lacked. But Volkonsky was quite a different matter. As a close friend and collaborator of that "arch-criminal" Pestel, he had been at the very center of the conspiracy; to Tsar Nicholas, his action was as incomprehensible as it was repulsive. For Sergei was the one who "belonged," who was virtually a member of the imperial family. Many from among the Decembrists came from old aristocratic backgrounds, such as the Trubetskoys, the Obolenskys, the Muravievs; some, like the Obolenskys and the Trubetskoys, had always been prominent in St. Petersburg society; but only Volkonsky *really* belonged; he had been around the imperial family all his life. Tsar Nicholas, who was nine years younger than Prince Sergei, well remembered when, as a boy of ten, he would ask the glamorous young aide to position his lead soldiers for him in the formation of Napoleon's armies at Austerlitz. Like his mother, "our dear Princess," Volkonsky was one of the innermost circle; his action, therefore, was a personal affront and a betrayal.

"You are a fool, Major General Prince Volkonsky! You should be ashamed of yourself," the tsar shouted at him when Sergei was brought into his presence in fetters, bleary-eyed and unshaven, out of the very bowels of the Peter and Paul Fortress. Then suddenly, in a change of tactics aimed at extracting a confession, Nicholas walked up to the unfortunate man and said, on a kinder note: "Your fate hinges on your sincerity. Be frank and outspoken with me and I promise to pardon you."

But Volkonsky was a man of honor above all else; he could not betray his colleagues, and in any case, he did not trust the new tsar, whom he knew to be a cruel and vindictive man. In vain did the interrogating officers, most of them former personal friends, invoke their camaraderie in the field, or the emperor's devotion to the Volkonsky family (Sergei's brother-in-law, Peter Volkonsky, had just been appointed court minister). Volkonsky kept hedging and admitted only what he knew was already known. The interrogation enraged the tsar. In Nicholas's reminiscences, written many years later, one can still sense his irritation with Volkonsky: "I felt like boxing his ears or striking him for being such an absolute idiot. He stood there before me with a sort of dazed look on his face—a revolting picture of flagrant ingratitude and arrant stupidity. No contrition! He paid for it!!!"

Not all the Decembrists behaved as honorably as Sergei. A number of them, after a few days in the foul, damp darkness of the Fortress, lost their initial fire and were ready to talk. The emperor soon had their measure. Prince Trubetskoy, the would-be "dictator," who had betrayed his colleagues on the Senate Square, now folded completely when brought in for interrogation. The mise-en-scène must have been intimidating. The towering figure of the tsar in full dress uniform, with the blue ribbon of St. Andrew spanning his chest, advanced toward the prisoner, waving his finger at him and speaking through clenched teeth: "Prince Trubetskoy, colonel of the guards, pah! Aren't you ashamed of yourself for being associated with such scum? The fate that awaits you will be terrible, terrible . . ." At first, Trubetskoy denied any knowledge of the plot. Then, when shown a draft of the manifesto written in his own hand, he threw himself at the emperor's feet, moaning: *"La vie, sire! De grâce, la vie!"* "It was a shameful spectacle," the tsar noted in his reminiscences.

But others such as Ryleev, Yakushkin, Baron Rozen, Alexander Muraviev, and the heroic Sergei Muraviev-Apostol, gave out nothing. "I can name no one, sire!" said Yakushkin at the end of a twenty-four-hour interrogation. "Have him clapped into chains so he cannot even stir!" was the emperor's angry retort. Yakushkin was given thirty years at hard labor.

Maria's first act on arriving in St. Petersburg was to obtain an audience with General Benckendorff, chief of police, old schoolmate of her husband, and brother of Princess Lieven, wife of the Russian ambassador to London, who was a good friend of the family. From her aunt's house in the Ukraine, she had also sent a personal appeal to the tsar, asking to be allowed to visit her husband in the Fortress. "I know the greatness of soul of Your Majesty and cannot believe that Sergei has sinned beyond forgiveness," she wrote. "I will be patient, but I must go back to my small child, that is why I address myself directly to Your Imperial Majesty, counting on his august mercy. I beg you, do not refuse my request."

Benckendorff, primed by Alexander Raevsky, Maria's brother, tried to dissuade her from the visit; he even suggested a temporary separation from her husband, who was "unworthy of her." But Maria would have none of it and turned to Alexander Orlov for help. After an agonizing ten days, her request was finally granted by the tsar. "I was still very weak," she recalled, "so the Emperor, who rarely missed an opportunity to display his magnanimity (as long as it was a small matter), decreed that I be accompanied by a doctor." In the end, it was Alexander Orlov, Mikhail's brother, who went with her.

The Peter and Paul Fortress was a terrifying place. The dungeon in which the Decembrists were held was the same in which, a hundred ninety years before, Peter the Great had his own son imprisoned and tortured to death; it later held Dostoevsky. It was like a watery grave, surrounded by the river on all sides, Stygian-dark, dripping wet, cells hewn out of rock like prehistoric caves, with iron rings for chains fastened to the walls. In those cells the conspirators—fastidious, highly civilized men— spent nights and days without end, in complete darkness and silence, without a book, or tobacco, without sanitary facilities or outdoor exercise, with only the bitter realization of the hopelessness of their dream and the totality of their defeat. The families of the prisoners were never allowed to see the cells; any visits took place aboveground.

"Led by Alexander Orlov, I slowly crossed the bridge to the

Fortress," Maria wrote. "We went into the commanding officer's house, and soon after, Sergei was brought to me under escort. This interview, with four witnesses in the room, was extremely painful for us both. We were luckily allowed to talk French and vainly tried to cheer each other up. I did not dare to ask him any questions, as we were under constant scrutiny, but Sergei managed to slip me his handkerchief. When I got home I rushed to see what was on it, but all I could decipher of the illegible scrawl were a few words of consolation. My mother-in-law plied me with questions; she wanted to know whether Sergei was being given preferential treatment, which he certainly wasn't; she also wanted to know how he looked, but she soon tired of these questions and declared that she was not going to visit him, for such an interview would kill her. She said that her first duty was to the Dowager Empress. Soon after, she left for Moscow, where preparations for the tsar's coronation were underway. I wanted to remain in St. Petersburg, hoping to see my husband again, and to await the arrival of Sergei's favorite sister, Princess Sophia Volkonsky, who was on her way from Taganrog, escorting the body of the Empress Elisabeth, Tsar Alexander's wife, who had died a short time after her husband. But my family had other plans."

Both the general and Maria's two brothers were determined to keep her away from St. Petersburg. Alexander, the "Demon" of Pushkin's verses, and a great friend of the poet, had never liked his brother-in-law. "Mashenka will never be happy with him," he often said. He was one of the first to realize the tragic implications of Volkonsky's arrest, and his foreboding increased as word reached them of Tsar Nicholas's fury at Sergei's refusal to talk. "He is behaving like a fanatic," Alexander wrote to his sister Ekaterina. "I see nothing good about him, never have . . . It is time for Masha to distance herself from him."

Playing on her anxiety about the health of her baby, the

family persuaded Maria to return to Countess Branitsky's house in the Ukraine, and Alexander set himself up as a barrier between his brother-in-law and his wife, in the hope that the marriage would eventually come apart. Not only did he arrange it so that she traveled by a different route from Princess Sophia Volkonsky, the sister-in-law that Maria was so anxious to meet, and who could have told her what the real situation was concerning her husband, but once at the Branitskys' estate he intercepted all letters from the Volkonsky family to Maria, including some from Sergei written from prison. He also stopped her from communicating with the wives of other Decembrists, lest she become influenced by them. In St. Petersburg she had been prevented from seeing Katyusha Trubetskoy and Alexandrine (Annie) Muraviev. Whenever one of them came to the Volkonsky Palace on the Moika, she was told by a servant that the princess was "not at home." It was only later, in Siberia, when comparing notes with the other wives, that Maria learned what had gone on. "In spite of it," she recalled, "Katyusha and I were the first wives to arrive in Siberia."

She spent the next two and a half months in the countryside with her baby in virtual isolation, without news and without any letters from her husband. Her own letters to him were of course never delivered—Alexander had so arranged with Benckendorff, the chief of police. Naturally, neither Sergei nor the Volkonsky family could understand her behavior and interpreted it as indifference.

In the meantime, in St. Petersburg, a judicial tribunal had been sitting since January to determine the guilt of individual conspirators. The severity of the verdict, announced on July 9, was greeted with amazement. Five hundred and seventy-nine people were brought to trial; of those, over two hundred were acquitted, a hundred and thirty-four were found guilty of minor offenses and, after military disgrace, were scattered throughout the various units as ordinary soldiers or sent to fight in the Caucasus. Of the hundred and twenty so-called leaders, five were selected as "the most guilty." In spite of the fact that capital punishment had been abolished in Russia by Empress Elisabeth, the court pronounced that the guiltiest five "should be quartered," a sentence that the tsar, fearing "adverse reaction from abroad," modified to hanging. The remaining hundred and twenty were to be exiled to Siberia for varying terms of hard labor, some for life.

The poet Mickiewicz, who was in Moscow at the time, wrote of "the shudder of horror that ran through Russian society at the draconian severity of the sentences." It seemed inconceivable that so many distinguished men of the realm could be sent to the gallows or to the mines of Siberia like common criminals. "People here are appalled and dismayed," he wrote, "mainly, I think, because it has all struck so close to the heart of the establishment. I am told that the young Empress Alexandra spends her time weeping in anguish, for many of the condemned men's families keep begging her to appeal to her imperial spouse for mercy, but she can do nothing, as the emperor won't be swayed. He himself has seen to all the details and has drafted a timetable for their execution."

The one person who remained silent throughout was Princess Volkonsky, Sergei's mother. A court lady of the old school, for whom etiquette was a dogma, she never uttered a word of entreaty. She merely "followed the Dowager Empress Maria with searching, imploring eyes." But even her ironclad composure broke down when she heard the verdict—fifteen years of hard labor, and exile to Siberia for life.

"Granny wept yesterday," wrote Alina Volkonsky, Sergei's niece, who had been to see her uncle in prison and later reported to her grandmother. "The Empress was with her and comforted her, but the Emperor came in and ordered her to calm herself.

He said it would have no effect on her career." (And indeed she was shortly afterwards awarded the much coveted Order of St. Catherine.)

The sentences were carried out at dawn on July 13 on the glacis of the Fortress of St. Peter and St. Paul. At two in the morning, the prisoners were led out into the quadrangle, which was ringed by troops. A bonfire was burning in the square to illuminate the proceedings. Delighted to be out of the fetid air of the Fortress, the condemned men stood talking to one another, trying to make out friends and acquaintances from among the crowd of diplomats, society people, and officials who had gathered in spite of the early hour. A Frenchman, Jean Ancelot, who had arrived at St. Petersburg the day before as a member of a special embassy sent for Nicholas I's coronation, noted that, "as Prince Volkonsky came out onto the quadrangle, he turned several times, obviously glad to be out in the fresh air, and, recognizing a few acquaintances, went up and greeted them, including myself; he was laughing and joking, lest we feel sorry for him. Benckendorff, his former classmate, and now the tsar's chief of police, was indignant to see him behaving so flippantly . . . But I remarked to myself that the man had great class!"

With the gallows visible in the background, the prisoners were stripped of their military uniforms, which were thrown on the burning pyre, their decorations were ripped off, their swords broken over their heads. Prince Sergei held an approaching orderly at arm's length; he took off his own uniform, carefully detached his decorations, then in a defiant gesture threw them on the brazier. They were all issued ill-fitting gray convict's clothes, "in which they felt totally ludicrous," and marched back to their cells to await shipment to Siberia.

Afterwards came the executions. The fiery Pestel; the gentle Muraviev-Apostol, the epitome of the romantic hero; young Bestuzhev-Ryumin; Ryleev, the poet, whose "jet-black eyes were lit with an unearthly glow"; and Kakhovsky, who so thrilled at the idea of "a glorious and beautiful death"—they were escorted to the gallows, their arms and legs pinioned with leather thongs, feet weighted down with iron fetters. As there was no professional hangman in Russia, one had to be brought over from Sweden. Even so, he botched his job, for three of the ropes failed, and Ryleev, Muraviev-Apostol, and Kakhovsky went crashing down into the pit. It had to be done all over again, and prompted Muraviev-Apostol's famous exclamation: "Poor Russia, they don't even know how to hang properly!"

"The scene was gruesome beyond belief," one of the eyewitnesses said. "Many of the onlookers turned away, while Father Peter Myslovsky, the chaplain, who had heard all their confessions, cried out: 'Lord bless the martyrs,' then he himself crumpled to the ground in a faint."

A few days after the execution, eight of the prisoners—those whom the tsar regarded as the most serious offenders: Volkonsky, Obolensky, Trubetskoy, the Borisov brothers, Yakubovich, Artamon Muraviev, and Vasya Davydov—were dispatched to Siberia by special convoy.

There was a ball that night at the house of Prince Kochubey, the minister of the interior. All St. Petersburg society attended. In the *salle blanche*, a room of dazzling splendor, the pillars were wreathed with flowers and standards. Three thousand candles produced the effect of daylight; the tall glass lusters, the abundance of flowers created the effect of a fairyland. The dance was in full swing when there was a sudden jingle of harness bells and four troikas swept into sight, escorted by a detachment of Cossacks. With horror, the dancers realized that these were the sons, brothers, cousins, and comrades of many of those present, who were being driven off in chains to Siberia. "For one fleeting second," wrote a contemporary, "the same candelabrum illuminated, upstairs in the white ballroom, the Emperor Nicholas dancing with the old Princess Volkonsky, and her son Sergei in the street below, huddled tense, pale, and in fetters between two gendarmes. Then the coachmen cracked their whips, the horses sprang forward, and the troikas were off again on their 4,500-mile journey to the east."

It was the formidable Prince Repnin, Sergei's handsome and powerful eldest brother, who finally broke through the barrier of silence around Maria. He arrived unexpectedly at her aunt's house, went up to her, and told her about the verdict and the executions that followed, about Sergei's sentence to hard labor and his imminent departure for exile, his loss of titles, possessions, and civil rights. "I have prepared your wife for everything and told her you will keep only your life," he wrote to his brother that same day. "She is determined to share her life between you and her son." Repnin also brought the Moscow and St. Petersburg papers, and a letter from their sister Sophia in which she expressed astonishment at not having heard from Maria for so long, and at her not coming to St. Petersburg to say farewell to Sergei. "If you delay much longer, dear sister, you risk not finding your husband here any longer; but of course Sergei will understand that you have to comply with your family's wishes."

Loyalty to her family prevented Maria from explaining to the Volkonskys why she had not gone to St. Petersburg. Details of her husband's noble and dignified behavior during the trial, which were now becoming public knowledge, of his martyrdom in the Fortress and his unflinching devotion to the cause—all this released deep chords of affection within her and reinforced her longing for him. Her mind was made up. Nothing would keep her from following Sergei to Siberia, even at the cost of breaking her father's heart. Her sister Ekaterina Orlov mentions in one of her letters that she had found Maria rereading Byron's poem *Mazeppa* on the day after Repnin left. Did she, with her vivid imagination, see herself as the Byronic heroine, breaking away from her father to follow her husband, who was much older than she? It could have been one of the images that had floated through Maria's restless, feverish mind at the time. Two years later, Pushkin wrote *Poltava*, based on Byron's *Mazeppa*. The heroine of *Poltava* bears a striking similarity to Maria. It was supposed to have been written for her, and it is quite likely that they discussed it together and reread Byron's poetic dialogue—"Husband or father, who shall it be"—when they met in Odessa at the Vorontsov house the year before. Undeniably, it had left a strong impression on her.

In the context of the times, and given the fact that she was not yet twenty-one, Maria's decision to take her fate in her own hands was both brave and unusual. In the first part of the nineteenth century, young women whose husbands happened to be absent followed the will of their fathers or fathers-in-law. General Raevsky was a god to his family. Even the cynical Alexander, the onetime rebel, now bowed to him and respected his wishes. There are constant expressions of concern in the Raevsky girls' letters to each other about the "terrible grief Mashenka is causing our father"; his grief seems of much greater importance to them than Maria's tragedy.

Their concern might have been justified, for the old warrior was undergoing his own personal purgatory. Face to face with himself, he knew that the responsibility for the dreadful misfortune that had descended on them was his. His son-in-law had been perfectly open with him. Long before the engagement, he admitted that he was a member of a secret society and had refused to leave it. He was in love with Maria, but he had warned his future father-in-law that, if he pressed, he would have to sacrifice her and his own happiness and withdraw from the marriage. It had all been so clear! But so dazzling was the match that the general had given in to temptation. And now his beloved Mashenka would end up being buried alive in Siberia.

"My darling, invaluable Mashenka," he wrote to her after Repnin's visit to Alexandria. "So now you know the full truth about your misfortune. I hid it from you to prolong your happy state of mind and because I wanted to be the chief messenger to my daughter. I had hoped that my tender parental love would give me the power to ease your sorrow. Darling Mashenka, I can say no more, since you seem determined to follow your husband. I write to you through tears, and these are not the first tears."

Clinging vainly to the one remaining hope that Sergei himself would forbid her to go to Siberia, he wrote to his son-in-law: "You know the devotion of your wife. Do not be her assassin. The power to stop her is *yours!*" He was furious at what he perceived as the Volkonsky family's efforts "to put pressure on Mashenka" to hurry her departure for Siberia. For example, the plan evolved by the old princess, whose behavior at the Kochubey ball had been widely criticized by friends and strangers alike. ("Imagine, the old mother goes to the ball and dances with the Emperor, to the great scandal of all the onlookers," noted Ancelot from St. Petersburg.) A few days after the ball, the old princess announced that she had decided to go to Siberia to keep her son company—since his wife had evidently decided to stay behind.

"You have seen the papers," Raevsky raged to his son Alexander. "The old woman says she is going to Siberia. Of course it is pretense, she has no intention of going . . . Let her, but I will not allow Mashenka to follow, though everyone will attack me for it."

It is doubtful whether the old woman ever actually contemplated the journey. She was cunning, and her object was indeed to hurry Maria's departure. She believed that her son would benefit from Maria's presence, and both she and Prince Repnin wanted Maria and Sergei's child out of sight; they were a constant reminder of the tragedy that had darkened the family name. She needn't have worried. Maria had all the courage in the world, and her mind was made up.

The family's opposition was not the only obstacle to contend with when Maria arrived at St. Petersburg. There was also the problem of obtaining permission from the tsar—and the money. Though Sergei's vast wealth had been confiscated by the state, a considerable sum had been set aside for his wife, their child, and for Sergei's maintenance in exile. (These sums were increased in later years, following petitions from the family.) But the bureaucratic process was slow, and Maria was in a hurry. Her father flatly refused to help. The Volkonskys, for all their urgings, remained silent now that she was ready to travel. "Many unpleasant things were said to me about my past silence, but not a word about helping me with the money for the journey," wrote Maria. "I finally pawned my diamonds, paid a few debts left by Sergei, and composed a careful letter to the Emperor asking for his permission to join my husband in Siberia."

She was encouraged in her petition by her new friend, Princess Trubetskoy, born Katherine Laval, a Frenchwoman who had married Sergei Trubetskoy, the ill-fated "provisional dictator" of the movement. Katyusha was small, round, and vivacious, with a homely face and incredible energy. She had remained in St. Petersburg after the uprising and had managed to visit her husband regularly in the Fortress. Childless and much in love with the weak and rather ineffective Sergei, she was determined to share his exile. Through mutual friends in court circles, the two women learned that they had an ally in the young empress, who had been heard to remark that she "would have done the same in their place." The empress's compassion for the unhappy wives, several of whom were among the greatest ornaments of her court, as well as dear personal friends, undoubtedly had a bearing on the tsar's decision to allow them to follow their men.

While Maria waited for imperial permission, the feud between the Raevskys and the Volkonskys raged on. Maria's family felt that the marriage should be annulled and deeply resented the Moika contingent's pressure on her to rejoin a husband who "has ruined his wife and therefore lost all rights to her heart." The Volkonskys, on the other hand, could not forgive the old general for keeping Maria in ignorance of her husband's fate for so long. The acrimony did nothing to lift Maria's spirits. She felt abandoned by all and depressed.

Only her sister Ekaterina was helpful. She was the lucky one, for her husband, Mikhail Orlov, had escaped punishment, although he was as guilty as the others. Ekaterina helped Maria with her most pressing financial problems, bought her warm traveling clothes, organized her medicine chest, and bought her a kibitka, a fast carriage, to travel in. "Don't ignore Mashenka's feelings," she wrote to her father, "don't hinder her. If she is prevented from going, she will be in torment. I say this as a wife myself. She can still find happiness in her devotion to her husband. Don't make her break her marriage vows. If—as I think —her mind is at present filled with *les pensées romantiques*, for she has always been a great reader, then time will cool her devotion and she will return to us. If not, let her meet her fate."

Maria had now been in St. Petersburg since mid-November, living in the Volkonsky Palace, in the same first-floor apartments overlooking the Moika Canal where Pushkin was to die eleven years later. Nikolenka, her eleven-month-old son, was with her; he was thriving, growing sturdy, and beginning to talk. ("Am teaching him how to say 'Papa,'" Maria wrote to her husband, who with the other prisoners was at Irkutsk awaiting shipment to the eastern shore of Lake Baikal.) Little Nikolenka had his father's blond hair and regular features, combined with his mother's liveliness and huge dark eyes. He was an enchanting little boy and the darling of the household. Everyone in St. Petersburg was concerned about his future, including the Dowager Empress. *"Cet enfant du malheur,"* she called him.

The tsar had let it be known some time before that there was no question of allowing mothers to take children with them to Siberia. His verdict was communicated to Maria by her brother-in-law Prince Peter Volkonsky, the court minister; it was hoped that she would now abandon the entire project and remain in St. Petersburg with her son. "My son is happy, but my husband is very unhappy and needs me more," Maria wrote to the emperor, renewing her plea for permission to travel. The long-awaited letter finally arrived on December 21. It was short, written in French on white vellum, with a huge red seal at the back:

I have, dear Princess, the letter you sent me on December 15. It has pleased me to receive the expression of the feelings you so kindly have conveyed to me. You are undoubtedly aware of the particular interest I have always taken in your personal welfare and it is because of this interest that I feel it my duty to warn you again of the extreme danger that awaits you once you have decided to travel beyond Irkutsk. Having said that, I leave the decision to you.

I send you my affectionate greetings.

Nicholas

The vellum envelope with the imperial double-eagled seal lay on the floor at her feet. Nikolenka, attracted by the red circle, seized it in his little hands and played with it happily; he couldn't have known that the letter condemned him to eternal separation from his mother.

"I warn you of the danger you will find beyond Irkutsk," wrote the tsar. Ominous words, and a warning Maria did not fully understand and blithely chose to disregard. The extent of the tsar's vindictiveness and of his spite did not become apparent to her until many weeks later. Tsar Nicholas was allowing Maria, Katyusha Trubetskoy, and Annie Muraviev to rejoin their husbands, provided they leave their children behind. What had been kept from them, however, was the fact that, once they passed beyond Irkutsk, they would never be allowed to return to European Russia, even in the event of the death of their husbands. "Let the thought of the fate of their wives torture the criminals in their lifetime," said the tsar. If the women wanted to share their fate, so be it, but it was going to be a one-way ticket for them, a journey of no return.

Would Maria's decision have been different had she known that the door was to shut behind her? "I am glad I did not realize it at the time," she admitted when writing to Ekaterina from Nerchinsk. Considering the exalted state she was in, the knowledge would probably not have been sufficient to change her mind. But it would certainly have made her family's opposition implacable. The only reason the old general allowed her to go was that he clung desperately to the notion that Maria, having left her baby son behind, would return in a year's time. Nor did Prince Sergei expect her to remain in Siberia. Most of his letters to Maria were withheld by Benckendorff's secret police on the tsar's orders, to further weaken the link between them, but it is clear from the ones that got through that the prince was unaware of the emperor's cruel deception. Though he longed for a visit from his wife, he truthfully described the hardships she would be likely to face and said that on no account was she to bring Nikolenka with her. He knew that there was a great risk in her coming, and he foresaw bureaucratic difficulties about the return journey. Yet he wanted her in Nerchinsk with him. "You yourself must decide what you should do," he wrote her. "I am placing you in a cruel situation, but, *chère amie*, I cannot bear the sentence of eternal separation from you." And he repeated a few days later: "Your choice is eternal separation from me, or temporary separation from your son."

Maria, meanwhile, had obtained the necessary permission and wrote to Sergei a few days before her departure: "I can tell you now that I had to bear a great deal to obtain this piece of paper. But at last I am ready. Without you, I am as without life; only my love and duty to Nikolenka prevented me from sharing your fate earlier. I am leaving him without worry; he is surrounded by guardians and will not feel his mother's absence; his dear, beaming face seems to tell me: 'Go, go and return to take me with you.' "

Before she left St. Petersburg, Maria had one more conversation with her father. For days now, the old man had been silent and unapproachable, but she had to see him once more to discuss the legal guardianship of her child. "When I showed him the Emperor's letter," she confided to her diary, "my poor father, unable to control himself, rose from his chair and, shaking both fists over my head, called to me in a voice choked with emotion: 'My curse will follow you to the grave if you don't return within a year!' How could I promise? I threw myself on a sofa and buried my face in a pillow. I could not bear to see him like that. My father, the hero of 1812, the most venerated man in Russia, who had once led his two teenage sons into battle, had the most tender of hearts. He could not bear to think of me in a prison."

On her last day in St. Petersburg, Maria dined with Peter Volkonsky, husband of Sergei's favorite sister, Sophia. It was an early winter afternoon; Prince Peter came to collect her in his carriage, and they drove along the pink granite quays near the river, under a pale, opalescent sky. Snow covered St. Petersburg; all the trees were powdered with frost. It suited the cold beauty of Polar Venice, blending with the pastel-colored palaces, a rainbow of pinks, yellows, pistachio, and flaxen blues, dominated by the reddish mass of the Winter Palace. It was shortly after 2 p.m. —the fashionable hour for dining and promenading along the granite quays after the daily military parade was over; the Exchange had closed for the day, and the commercial business of the city had ceased. All the *beau monde* could be found strolling by the river on the English Quay in front of the Admiralty, hoping to catch a glimpse of the emperor, who was often seen promenading among his subjects, or of the pretty young Empress Alexandra Fedorovna, who loved shopping and was always followed by two gigantic lackeys dressed in purple coats and fur hats whose duty it was to carry her parcels and open doors whenever she chose to grace a merchant with her patronage.

Along the wide prospects walked people from all nations of Europe and most of Asia: black, white, yellow faces, all races and costumes. There were British and American sea captains, blond Norwegians, Bokharans and Persians wrapped in silks, Indians, Chinese with long pigtails, sturdy Germans. And among the chattering, gesticulating crowds dashed the droshkies, the tireless St. Petersburg droshkies, galloping across the wide expanses of the great city, driven by coachmen in long, padded, red or blue caftans fastened with silver buttons and cinched with Circassian belts, wearing low, furry hats with rounded crowns, full beards spread over their chests, arms outstretched, a rein in each hand—proud, independent, and tough. They were a tribe to themselves, a tribe that set its own rules; horses were led by voice alone, for no self-respecting coachman used a whip.

Prince Peter glanced at the lovely young woman next to him. She was dressed in a long, green velvet skirt, a tight-fitting jacket edged with sables, her dark, curly hair spilling out from under the fashionable fur bonnet. In spite of the strain of the last year, she had retained her dazzling complexion and ready laughter. But the magnificent dark eyes were wistful as she contemplated the lively scene around her. She thought of Pushkin's words: "I love you, city of Peter's creation."

Prince Peter was privy to many a court secret, and it is likely that he knew or guessed what awaited Maria beyond Irkutsk. Was that why he seemed so perturbed, Maria later wondered. If he knew, it must have seemed wrong to him that a girl so young and so alive should be sent to live in a wilderness. There was still time for her to change her mind. "Are you certain that you will be allowed to come back?" he asked. The question surprised her and she was silent for a moment. "I don't even desire it, unless I am allowed to return with Sergei," she finally said. "But for God's sake don't worry my father with that."

She thought about Prince Peter's warning on her way to Moscow a few days later. What exactly was her brother-in-law trying to tell her? Did he know what was in the tsar's mind? It was no use to speculate, she decided; she would soon find out. Next morning, having commended her son to the care of her mother-in-law, Maria left St. Petersburg for Moscow, the first leg of her long journey.

7

The Journey

THE ROAD BETWEEN ST. PETERSBURG AND MOSCOW was reputed to be the best in the realm. Constructed in 1816, it was at the time of Maria's travel in the final stages of completion—677 versts (about 450 miles) of well-kept highway, where before only tracks had existed, worn out by generations of cart wheels and weary feet.* Even so, the indefatigable Marquis de Custine, who traveled on it several years after Maria, found that "during long periods it gave the same sensation as experienced when riding a roller-coaster in Paris." Unfortunately for him, Custine was traveling in August in a high-back wheel carriage during the rainy season; Maria's sleigh, on the other hand, seemed to fly in the snow, covering an average of ninety to a hundred miles in twenty-four hours. Stopping at the relays only long enough to change horses, she arrived at the great plain before Moscow on the morning of the fifth day of travel. It was a day of dazzling sunshine, so different from the murky grayness of St. Petersburg.

---

* It was in the later stages of Nicholas I's reign that main roads began to be built linking provinces and cities throughout Russia; all of them were constructed by slave labor.

Before her spread the golden panorama of the old capital: the bulbous domes of the churches, the airy spires, the palaces and the convents, the minarets and gilded roofs, the green porticoes of the medieval monasteries. They crossed over the bridge on the Moskva River, opposite the crenellated red mass of the Kremlin, and could now hear the pealing of endless bells, led by the chimes of the great clock over the Spassky Gate. It was market day, and outside the citadel milled crowds of people from every corner of Europe and Asia—exotic, bright-colored, shouting, gesticulating, nibbling sunflower seeds, loitering by the booths.

Princess Zenaida Volkonsky's palace was on the Tversky Boulevard. As the sleigh drove into the enormous courtyard, the coachman cracked his whip with a flourish to announce their arrival, and the noble gates of the house swung open to admit her. She was home with her favorite cousin.

At the time of Maria's visit, Zenaida Volkonsky was thirty-seven years old. Fair, blue-eyed, a classical beauty, she was remembered as the close friend of the late Emperor Alexander, but above all was admired and respected as a writer and as the leader of the foremost literary salon in Russia. Since Maria had stayed with her in Odessa, the princess had traveled to Italy and been to Paris, had published two books of short stories in French, and had even written an opera in Italian. When she returned to Russia from her travels, she found, much to her satisfaction, that her reputation as a writer had preceded her. She became the first woman to be elected a member of the Society of Russian History and Antiquities and of the Moscow Society of Lovers of Russian Literature. Her classical salon, from which she reigned over the Moscow literary scene, is described by Adam Mickiewicz, a regular guest, in his reminiscences:

> It was a huge room in neoclassical style, painted white, with Greek columns and Greek statuary. One end of it was a library

filled with books in Empire-style glassed-in cases; there were works by Voltaire, Rousseau, Chateaubriand, André Chénier, by Bernardin de Saint-Pierre, Madame de Staël, and many other, both recent and classical, French and English writers. Alfred de Vigny and Musset occupied prominent positions in the nearest bookcase by the window—and so did Byron. There were some splendid pieces of furniture by renowned French cabinetmakers, and many comfortable armchairs, in which dozed elderly relatives and assorted aged visitors—reminiscent of the days of Catherine the Great and Potemkin. The other end of the great salon was dominated by a piano, which seemed to be in constant use; it was the rallying point in the room. Flowering orange trees, chrysanthemums, and hothouse plants in huge tubs filled the air with a most pleasing aroma . . . Waiters in white gloves, blue-and-gold livery, and red slippers moved silently among the guests with trays laden with food, champagne, and drinks of all sorts . . . It was a most luxurious ambiance . . . From the fertile soil of central Russia and the labor of thousands of slaves flowed the money for the Moscow salons. Nevertheless, it was a joy to go there, for the princess collected all the artistic and literary lights of her day, and her charm and hospitality made these gatherings unique. She made only two demands on her guests: a modicum of talent, and punctuality at meals.

Music, theater, and poetry were Princess Zenaida's natural elements. Though nicknamed the Corinne of the North by her admirers, she was far prettier and more feminine than Mme de Staël, and less interested in politics than the famous "Mistress to an Age" had been in her time. The comparison never failed to annoy Zenaida. She much preferred Pushkin's admiring description, "Queen of the Muses and of Beauty," or the poet Venevitinov's loving confession that "she suffused his poetry."

The Corinne of the North was anything but a bluestocking;

gay, affectionate, intensely human, she now greeted her unfortunate cousin with a warmth that none of the other Volkonskys had ever shown her. Worried by what awaited Maria in Siberia, Zenaida was determined to do everything in her power to make her cousin's stay in Moscow memorable. "I shall never forget Zenaida's wonderful welcome," wrote Maria. "She was all tenderness and delicate thought. Knowing my passion for music, she collected the best of Italian talent in Moscow at the time. I was transported with joy to hear such bel canto. Many of the arias I had studied myself recently and would have sung with the artists, but unfortunately I had contracted a bad cold on the journey and my voice had completely left me. So I just sat there and listened, clapping my hands and asking for more." Then, on a more personal note, she continued: "Pushkin, my childhood friend, was in the room; he never left my side all evening . . . Unusual for him, he was silent and grave. But we understood each other without words."

It is interesting to see how others among the guests saw Maria that evening. In a fragment from his diary, found by his son in the papers of the poet Venevitinov, there is the following description: "Yesterday I had an unforgettable evening. I saw for the second time and found out more about the unfortunate Princess Maria Volkonsky. She is not as beautiful as her cousin [Venevitinov was in love with Zenaida], but her eyes are extraordinarily expressive. Two days ago, she was twenty [Maria was just twenty-one]—too young to be stricken with woes—but this attractive and capable woman proved to be master of her misfortune. She overcame it and shed all her tears. She has accepted her fate and the decision has left her calm. Remember, she is a mother and has doomed herself to sacrifice as Christ did . . . She greatly loves music. Music alone can harmonize with her feelings at present, for what is more appropriate than music to soothe the soul? . . . She listened to the singing all evening, and when one song was finished, she requested another. She didn't go into the main drawing room until midnight, because Princess Zenaida had many guests, but she sat behind a screen listening, while her hostess attended to her with great concern for her comfort. A piece from Maestro Paer's *Agnes* was cut short at the point where the unfortunate daughter begs her unhappy father for his blessing. The unintended coincidence caused Princess Zenaida much distress; she ordered the singing to stop and rushed out to her unfortunate sister-in-law, who had to leave the room because her tears were overflowing and she didn't want it noticed, as everyone would then have come to her . . . The rest of the evening was sad, in spite of attempts to break the gloomy silence with lighthearted duets. When everyone had gone and only Princess Zenaida's dearest and closest remained—including Pushkin—the Princess sat near the piano and continued to listen to the music, enraptured. She moved closer to the clavichord, tried a few notes, then sat on a divan, spoke a little in a quiet voice, smiling now and then. Sometimes a cloud would pass over her eyes, a memory or anticipation, then she would hide her head in her hands to cover her emotion. She asked each one of us to sing her something, assuring us that the memory would lighten her difficult road to Siberia. When my turn came, I couldn't refuse and somehow stumbled through a duet from *Don Juan*. She thanked me, as did the others, not out of empty courtesy, but with her heart. I wish I could have captured the expression on her face to preserve it forever. It was late, and Princess Zenaida ordered supper to be brought in. During the meal, the sad Princess tried to turn our attention to something else, talking of various topics, to make us feel cheerful. I left at 2 a.m. and returned home with my heart overflowing; I shall never forget that evening."

Everyone in the room had noted Pushkin's silence—so unusual that it provoked endless comment. Tears came to his eyes when he heard Maria whisper to one of the singers: "Again, sing that again! To think that I may never again hear music." Pushkin was deeply moved, both as a poet and as a man. It was five and a half years since that radiant May morning in the Crimea when Maria had first captured his imagination—the graceful, lithe girl with the huge, expressive dark eyes, happily playing with the surf on a crescent-shaped beach. How young and brimming with life she was! Since then he had become Russia's foremost poet; many called him a genius; he had since known many beautiful, sophisticated, clever women, his love affairs were legion, but somehow Maria's memory dwelled within him. He had resented her marrying Volkonsky—was it plain jealousy, or a poet's premonition? And now here she was in this room—more beautiful and alive than ever, an angel of abnegation and courage, sharing her last hours of freedom with him.

"He held my hand through the evening," wrote Maria, "and he told me that he admired my devotion and that he would come and visit me beyond the Urals. He planned to write a long poem about Pugachev's rebellion and then continue east to see me. He wrote his splendid poem, but he never came to Siberia."

Pushkin would not have been allowed to go to Lake Baikal even if he had wanted to. In future years, though marriage and life intervened, he never forgot Maria. A few days after her departure from Moscow, when the wife of Nikita Muraviev was in turn leaving town to join her husband in Siberia, Pushkin—oblivious of Benckendorff's spies around him, and risking severe punishment for unauthorized correspondence with political exiles—gave her a warm personal message for "the little Maria," and a poem written for his friends, now exiled:

> In the depths of the Siberian mines
> Keep that proud patience.

> The heavy chains will fall,
> The prison gates will open wide.
> Outside, freedom awaits you.

Pushkin had only eleven more years to live. He died on a snowy January night in St. Petersburg, killed in a duel provoked by his wife's infidelity.

Ekaterina Orlov came to call the next day—affectionate and attentive, conscious of the injustice of their fate. She brought a bearskin rug, books, drawing paper, wool, knitting needles, and money, for the sums reluctantly disbursed by the Volkonskys would have hardly lasted Maria beyond Irkutsk. In a final gesture of concern, Ekaterina took off her fur-lined pelisse and threw it around her sister's shoulders. *"Leurs adieux furent déchirants,"* noted Princess Zenaida.

When Maria's presence in Moscow became known, relatives of other deported prisoners arrived, bringing letters, parcels of clothing, and medicine. "There was so much of it," wrote Maria, "that I had to buy another kibitka to fit it all in." There was no time to recruit a family retainer from Boltyshka, so she was obliged to find domestics who would be willing to accompany her to Siberia and who were in possession of a passport.* As it turned out, both the manservant and the maid she so hurriedly engaged in Moscow proved to be unreliable and dishonest and had to be returned to Russia, undoubtedly much to their satisfaction, as they were appalled by conditions in Siberia.

* Until 1861, the year of the emancipation of the slaves, peasant serfs were not permitted to move freely about the country or work for a master of their choice. They all had to have a passport issued by their current owner.

The night before her departure, Maria received a letter from her father: "I am writing to Moscow, my dear Mashenka, on the off-chance that this will reach you there. It is snowing. Your route will be good, and weather favorable. I pray for you, my poor innocent victim. May God strengthen your soul and comfort your heart."

She wrote back: "Dear, adored family! I am leaving this minute; the night is excellent, the road marvelously smooth . . . My sisters, my dear wonderful sisters . . . I am happy because I am at peace with myself . . . Farewell, my beloved parents . . . farewell."

Day after day, the sledge raced onward into the endless horizon. Enclosed as if in a time capsule, Maria was in a state of feverish elation. There was a sense of unreality to the journey: lack of sleep and little food. She stopped only at an occasional relay for a glass of hot lemon tea dispensed from the ever-present brass samovar. The intoxicating speed of the sleigh, pulled by three plunging horses, devoured the empty distances at a gallop, "*Poidi!*—onward . . . forward!" shouted the drivers, dashing on as great plumes of snow rose from under the horses' hooves, and harness bells jingled relentlessly, warning of the approach of the vehicle.

Like all Russians, Maria loved speed—*le vertige de la vitesse*, they called it. It was a national craving, derived from the vastness of the land, to which everybody, including the tsar, succumbed. And the best expression of it was the troika—the "bird troika," as Gogol was to call it, driven by Russian horses, "with the whirlwind sitting upon their manes."

The distances on the road were computed by striped black-and-white guardhouses topped by imperial eagles, and were punctuated every twenty-one versts (fourteen miles) or so by relays, at which the horses were changed. There was an occasional inn—a *korchma*—most often primitive and lice-ridden, with greasy tablecloths, rows of bottles, huge tureens of cabbage soup, mounds of blini, and the inevitable samovar, and crowded with peasants, merchants, or traveling officers playing cards and drinking vodka and the local brandy. One could curl up on the warm shelf by the stove and fall asleep, but Maria firmly refused to make a break in the journey. Only when the distress of her servants became acute did she consent to an overnight stop. Being afraid of the bug-infested walls of the *korchma*, she remained outside in her sleigh with the leather cover drawn over her head. She slept wrapped in Ekaterina's bear rug, with her sable-lined pelisse as a blanket. On the third day of their travel, they entered the old Tartar city of Kazan on the Volga, the ancient capital of the Kingdom of the Khans of the Golden Horde, captured for Russia by Ivan the Terrible. She was weary, and because it was New Year's Eve, they decided to stop at a hotel for a few hours.

"My hotel was in a wide, walled courtyard right next to the Kazan Nobility Club, whose drawing rooms were brilliantly lit in preparation for the New Year festivities; I saw groups of masked dancers gaily getting out of their sleighs, chatting, laughing. I couldn't get over the contrast: here were people, normal, ordinary people like myself, enjoying themselves, while I was descending into an abyss . . . All is finished for me, no more singing or dancing, no more carefree enjoyment . . . My elation vanished: I felt intensely unhappy and very frightened . . . I should have been ashamed of myself, but after all, I was only a few days past my twenty-first birthday and had not really lived! . . . While I was thus grappling with my emotions, an officer from the staff of the Governor of Kazan appeared in the hotel and, after introducing himself, informed me in a rather brisk and unpleasant manner that I would do better to turn around and go home; he said that Princess Trubetskoy, who had preceded me on this journey by a few weeks, had been ordered to stop at Irkutsk and would not be allowed to proceed beyond. I answered that His Majesty the Emperor had given me permission to join my husband and that I was traveling on his orders. After inspecting my papers, the officer left, shrugging and telling me I would come to regret my decision. His was just another attempt—very clumsy, at that—to make me change my mind. I was to run into it again and again on my journey." She left Kazan just before midnight, while the reveling was at its height. It had started to snow heavily and the hotelkeeper tried to convince her to wait until the blizzard abated. But Maria decided to go on. "I will have to brave far worse conditions than this in Siberia," she told him.

The coachman lowered the leather roof cover of the sledge and set off in the blizzard. "It was foolish of me to have insisted," she recalled. "I did not know the ferocity of the wind on the steppes of Kazan. The snow began to pile up on the flimsy leather roof over my sledge—there was a mountain of it between me and the coachman—the night was dark; no moon, no stars could be seen through the blizzard. My little traveling clock marked midnight, and so I made it ring to usher in the New year. It was New Year's Day—the start of the twenty-second year of my life." As no one else was about, she turned toward her maid with the traditional New Year's greeting, but "she answered in such a disagreeable manner that I addressed myself to the coachman. 'I wish you a Happy New Year,' I said, and my thoughts flew home to Boltyshka, to my youth, to my wonderfully happy childhood. It had always been such a festive time." She imagined herself attending New Year's Day services in Kiev's St. Sophia Cathedral as she had done so often with her family in years past: the glorious chanting, the jeweled icons, the opulent vestments, and the all-pervading smell of incense mixed with flowers. She should have stayed the night in Kazan, gone to church, prayed for God's help in this frightening new year which was about to unfold! But soon her thoughts veered back to her husband. "Poor Sergei, where is he? what is he doing at this moment?" Stark reality overwhelmed her; how will it all end? "I forgot about the danger of the road," she recalled. "All I could think of was my poor husband and what awaited me beyond Irkutsk."

They had been traveling for over an hour when the coachman informed her that it was impossible to go farther—the horses were exhausted and he did not know where he was; they had, in fact, lost their way. Someone spotted a woodsman's hut in the forest, and they spent the rest of the night huddled by a small fire; the wood was wet, the fire smoked, and jackals howled in the distance. "A most depressing sound, and a dismal beginning to the New Year," noted Maria. Next morning, the tempest had abated, the sky was clear, and they were able to continue their journey.

"The cold was so intense that I barely dared to stick my face out, so I saw nothing. I passed the time singing and reciting poetry to myself—anything in French, Italian, or English that my memory could dredge up. Then I went through the Russian ballads my *nyanya* had taught me in my now, oh, so very distant childhood. One day we came to a village in the foothills of the Urals and saw two huge bonfires blazing in the middle of the square. People were milling around a large caravan escorted by military guards." It turned out to be a transport of silver from the Nerchinsk mines, being conveyed to the capital. Wasn't Nerchinsk her husband's place of detention? Maria set off at once to question the officer in charge of the convoy, for he must have seen Sergei and his fellow prisoners. "I went into the post office to gain time and tidy up. I was determined to talk to the officer in charge, but the man turned out to be a brute . . . I knew

[1 3 9

it the moment I saw him, for he came into the room without taking his cap off, smoking a horrible cigar—the nauseating kind, the fumes of which made me quite ill . . . I nerved myself to ask him news of the state prisoners, whereupon he gave me an insolent look and replied: 'I have not seen them, and I have no desire to know anything about those rascals.' (His name was Fitinov, and I learned some years later that he ended up in jail, convicted of some gross misdemeanor.) I was furious, but my spirits revived when a few moments later I was approached by a young soldier who had witnessed the incident and obviously felt ashamed for his officer. 'I saw the prisoners at Nerchinsk,' he whispered. 'They are all well, don't worry, none of them has been ill.' I was much heartened by this news and grateful to the good man, so much more human and sensitive than his chief. A good Russian!"

After two weeks, they arrived at the Ural Mountains. Beyond them stretched the enormous land mass of Siberia, one fourth of the Asian continent, bigger than the United States, Alaska, and Europe put together. To most Russians in the first part of the nineteenth century, the Urals represented the limits of the habitable Christian land, and as such were a great psychological barrier. This was the official frontier of Europe, beyond which lay wilderness and pagan tribes. Strange tales abounded of the Samoyeds, so wretched and poverty-stricken a tribe that they turned cannibal and ate one another to sustain life in the depths of the winter; of Ostiak and Buriat tribes, who rode reindeer in the deep snowy forests, slept in a trance through the winter months, and woke with the first rays of spring, to worship the bear as it came out of its hibernation. According to the caravans plying between China and European Russia, Siberia was an inhospitable land of eternal cold, "somewhere at the frontier of

an unpeopled realm, where human existence was intolerable."
One Decembrist, Basargin, on hearing where he had been sentenced, considered himself "no longer an inhabitant of this
world."

Yet there were others in Russia who were attracted to the
country, to whom Siberia was a land of opportunity, comparable
to the United States of America, a place where serfdom did not
exist and where a great deal of money was to be made. As early
as the middle of the sixteenth century, Grigory Stroganov,
founder of the famous family of merchant adventurers, established the first settlement and trading post on the Upper Kama
River in the Urals. Baron Rozen, one of the Decembrists, after
ten years of exile in Siberia, predicted that, "with its fabulous
mineral resources, comparable to those of the United States,
Siberia is bound to become a great and prosperous state."
Rozen, like other Decembrists, hoped that, "just like the United
States, Siberia would one day become a haven for all refugees
from political and religious persecutions." Many dreamed of a
free Siberia federated with the United States.

To Maria, in her state of exalted anticipation, Siberia appeared as a promised land in which she was to be reunited with
Sergei and in which she was to assume the romantic role of
guardian angel, nurse, inspiration, and general protectress of the
exiled men. She would become a legend in her lifetime, the
heroine of local ballads, immortalized by her friend Pushkin and
other poets. Locked inside her kibitka, propelled over the endless snowy tracks across primeval forests by the ever-rushing
teams of relay horses, she retreated into a timeless make-believe
world in which the only reality was the agonizing exhaustion of
her body. As they were coming down the slopes of Mt. Altai in
the Urals, an unruly team of young horses broke their harness
and ran off, leaving the kibitka helplessly careering toward a
precipice. Jolted out of her reverie, Maria forced open the door

and jumped out into the deep snow, where she clung to the branches of a cedar tree until the coachman was able to summon help. Luck was with her, for the sledge, with her maid and luggage inside it, was recovered intact several hundred yards down the slope, its fall arrested by a stack of firewood. All around her, the mountains were covered with forests, spreading over the protruding cliffs, rising steeply from their bases. Silence reigned, and the cold was beyond anything she had ever experienced. To the east, heavy clouds forecast a big snowfall. After what seemed an agony of waiting, a distant jingling announced the arrival of relief horses. They repacked the heavy sledge, calmed the hysterical maid, the coachman climbed on his seat, and they were off again along the primitive track heading east.

Perm and Ekaterinburg passed unnoticed. While they were changing horses in Ekaterinburg, the center of Siberian mining, local merchants tried unsuccessfully to draw the "rich princess's" attention to amethysts, opals, chalcedonies, topazes, aquamarines, emeralds, and other varieties of rock crystal, all exhibited on the counters in huge mounds. Magnificent malachite doors like those in the Winter Palace, superb urns, vases, malachite tables and stools could be bought at incredibly low prices, a king's ransom for some enterprising merchant. But what use would they be to Maria? She looked utterly indifferent and ordered the coachman to speed on.

Tobolsk, the capital of western Siberia, nearly twelve hundred miles from St. Petersburg, seemed like the end of the world to Maria. Yet she was not even halfway to her destination. This ancient city was situated at the confluence of two powerful rivers —the Tobol and the Irtysh, which join the mighty Ob farther north and empty into the Arctic Ocean. The city was forever associated with Ermak, the Cossack chieftain who discovered and conquered Siberia. His tomb and monument were there, dominating the ancient Upper Town; his legend lived on throughout Russia and particularly in the Cossack ballads of Maria's native Ukraine. As a child, she had often heard the story from the family coachman, who liked to recount Ermak's exploits as he polished the brasses in the harness room at Boltyshka, and traveling bards sang Ermak ballads to the accompaniment of a lute at the autumn campfires on the Dnieper. Ermak's conquest of Siberia in the latter part of the sixteenth century was a feat of imagination and daring on a scale comparable to the exploits of the Spanish conquistadors. It resulted in the transformation of Russia from a fledgling state—loosely grouped about the Tsar of Muscovy, who only recently had ceased to pay yearly tributes to the Tartar khans—into an Oriental power occupying one quarter of Asia, whose writ was to run from the Urals for three thousand miles to the Pacific, and whose shadow would eventually fall as far as Alaska and California.

With a force of about a thousand men, armed and equipped with muskets by the Stroganovs, who controlled the Russian frontier along the Urals, Ataman Ermak defeated a detachment of thirty thousand cavalry of the famous blind Mogul chief Kuchum Khan, who considered himself heir to the great Genghis Khan. It was not only a triumph of foot soldiers against massed cavalry forces and of fire power against primitive bows and arrows, but also a triumph of Ermak's superior tactics. Taking advantage of a peculiar feature of Siberian geography—a network of interconnecting rivers and streams which form a spiderweb across the continent, Ermak embarked his army on rafts and floated with them downstream, transferring from one river basin to the next by easy portages. He and his men thus penetrated into the heart of enemy territory. "When Ermak and his Cossacks launched upon the upper headwaters of the Tagil," goes the seventeenth-century *Remezov Chronicle*, "it was as if a new virus had been injected into the circulatory system of northern Asia. It became obvious to Kuchum Khan that unless the Cossacks were stopped, they would spread through the rivers into every corner of Siberia." Eventually, Ermak's genius as a tactician, together with the firepower of Russian muskets, triumphed over the enemy's numbers. The blind khan and his retinue of Mongol princes abandoned their capital, Sibir (after which the country was named), and fled. Ermak fortified Sibir and sent his deputy, Ataman Koltso, back to Moscow with a sumptuous tribute of furs to the tsar as living proof of Siberia's riches. He placed the conquered territories under his empire's rule. Ivan the Terrible, dazzled (at that time, furs were a priceless commodity in Russia), ordered Moscow church bells to be rung in celebration. He also dispatched reinforcements to help Ermak consolidate his gains.

Ermak was killed in an encounter with the Tartars, drowned in the river Irtysh, weighed down by the splendid golden suit of armor given him by the tsar. Like King Arthur's sword, this armor passed into the realm of myth. According to local lore, it reappears in the waters of the Irtysh on the shortest night of the year, "one arm covered in golden chain mail, but vanishes immediately if anyone tries to seize it."

By the end of the seventeenth century, all Siberia, right to the Pacific Ocean, was opened up and most of the local tribes subjugated: the gentle reindeer-riding Chukchi, who "could be seen traveling through the forests like strange jockeys on antlered mounts" and worshipped the storm spirits of Lake Baikal; the Tungus, who sewed their dead in a bag of reindeer skin and hanged them in trees, because the ground never thawed; and the Mongol Buriats, who worshipped the bear when he came out of hibernation—all these tribes became subjects of the tsar. It was Peter the Great who demanded to know what lay in the farthest northeastern part of the country. Was there a body of water suitable for navigation to serve as a highway of commerce with China and all the way to India? What was the mysterious land talked about by missionaries and Chinese traders which lay beyond that sea passage? If there was such a land, let it become the dominion of the Russian tsars! "I want to know where America begins," he exclaimed as he lay on his deathbed at St. Petersburg. He summoned Vitus Bering, a Danish captain in the service of the Russian navy, and ordered him to mount a naval expedition from Kamchatka to establish whether Asia and America were connected. The result of Bering's two voyages was the colonization of Alaska, and a Russian presence on the northern coast of California, an achievement the Ataman Ermak would have approved of.

The Governor General of western Siberia, Prince Gorchakov, who had served under General Raevsky at Borodino, received Maria in the governor's mansion. Tobolsk was far enough from St. Petersburg for Gorchakov to feel that he could entertain whom he wished. In the social desert around him, the arrival of a lovely young woman two weeks out of St. Petersburg was a pleasing event, certainly not to be missed. By then, Maria's exhaustion was so great that the idea of a comfortable bed and decent food seemed something straight out of paradise. The two days were a welcome break; she felt close to her family, as the governor talked to her of her father, of his admiration for him, and showed genuine concern for her future. How could this beautiful young woman be allowed to proceed beyond Irkutsk? Tobolsk was bad enough, but Lake Baikal? Surely this was no place for the daughter of the man "whose name alone had been worth battalions to the Russian army." But Maria's determination never wavered. She enjoyed Prince Gorchakov's hospitality, and the restful stay restored her strength. On her last day, after attending a religious service in the Tobolsk Cathedral in the company of the governor and his wife, she climbed the steep narrow path to Ermak's tomb, a sacred place for the local inhabitants, over which "a ghostly light was supposed to flicker most nights." In a strange way, Ermak was a link with her childhood, going back to the tales told by Bogdan the coachman at Boltyshka and the ballads sung by the Cossacks on the Dnieper; she was ready to continue her journey into the limitless land he had conquered.

She sped past Omsk and Tomsk. Days and nights again merged, like the forests and steppes that slid past. For long stretches, no life showed in the unchanging emptiness; and when it appeared, it was foreign, like the Buriats, with their slit eyes, dressed in roughly sewn reindeer skins, mounted on toy-like, shaggy, blunt-nosed horses, or the Chinese merchants on their way eastward to Kyakhta, who so kindly provided her with bread, tea, rum, and sugar and wondered what this young woman was doing traveling alone in the heart of the Asiatic countryside. Asia was closing in around her; even the soldiers at the relay stations looked Asiatic.

The wavering track along which she was traveling was the so-called imperial *trakt*, later known as the Great Siberian Post Road. It would be trudged by generations of convicts and political exiles. In Maria's day, the road was still undefined and it was hard to see the way forward. Small clumps of evergreens, their branches contrasting with snow, were placed on both sides of the road, to direct drivers. On some sections, silvery columns of birches fringed the route.

Krasnoyarsk provided a welcome relief from emptiness. A large and opulent town on the direct route of the caravans leading east, it offered a variety of shops, bazaars, and relatively clean hotels. The crossed the frozen Enisei, more than three miles wide at Krasnoyarsk, on a sledge ferry crowded with

Buriat tribesmen and their beasts. Before them lay the grandiose spectacle of a primeval river cutting through cliffs of porphyry, amid steep, towering banks of pink granite. Maria heard, while they awaited the ferry, how in the terrible depths of the Enisei seventy-pound sturgeons and other huge fish collect in pools in the winter and how local fishermen drill holes in the ice near the shore, ringing the deepest pools with their nets and pulling out fabulous hauls. She saw the "holy islands" on the water—little outposts of rock and birch trees, where shamans and priestly sorcerers were said to dwell. As the ferry slowly wound its way toward the eastern shore, a chain of blue mountains appeared on the distant horizon—the mountains of Transbaikalia. Beyond them lay the great inland sea, Lake Baikal.

They were now in eastern Siberia, having crossed a small river ominously called the Styx by the convicts exiled to Transbaikalia. Driving over the Bratsky steppe before Irkutsk, they were suddenly surrounded by herds of wild horses and horned cattle that were unfamiliar with humans. Many of them came close to gaze at the sleighs gliding over their native habitat.

On the morning of the twenty-third day after leaving Moscow, having covered approximately four thousand miles, they saw, looming out of the snowy atmosphere, a multitude of gold-domed churches and monasteries and the ornate, turreted houses of the rich merchants, their tin-and-copper casings reflecting the morning rays of the sun. It was Irkutsk, the capital of eastern Siberia, the city where Maria's fate was to be decided and where, in the years to come, she was to leave the imprint of her powerful personality.

8

Point of No Return:

Irkutsk

"I FOUND IRKUTSK ATTRACTIVE," wrote Maria. "Its position is lovely and the Angara River magnificent, even when covered with ice. My first act on arrival was to go into a church and ask for a service of thanksgiving, for the more I reflected on my journey, the more grateful I was to God for allowing me to come this far safe and healthy. The priest who accepted my offering was a Father Peter Gromov, who by a strange coincidence was some years later assigned as chaplain to our prison in Petrovsky Zavod; he was a wonderful man and became a lifelong friend. After a fervent prayer that I soon be reunited with Sergei, I drove to the large hotel by the river and gave orders to unpack the kibitkas."

Irkutsk, which in St. Petersburg was ironically referred to as the "Paris of Siberia," grew out of the winter quarters established in 1652 by Ivan Pokharov, a Russian customs official, for the collection of the fur tax from the Buriats. At the time of Maria's arrival, it counted fifteen thousand inhabitants, a dozen churches, two monasteries, a number of fine merchant houses— built of brick—and several imposing public buildings, dominated by the huge white stone governor's mansion on the banks of the Angara. The streets were wide and ran at right angles, but except for the main roadway, the rest were unpaved, petering out into snow, slush, and mud. It was the time of the Russian winter carnival, the *maslenitsa*, which in this Asiatic emptiness was celebrated with particular gusto; jostling crowds filled the streets and the Oriental bazaars, preparing for the festivities ahead.

A pleasant surprise was waiting for Maria when she returned to the hotel to supervise the unpacking. Attached to the back of her kibitka, covered with layers of sheeting and furry rugs, and well hidden under the numerous cases and trunks containing personal effects was a lovely small piano! It was a present from Princess Zenaida, and had been fastened to the back of the carriage during Maria's last night in Moscow, while she slept. Only one other piano existed in eastern Siberia at the time; it was in the governor's mansion, and as no tuner had yet dared to undergo the long journey to Irkutsk, it remained unused.

"I was thrilled," Maria recalled, "and the more so when I realized that my piano had survived the vicissitudes of the journey extremely well; it was so cleverly packed! I immediately started to play and to accompany myself singing. I was not alone any more, I had my music. Dear, beloved Zenaida, how like her! She knew this was the one thing that would cheer me in whatever awaited me in the future."

She had hardly had time to unpack and change clothes when General Zeidler was announced. General Friedrich Zeidler, Governor of Irkutsk, was a German in the service of the Russian tsar. Since the days of Peter the Great and his passion for everything Western, there have always been many foreigners and particularly Germans in the officers' corps of the Russian army. The Germans were the lawgivers in military science, and most Russian military textbooks were written by Germans in German and then translated into Russian by other Germans. In the 1820s, half of the higher dignitaries in Russia were of German stock, or at least had German surnames (only a quarter were Russians); German officers commanded prestigious regiments and filled far-flung administrative posts throughout the empire. Their arrogant efficiency, combined with their preoccupation with exactitude, symmetry, and hierarchy introduced a modicum of order in the country; it was also responsible for creating gigantic bottlenecks, when it collided with the slovenly and corrupt ways of minor Russian officials.

Friedrich Zeidler had spent his life in assorted administrative posts. Born in East Prussia, he joined the Russian army in his twenties and filled a number of military and administrative posts, without ever quite reaching the top. Now in his early sixties, he looked forward to retirement in his native East Prussia; he knew that his pension would depend on how well he performed in his present job.

Maria saw before her a gray-haired man with light blue, expressionless eyes; his dark green general's uniform, with its heavily gilded epaulettes, showed signs of wear. (She noted that it was "slightly yellowed in the creases.") He addressed her in heavily accented French. After congratulating her on the extraordinary rapidity of her travel—"almost as fast as an imperial courier"—the governor adopted the stance of a benevolent uncle, trying to dissuade his favorite niece from the folly of continuing her journey beyond Irkutsk. Her husband was nine hundred versts away (six hundred miles), he pointed out; the roads were dangerous and impassable in most places. Of course he understood the emotions that prompted her to leave St. Petersburg and embark on this heroic journey to the east, and so, he said, did the tsar. But now that she was in Irkutsk, the last outpost of the civilized world, it would be very much better for her and her family if, after a decent rest and an exchange of letters with her husband, which he himself would speedily arrange, she was to turn back and rejoin her small son. She had fully discharged her duty as a wife in coming as far as she had, her husband would appreciate it, but it was the emperor's dearest wish that she should not proceed farther. "Governor Zeidler repeated himself like a parrot," was Maria's spirited observation. "I had heard the same speech many times along the way; he, of course, was following his instructions, just like the others. His Majesty the Tsar did not at all like the idea of us young wives following our 'criminal husbands' into exile. It stirred up the public's interest in their fate, whereas the Tsar wished them to be forgotten, presumed dead. There would have been a good chance of that happening, for the prisoners weren't even allowed to correspond with their families and friends back in Russia. But how could the Tsar forbid us wives to write and maintain contact?"

As none of General Zeidler's arguments made the slightest impression on Maria, their animated conversation abruptly drew to a close. Realizing that he was wasting his time, the governor rose to his feet and addressed her in the cold tones of a government official. "Before I allow you to proceed," he said, "you will have to sign this document. Please read it!" He pulled out a long sheet of official paper with the double-headed imperial eagle at the top; the writing ran into several paragraphs. She signed it without a glance at the contents.

It took Maria a long while to grasp the meaning and implications of the cruel document, which now lay on the table before her; its copy had been left for her to reflect on by an angry General Zeidler, who departed shrugging his shoulders, much annoyed at the prospect of having to report to St. Petersburg that his arguments had turned out to be unconvincing.

There were five clauses to the document:

1. A woman who follows her husband to Siberia and continues to live with him as his wife must share his fate. She must renounce all rights to her previous position and will henceforth be considered as the wife of a state criminal. It goes without saying that she will naturally have to bear the consequences of her status, no matter how painful they might prove to be. It is understood that the authorities themselves will not be in a position to protect her against any insults or attacks from various depraved criminals, who quite naturally will expect to go unmolested if they offend and even assault the wife of a fellow convict. Hardened criminals do not fear retribution, and they will soon realize that no punishment for this sort of misdemeanor is likely to be forthcoming.

2. Any children born in Siberia out of such a woman's union with her criminal husband will have to be registered in the category of peasant serfs and will become the property of the crown.

3. She will not be permitted to keep any valuables or sums of money—such an order being issued for her own good, as the countryside abounds with bandits.

4. She will lose the right to the services of any domestics or serfs she may have brought with her to Siberia.

5. She will never be allowed to return to European Russia—even on the death of her husband.

So this was the meaning of Tsar Nicholas's warning: "I warn you of the danger that awaits you beyond Irkutsk." This was what Prince Peter, her brother-in-law, was thinking of when he looked at her with such regret and concern as they drove through

St. Petersburg. With a flash of her pen, she had just crossed the river Styx and entered the land of perpetual darkness. She would never see Nikolenka again. Her Highness Princess Maria Volkonsky, wife of a peer of the realm, mother of an infant prince, daughter of a heroic general, had formally ceased to exist. At twenty-one, she was left with nothing but her memories. Maria recalled that when her hitherto sour maid read the paper, she burst into sobs and begged her to rush to the governor and retract the unfortunate signature. "What have you done, Princess? Do you realize what is being demanded of you?" Maria told her to be silent and prepare for the last stage of their journey.

But it was not so easy to leave Irkutsk. An authorization for travel to Transbaikalia was required from the governor, and General Zeidler decided to take his time issuing it. He was determined to punish Maria for her outright rejection of his plea. His annoyance was made worse by the fact that only a few days previously he had met with a similar rebuff from Princess Trubetskoy, who, unknown to Maria, had left Irkutsk the day before Maria's arrival. (Katyusha Trubetskoy left Moscow a month ahead of Maria, but traveled in very slow stages.) Still, Princess Trubetskoy had no children; her situation was quite different. Zeidler had cherished high hopes of influencing Maria and thus scoring in St. Petersburg.

Having signed away her social status, Maria was now required to join the long queue of petitioners in the governor's anteroom and had to wait for two days to be finally admitted into his presence. His manner was now barely civil; he did not ask her to sit down and this time he addressed her in Russian to point out how low she had fallen. He could not issue travel orders in her own name, he explained, since in the eyes of the law she had ceased to exist. They had to be made out in the name of her Cossack driver, who would accompany her to Nerchinsk. She was to obey his instructions at all times, "even if they appeared insulting to her." (In fact, the driver turned out to be a kind and good man, and Maria was grateful for his company.) The general's parting shot was to order a detailed inspection of the luggage.

"He sent me an entire detachment of his dreaded *chinovniks* [customs inspectors]," noted Maria. "They went through every single personal item I possessed, leaving everything in a mess; they opened the cases of tea, flour, and clothing destined for Sergei and his fellow prisoners, liberally helping themselves to tea and flour and taking a sack of sugar with them. Luckily, they did not notice my piano; they must have thought it was part of the room's furnishings. As for money, it had all been skillfully sewn into the hem and the sleeves of my traveling costume by Zenaida's wonderful maids. I wore it in Irkutsk every day."

This final indignity infuriated Maria and made her feverish to leave. She reasoned that, as she was never going to see her son, her family, or European Russia again, she might as well hurry forth. Her husband, Prince Volkonsky, was now a laborer in a silver mine in Transbaikalia, and her place was with him.

"I am glad I did not know what awaited me here," she wrote to her sister. "It would have made my decision to leave Nikolenka and the family very much harder."

The approach to the unfathomable Lake Baikal, the deepest inland lake in the world, is a grand sight. On all sides, the lake is fringed by bold, craggy mountains of the most extraordinary colors and shapes; their strange romantic forms have inspired pagan worship and since time immemorial have spawned tribal legends. Four hundred and thirty-seven rivers are said to empty their waters into Lake Baikal, but only one—the Angara, "the bride that got away"—flows out of it, merging with the Enisei in the Arctic north.

Gliding along a narrow track, which was cut through a forest of pines, their sleigh coasted along the shore of the lake for thirty miles before reaching the crossing point. As they turned toward the water's edge, the forest suddenly opened, revealing an immense expanse of shimmering ice and a chain of blue mountains in the distance. "It was a magic sight," recalled Maria, who, in spite of the terrifying cold, could not help but be awed by the spectacle. "The ice was clear, almost transparent, and extraordinarily slippery, yet our horses seemed to be so accustomed to it that they launched themselves upon the surface of the lake without hesitation and we crossed it in less than three hours." They were lucky, for a horse, once fallen on the clear ice, is unlikely ever to get up again. Nor is it possible to stop a vehicle once the horses have started to move; many accidents on Lake Baikal were caused by sledges moving faster than horses and overtaking them, so that the reins became entangled and the carriage went out of control.

Leaving the lake behind them, they turned east, in the general direction of China, which was not far away. In Verkhneudinsk, a trading post on the right bank of the Selenga River and an old stopping place for caravans plying between Irkutsk and the Chinese border, the local town major showed her hospitality and great kindness, providing clean, comfortable lodgings and food. She sensed a change of atmosphere around her; it seemed that the deeper she went into Siberia, the more concern she encountered for her personal welfare and sympathy for the cause for which her husband had fought. The institution of serfdom did not exist in Siberia; most of the peasants were free settlers, the merchant class was prosperous and independent-minded. The tsar was far away in St. Petersburg; his arm could not reach into every corner of the realm. Governors made only occasional tours of inspection. And as far as the minor officials—the *chinovniks*—were concerned, a bribe was the answer to any problem they might pose.

This more relaxed atmosphere colored the remaining stops on her journey. At Selenginsk, she spent an agreeable evening, staying with a family of Polish farmers transplanted to that far corner of the earth in the days of the Empress Catherine and then forgotten. Unable to return to their own country because their papers had been mislaid by a local official, they resigned themselves to perpetual exile, married local girls, raised children, and became famous throughout the province for the excellent quality of corn they raised in spite of the inhospitable climate. Their secret was that they applied manure to the land; they suggested it to others, but they were still the only farmers in that part of Siberia who did it.

On the last stretch of her journey, Maria had to abandon the sledges, for in spite of the perishing cold, the sandy, porous soil of the land bordering Mongolia absorbed the snow so rapidly that there was none on the road. She regretted leaving the Moscow kibitkas behind and worried how her piano would fare on the telega—a four-wheeled vehicle without springs, where one sat wedged among one's belongings, with only a flimsy leather for protection from the elements. "I never imagined how fiendishly uncomfortable this new mode of travel would turn out to be," she recalled. "All my bones ached and my chest began to hurt terribly. I had to order the driver to stop from time to time so I could breathe." She also suffered from hunger, for she had now entered the territory of the Buriat encampments, where the only available food was raw meat and brick tea—a beverage made of fat and an inferior-quality tea steamed together into the shape of a brick.

She reached Nerchinsk, the end of her journey, on the morning of the tenth day after leaving Irkutsk. It was not much of a town; grouped together along the Ingoda River, there were a few Buriat and Mongol settlements, a Cossack village, a few houses inhabited by officials of the mines, and a prison stockade surrounded by a strong guard. The countryside was magnificent. The site itself would have been picturesque if the forests within a radius of several miles had not been cut in order to prevent the prisoners from escaping.

As her bone-shaking telega turned into the Nerchinsk main street—a track of frozen mud lined by small peasant houses—Maria heard her name called. Striding toward her, she saw the small, round figure of Katyusha Trubetskoy, dressed in her fashionable fur coat and plumed hat. She looked as if she had never left St. Petersburg. Maria was overjoyed. Here at long last was a friend, a sister-soul with whom she could talk, exchange ideas, and from whom she could ask advice. For weeks now, she had had no female company except her disgruntled maid. The two women, who had never been close friends in St. Petersburg, now fell into each other's arms. Katyusha, who herself had arrived only two days before (she took twice as long as Maria to reach Nerchinsk), had already managed to see her husband and had gathered a bit of information about the place. Both husbands were working in the same mine, ironically known as Blagodatsk (Bliss), just outside Nerchinsk. Maria could arrange to visit Sergei the next day, but first her travel permit had to be checked and she had to present herself to the commandant of the mines. He was a most unpleasant fellow, Burnashev, coarse and loud-speaking, who smelled of bad cigars and drink. He obviously considered the arrival of the two women a great nuisance and was determined to show it.

Lounging in a greasy velvet armchair behind his desk, he gruffly pushed a sheaf of papers toward Maria, ordering her to sign them standing up. "I promise not to attempt to see my husband more than twice a week and always in the presence of an officer and a guard," said the first paper. The others read: "I promise never to take him wine, beer, or any alcoholic beverages," and "I promise never to leave Nerchinsk without the permission of the commandant of the prison or his deputy."

"There were many other formalities to cope with," recalled Maria. "They seemed endless. After traveling for thousands of miles, leaving my son and family behind, renouncing all my rights as a free citizen, including the protection of the law—such as could be expected in this godforsaken land—I would have signed anything that was demanded of me. Had I balked at one single paper, my journey would have been in vain. So I went on signing and signing, until I found myself on the floor, having apparently fainted from exhaustion."

She moved into a small room Katyusha had rented for them in the shack of a local Cossack. The oven smoked, the windowpanes were not glass but fish skin, which barely let through any daylight. They spread their fur rugs on the floor, and the only way they could find space to sleep was if one head was propped against the wall, with the feet reaching the door.

Next morning at dawn, Maria set off for the mine, escorted by Burnashev and two guards. "Prepare yourself for the worst," warned Katyusha, but nothing could have prepared her for what she found. "I stepped down into total darkness," she recalled. "Gradually, as I extended my hands, I began to feel that I was in a tiny cell, like a kennel, and that someone was slowly dragging himself toward me; I heard the clanging of iron on the stone floor. My husband stood before me and I saw that his legs were bound by heavy chains. No words can ever describe what I felt when I saw the immensity of his suffering. Only then did I fully realize the sacrifices required to fight for liberty in our country. A feeling of exaltation and great pride swept over me. To the bewilderment of the guards, I knelt on the filthy floor and kissed the chains."

PART TWO

9

Descent into Hell

"THE NADIR OF MISERY" was how Maria described the spring
of 1827. And no wonder, for it was then that brute reality
displaced the romantic illusion which had been her staple diet
from the moment she heard of Sergei's arrest. All that time,
though desperately worried and unhappy, she had lived in a
trance-like state of half fantasy, half expectation. In spite of all
the hardships on the journey across Asia, her mood had been
one of elation, almost rapture. Somewhere beyond the endless
horizon was her husband, and she was speeding toward him.
Maria's imagination did not project itself beyond that point. But
now that her ardent wish had been granted and she had finally
arrived at her destination, what did she find? Her husband—
His Highness Major General Prince Volkonsky—a convict, had
been turned into an emaciated human wreck, covered with
verminous rags, dragging his chains. And her home? A cell-like
room in a primitive dwelling in a godforsaken town of unpaved
streets, ruled by an uncouth, cruel official. Was the rest of her
life to be spent among illiterate peasants and drunken soldiers in

a frozen wasteland? Standing in front of the miserable Cossack hut in which she shared a room with Katyusha, she met the insolent stare of her maid, who had lost all respect for her mistress when she grasped that these were the conditions the princess would be forced to live in from now on. She refused to unpack Maria's belongings and was carrying on unashamedly with the local soldiers. She would soon be returning to Moscow, as the wives of state criminals were forbidden to retain servants.

In spite of the maid's disagreeable nature, her departure would make life even harder for Maria, who knew no practical skills and since earliest childhood days had been surrounded by loving family retainers.

Sergei's father, the old prince, had described Maria as "immensely brave, like Raevsky; proud and imaginative, like Potemkin"—when he met her at the time of her engagement to his son. In years to come, these attributes would move more and more to the fore, as Maria's character was tested to the full in the Asiatic wilderness. But at first she almost caused a crisis in the prison.

Two days after her arrival at Nerchinsk, disregarding the commitment made to the commandant of the camp that she would not attempt to visit the detainees on her own, she decided that she must see for herself the mine in which her husband was made to work. She also wanted to deliver letters she had brought from Moscow and St. Petersburg from assorted relatives of his fellow prisoners.

"I got up at daybreak," she recalled, "and went for a walk in the village to try to discover where it was that my Sergei was digging. The town seemed to consist of only one street, running along the foot of the mountains; here and there the rocks were pierced by large openings. I noticed something that looked like the entry to a large cave; a soldier, armed with a halberd with a steel pike mounted on the end of a long shaft, was guarding the door. 'This is the door through which the Gentlemen Princes go,' whispered a peasant woman who passed me, carrying a bundle of firewood on her back. The soldier was young and looked pleasant; he obviously had not been given his orders, and had no idea who I was. He must have taken me for the wife of a prison official, so he made no objections when I asked to go in; he gave me a kind of torch, like a huge candle, so I could see my way in the dark. I plunged into the Stygian labyrinth; it wasn't cold, but the air was close and oppressive; it hurt my chest. When I saw lights flickering far in the distance, I guessed that this was the place where the 'Gentlemen Princes' were working. Suddenly I heard someone yelling at me to turn back; it was the officer in charge, who had just discovered I was there. I blew out the torch and ran, stumbling a bit but as fast as I could, toward the lights in the distance. I came to a little platform hewn in the rock and saw my Uncle [Vasya] Davydov standing there; the others were digging below. Uncle Vasya quickly got hold of a ladder and we let ourselves down, taking the ladder with us.

"My Sergei, Obolensky, and Trubetskoy were working somewhere else that morning, but Artamon Muraviev, the two Borisov brothers, Yakubovich, and Uncle Vasya were overjoyed to see me. I delivered the letters—the first direct communication from their families since the day they left Russia—and quickly gave them all the news I could think of. By now the officer had arrived on the platform and was shouting furiously at me to come up. I made him wait quite a while, for I had a lot to tell our friends, but finally climbed back up the ladder and let him escort me out of the mine. There was much talk of insubordination. Strict orders were issued the next day to stop any of us from entering the mines. But the prisoners were delighted, and Artamon Muraviev described my subterranean foray as 'Maria's descent into hell.' "

Prison regime called for work in the mines to begin at 5 a.m.

and carry on until eleven in the morning. The norm was to excavate three poods (approximately fifty kilos) of ore daily. It was not excessive, but onerous for middle-aged men unused to physical labor and weakened by months of internment in the Fortress. Trubetskoy had begun to spit blood, Volkonsky suffered from prolonged pains in the chest and was quite weak, Obolensky had scurvy, and the elder of the two Borisov brothers showed signs of madness. Tsar Nicholas had decreed that the "state criminals be occupied, but not worked to the detriment of their health"; he did not want martyrs on his hands.

Burnashev, the Blagodatsk prison commander—the "executioner," as the women called him—raged at the restrictions placed upon him: "The devil take them! What stupid instructions! Keep them working, but at the same time watch over their health? But they are useless as workers . . . If it wasn't for this laughable stipulation, I would have had them all shot long ago." Burnashev was not only a cruel man, but Nerchinsk was a long way from St. Petersburg. Several of the wardens were brutal by nature and could easily become worse; the prisoners were entirely at their mercy. A fatal accident could happen at any time and there would be plenty of plausible excuses to cover it—had it not been for the presence of the women.

One day shortly after Maria's arrival, the worst almost did happen: Burnashev's assistant, Rieck, a rough, stupid, mentally unbalanced fellow, decided, on a sudden whim, to forbid the Decembrists to assemble after work in the prison's dingy common room where they took their meals together. He ordered them to return to the cells immediately after work, before noon, and remain in solitary confinement, without light, until dawn the next day; he also suppressed the distribution of the daily ration of candles. The prisoners were outraged and decided to go on a hunger strike. Fuming with fury, Rieck called it "an attempt to mutiny," which of course was a most serious offense. The situation was tense and turning uglier. Learning that the "secret ones," as the prisoners were called in Siberia, were about to be tried by a summary court, Maria and Katyusha positioned themselves on a boulder right in front of the prison gates. They remained at this spot without sleep for two days and three nights, watching the goings-on in front of the prison and gleaning snippets of information from the guards. Strangely intimidated by their presence, Burnashev, the commandant, canceled his subordinate's instructions and eventually dismissed him. Rieck was succeeded by an older man, a disciplinarian, but not a sadist. After it was all over, the two women called on Burnashev to inquire how such an incident could have happened. "It is nothing, absolutely nothing," he assured them. "My officer turned a molehill into an elephant."

The women hovered over the prisoners like guardian angels. In the end, Burnashev had to resign himself to the fact that with their arrival his arbitrary rule had come to an end. He knew they had powerful connections at court, and they could not be silenced.

As for the prisoners themselves, the presence of the two wives—to be followed, they hoped, by several others—was the difference between despair and the beginning of adjustment to a new life. Their arrival brought benefits to all, the most important of which was the reestablishment of contact with their families. No detainee was allowed to send letters or request packages and money, but no one could forbid Maria and Katyusha to do it for them. Soon a steady flow of packages and much needed money began to arrive from relatives all over Russia.

The prisoners' food was terrible, often putrid, and the men had lost a great deal of weight. Sergei, always delicate, suffered from an acute liver condition and diarrhea; Obolensky's scurvy was getting worse. "We must feed them," declared Maria. But how? The maids had already left for Russia, and neither Maria nor Katyusha had experience as a cook. A local Cossack woman was engaged, but her culinary skills were almost as limited as Maria's. At that moment Katyusha's French blood and practical sense took over; she had brought along several cookbooks and on the primitive wood-burning stove soon began to produce meals reminiscent of those of the chefs in the Laval household; they were carried to the prison each day by friendly guards bribed to act as messengers for the two princesses.

But everything in Siberia was expensive and quality food cost a fortune. Maria and Katyusha realized that they would soon run out of money. On Governor Zeidler's orders, Katyusha had left all her money in Irkutsk; Maria was asked to do the same, but wisely kept the eight hundred rubles she had had sewn into her traveling costume. This is what the two women were living on and what they were feeding eight hungry men with every day. "We decided to go on a diet," recalled Maria. "From now on, our own meals would consist only of kasha and kvass [a drink distilled from fermented yeast]. But one day one of our messengers spilled the beans and told Trubetskoy that his wife ate 'nothing but black bread and only drank kvass,' and that the Princess Volkonsky never ate supper any more. After that, the men categorically refused to accept our food. Finally a compromise was arrived at: the prison guards, who by then had collected a tidy sum from our bribes, offered to share their own food with the prisoners, if we would occasionally supplement it, 'for a small fee.' The system worked until we finally managed to extract our withheld money from the commandant."

The days settled into a dreary routine. The two women took on all the housework and the cleaning. Maria wielded the broom, dressed Katyusha's hair, washed the floor. There was always a lot of sewing to be done (no needles, only fishbones existed in Siberia), and the men's worn linen had to be replaced. Left entirely to their own devices, the two women derived much consolation from each other's company and came to depend on it.

The two were as different in character as they were in appearance, and in normal circumstances would probably never have become friends. Whereas Maria was tall and graceful, with a proud bearing and a naturally commanding manner, Katyusha was small, vivacious, and easily upset. She had a round, homely face, a rapid and lively speech; she radiated warmth and had an endearing, spontaneous way about her. Maria was by far the more intelligent, and Katyusha looked up to her as a leader.

Prison visits to husbands were restricted to two a week, but each day, whatever the weather, Maria and Katyusha went and sat on the boulder just outside the stockade, where they could easily be seen from the prison and with luck exchange a few words with their husbands or friends from a distance. The sight was the exiles' only link with the outside world, and a source of enormous comfort.

Often, Maria went for a walk with Katyusha. At first, they only ventured as far as the local cemetery, about two miles distant. "We used to ask ourselves, 'Are we going to be buried here?'" recalled Maria. The thought depressed them so much that they gave up going in that direction and walked in the wild countryside, as much as eight or ten miles a day. In spite of Governor Zeidler's predictions, they were never bothered by common criminals, whose prison adjoined that of their husbands. But Maria was upset to see these men walking about in rags within the compound. She bought some cloth and had shirts made for them in the village.

When her money was about to run out, Maria decided that it was time to tackle the dreaded Burnashev at the mine headquarters—the Zavod—twelve miles away. "I dressed as if for a visit in St. Petersburg, complete with a hat and veil, hired a cart, and asked the local sweeper to accompany me for protection.

Katyusha and I were always careful to dress well and look dignified; it was important for our standing with the local people; they could see us coming from afar and always saluted us with respect." Not for a moment did it occur to the two women to let down on their appearances. (Davydov's memoirs describe how the princess, wearing a hat with a long, flowing veil and sitting on two large sacks of flour and potatoes, was seen driving in the cart through the village, acknowledging the respectful salutations of the peasants.) "I presented my accounts to the commandant," wrote Maria, "and asked that more of my money be made available for our expenses. I gave him all the accounts; he went over every item in great detail, and glared at me furiously when he saw that I had had shirts made for the common criminals. 'You have no right to dress serfs, who are the property of the crown!' he shouted. 'If you want to distribute alms, give ten kopecks to the beggars in church.' 'Well, monsieur,' I answered, 'then you had better dress them yourself, for I am not in the habit of seeing naked men around me.' My reply seemed to convince him, for he smiled and told me that I was 'as frank as a child' and that he liked me better than he liked Katyusha, who was 'too subtle.' I returned with a good sum of money and provisions."

When the weather got warmer, Maria borrowed a horse from a local Cossack and had a sidesaddle fashioned to her order. From then on, she rode every day, venturing sometimes all the way to the Chinese frontier fifteen miles distant, where Buriat tribes traded their modest supplies of flour and animal skins for brick tea and Chinese millet. She surprised Burnashev one day by arriving for her scheduled interview riding sidesaddle. Unused to such an elegant sight, the dreaded commander reluctantly admitted to his aides that here was a "fine aristocratic figure of a woman."

The real criminals—thieves, brigands, and murderers—were

not only housed next to the prison where the Decembrists were held, but their leg irons were heavier, and they were made to work much harder. Orlov, the best known among them, was a kind of Robin Hood; he never attacked poor people, concentrating his assaults on prosperous merchants and on the dreaded *chinovniks,* state officials, who grew rich extorting bribes from the population. He had a magnificent voice and organized a prisoners' choir. Every evening at sunset, their powerful voices rang through the surrounding emptiness. One of their chants in particular affected Maria: *"Volya, volya, dorogaya"*—"Liberty, liberty, beloved liberty." It was mourned in vain, for most of them were serving life sentences. She would walk over to the prison fence in the evenings to listen to their singing—the only distraction they were permitted to enjoy—and encouraged them to find new tunes and develop their voices. As time went on, an almost affectionate rapport developed between the deeply human princess, who loved music, and Orlov, the ex-murderer, and his band of seasoned criminals. "It just shows how wrong people can be about our good Russian folk," wrote Maria in one of her letters home, in a sudden burst of patriotic feeling. "Everybody in Irkutsk warned me about the dangers I ran of being insulted, killed, raped, etc., by these tough criminals, and how the authorities would be unable to protect me. And here I was living among them—the dregs of humanity, as they were called—and I found myself surrounded by the greatest respect; even more, for Katyusha and I had become objects of a cult. They always referred to our political detainees as 'our princes' or 'our masters,' and whenever they happened to be working nearby, they surreptitiously managed to help them in their work, and brought them potatoes cooked in ashes. Those wretched people, after serving out their sentences, often settled down somewhere in Siberia as farmers or shopkeepers, got married, and led decent lives, though they rarely ever became free. I am sure that there are not many criminals in England or France who behave as well as the ones in our country."

With the approach of spring, Maria noticed a marked nervousness among Orlov's singing companions. Rumor had it that one or two of them contemplated escaping into China—a perilous undertaking, as the Buriat tribes on the frontier were adept at hunting ex-prisoners and received substantial rewards for delivering them to the authorities. One morning the news came that Orlov and three of his companions had disappeared; every effort was made to locate them. Two days later, as Maria was out walking near the prison, she was approached by one of the criminals—an ex-Hussar with a good baritone voice—who whispered that he had a message for her from Orlov, who was hiding in a cave in the mountains behind her house. He begged her to give him some money so he could buy a pelisse, as the nights were cold on the mountain. Maria was terrified of being discovered; aiding a prisoner to escape was a serious offense. But how could one refuse help to a man with such a wonderful voice as Orlov's? "I went into the house," she recalled, "took ten rubles out of my bag, and told Orlov's friend, who was supposed to be carrying water for the prison, to watch from the distance where I put the money—out of sight, under a reddish rock, near a fir tree. Of course he found it at once and disappeared. About a week later, I happened to be alone in my room, playing the piano and accompanying myself singing. Katyusha was having her biweekly meeting with her husband. Dusk was falling when I saw a tall figure sneak into the room and fall on his knees before me. I realized it was Orlov, dressed in his new fur-lined pelisse, with two cutlasses dangling from his belt. 'I have come to you again,' he said. 'Please help me, I am starving. God will repay you, your Highness.' I gave him five rubles and begged him to disappear as fast as possible. When Katyusha came back, she was terrified at what might have happened and accused me of being reckless. I, too, felt uneasy, remembering what Burnashev had said when I had got the shirts made: 'You are trying to interfere with the state criminals.'

"In the middle of the night, we were awakened by repeated gunshots. I woke up Katyusha and we dispatched the sweeper to the prison to find out what was happening. By then the entire village was up; it turned out that the escaped prisoners had been captured, with the exception of Orlov, who disappeared through the aperture in the chimney. The idiot! Instead of getting bread, he and his companions decided to celebrate their new wealth by buying vodka, getting drunk, and of course falling into the police's hands. Next morning Orlov's companions were flogged and an investigation got underway to discover where they had got the money to buy drink. No one betrayed me; Orlov's friend, the ex-Hussar, in order to protect me 'confessed' that he had stolen the money from a guard. He was flogged, but no suspicion was ever cast on me. It just shows that there can be gratitude and devotion even among men who are officially categorized as 'monsters.' "

As the cold gradually subsided, a new plague attacked the state prisoners: an invasion of fleas. "It was like the Chinese torture inflicted on the worst criminals," recalled Trubetskoy in his memoirs. "We covered our bodies with turpentine, but it brought little relief." Maria and Katyusha would return home from their eagerly awaited prison visits covered with fleas; they had to rush back and shake out every item of clothing; even so, there seemed to be no way to keep the fleas from invading their dwelling.

The women's interviews with their husbands always took place in the presence of a guard or a non-commissioned officer. These varied from lazy, good-natured, easily bribed individuals to men who were cruel by nature, eager to win the attention of their superiors by reporting unfavorably on what was going on. The cause of many difficulties was the fact that—strange as it may seem—neither Katyusha nor Maria spoke fluent Russian. Katyusha Trubetskoy, born Laval, daughter of an émigré French aristocrat and the immensely rich Russian Countess Kozitsky, had been brought up and educated in Paris, where she met and married Prince Trubetskoy. She had never addressed her husband in anything but French, which was the commonly used language in St. Petersburg society; her Russian was strictly the nursery kind. Maria, who had been brought up in the Ukraine, was much closer to her native soil than most young women of her class, but even she knew only the elementary kind of Russian used to communicate with the servants and the peasants at Boltyshka. Her operative language was French. Such was the established custom among upper-class nineteenth-century Russian women, and in normal circumstances there would have been little need to use one's native tongue, except when addressing servants, laborers, or small shopkeepers; the more important merchants prided themselves on their excellent French. Maria's family conversation and correspondence were always conducted in French. The men's Russian was generally quite fluent—it was essential for officers in the army and for running country estates —but even the men preferred to converse in French among themselves, not only because it was the fashionable thing to do, but often so as not to be understood by the servants, who were always about. It was not necessarily good French. Many hybrid words were introduced that a Frenchman would have found difficult to understand, and the spelling was often unorthodox— "fantaisie," as Tocqueville remarked—but, nevertheless, French would most commonly be used in all intimate conversations between an aristocratic Russian and his wife. The trouble in Siberia was that the guards were supposed to listen, but they could not understand what was being said. A lazy guard generally let it pass; he would yawn, shake his head, and go to sleep, or contentedly pocket a small bribe. But there were others who brusquely interrupted the conversation and demanded that only Russian be used. The husband–wife exchanges would then be reduced to an elementary level, or to a one-sided monologue by the husband in Russian, uttered slowly, using the simplest of words, as if he were addressing a child, not a wife. "It was a ridiculous situation," recalled Maria. "Here we were in the depths of the Asiatic wilderness, in the heart of the Russian empire, and we insisted on communicating with each other in French. It had to stop!" Obolensky had a library of Russian classics and a copy of the Scriptures. Maria set off to study it and within a few months proudly announced that her Russian was now perfect. It was not, but great strides had been made and there was no need for stilted conversations in the prison any longer.

Preserved in the police archives of His Imperial Majesty in St. Petersburg are the weekly reports on the conduct of the first eight political detainees in Siberia, compiled by the commandant of the Nerchinsk mines. The reports are accompanied by a daily journal recording the conduct, occupation, and state of health of each individual prisoner. They provide a vivid insight into their existence.

"The prisoners have behaved well all through their work," reads one entry. "They uttered no revolutionary slogans; they obeyed all commands; when in lodgings they are affectionate toward each other and there is much mutual self-help."

An entry of December 27, 1826, notes: "Trubetskoy suffers from what appears to be a malady of the lungs . . . He is spitting blood."

February 16, 1827: "Both Trubetskoy and Volkonsky appear visibly more cheerful since the arrival of their wives."

February 26, 1827: "Sergei Volkonsky had an interview with his wife and was allowed off work on that day."

April 1, 1827: "Volkonsky has been ill for more than a week . . . Typhoid fever suspected . . ."

April 10, 1827: "Volkonsky appears better . . . Both he and Trubetskoy seem to be getting used to conditions in prison, but because of his fragile health Volkonsky often appears silent and depressed . . ."

April 12 1827, in the column headed "Artamon Muraviev": "Since receiving his wife's letter on March 27, Muraviev appears to be in great distress." He learned his wife's arrival would be delayed.

April 18 1827, in the column headed "Borisov": "The prisoner suffers from the aftereffects of a head wound received in the Caucasus, aggravated by the damp air of the mine; he also suffers from chest pains; he alternates between gaiety and depression."

April 30, 1827: "Sergei Volkonsky and others worked in the mountains today, digging near the Kreshchensky cave; they worked well together, with patience and application."

Vasya Davydov, the charming heir of the great Kamenka estate, formerly always cheerful, was described as "rarely gay, mostly silent; spends much time reading Scriptures . . ." The guards' general impression was that they all "get on well together—they share everything, food, tobacco, and linen, which are supplied by the Princesses Volkonsky and Trubetskoy."

Dr. Vladimirsky's medical records tell us that Volkonsky was "very weak in the chest, that Borisov's wounds were bothering him, that Obolensky had scorbute and suffered much because of his teeth."

There is also an entry explaining that "following the request

presented to us by the Princess Volkonsky, wife of the condemned political prisoner Sergei, the depot is being requested to
locate among the objects belonging to the said Volkonsky and
deposited in our safekeeping one lined overcoat in fine English
material with a beaver collar and cuffs, and a meerschaum pipe
with a silver band. The coat and the pipe, less the band, which
is to be returned to the depot, are to be forwarded to Blagodatsk
in care of Lieutenant Rezanov; the coat will be sent to the Princess Volkonsky, to be altered and refashioned for her personal
use; the pipe, less the silver band, will be given to the condemned political criminal Volkonsky . . ." The entry was signed:
Burnashev.

Easter came—the greatest religious festival in the Orthodox
Church. In spite of the two women's entreaties, Burnashev refused to allow a priest to visit the prisoners so they might perform
their Easter duties. But as there was no church at Blagodatsk, he
did grant Maria and Katyusha permission to visit an Orthodox
monastery on the Shilka River, just beyond the Bolshoi Zavod,
headquarters of the Nerchinsk mines. They went early, at the
beginning of Holy Week, traveling in a peasant cart, dressed
smartly, as befitted the occasion of going to church. "It was a
great comfort to us," recalled Maria, "to partake in a religious
ceremony again. We derived strength from being in church,
amid the familiar ritual. The monastery itself was in wild and
beautiful surroundings; the monks—not the ascetic kind (apparently, they kept concubines)—were generous; they presented
us with two bottles of madeira wine, three of *nalivka* [fruit
brandy] of their own make, for which they have always been
famous, and a dozen gaily painted Easter eggs. We returned to
Blagodatsk on Easter Day and immediately repaired to our
boulder outside the prison. Our men had a day off because of

Easter, and one of the guards agreed to take a basket of Easter eggs to them. All we could do was murmur the joyous Easter salutation *Khristos Voskrese* [Christ is risen] and wave to them from the distance ... I was sad, so I spent the afternoon playing with some of the Buriat children whose tribe had set up camp near the village. Using the simplest of words, I told them the story of the Resurrection ... They listened to me spellbound."

After Easter came the first letters from home, much delayed because of the triple censorship: first, Benckendorff's office in St. Petersburg; then the governor's staff in Irkutsk; and finally the office of the commandant of the mines. Since her arrival, Maria had received only two letters from the family: one from the old princess, mostly destined for Sergei and full of Volkonsky family and court gossip, but enclosing an all-too-brief and general account of Nikolenka—the item of news that Maria longed to hear above all. There was a short, dry, formal note from her own mother, which startled Maria. It referred to her request, made before she left Moscow, that Maria's favorite diamond bracelet, a wedding present from her husband, be given to young Princess Repnin, Sergei's niece, since Maria had no use for it in Siberia. "I have been in touch with the Repnins," wrote Mme Raevsky. "They declined. No one wants to have a bracelet which has anything to do with Sergei. It might bring them bad luck."

Mme Raevsky's harsh words to her daughter six thousand miles away reflected the family's feelings of exasperation with Sergei, the cause of Maria's misfortune. These feelings were symptomatic of the prevailing atmosphere in Nicholas I's Russia following the Decembrist uprising. "It was as if a pebble had been dropped into a pond—a few ripples and then silence," wrote a contemporary. Of the 578 men implicated in the Decembrist cause, nearly 130—an entire generation—vanished for a lifetime, and their disappearance went virtually unnoticed. The pendulum had swung back from Alexander I's humanity to Nicholas's despotism, which was reminiscent of his father, Tsar Paul. For the next thirty years, Russia was to be a silent country in which all traces of enlightened opposition and criticism were forbidden by a tyrant who abhorred independent thought. "I know nothing so terrible," wrote Herzen a few years after the Decembrist uprising, when describing Nicholas I, "nothing which could so banish hope as those colorless, cold pewter eyes . . ." (Queen Victoria, after meeting the tsar at Windsor in 1844, was also unfavorably impressed by what she called his "wintry eyes.")

Tsar Nicholas wanted the Decembrists forgotten. Having deported them to a faraway land where they would be made to eke out an existence for the rest of their lives, like shadows in some subterranean kingdom, without hope of redemption, without hope of ever returning to the land they belonged to, he was sure that their families, most of whom had much to gain from imperial favor, would soon forget their unfortunate offspring. Many couldn't, though they rarely sympathized with their cause. They kept in touch with the exiles and showed many instances of personal devotion. For the most part, friends offered only embarrassed compassion, and the subject was seldom discussed. But others, motivated by vindictiveness or hypocrisy, behaved in a despicable way. Nicholas Bestuzhev recalls in his memoirs how his cousin, old Bestuzhev-Ryumin, the father of the heroic twenty-one-year-old Mikhail, the hero of the southern uprising, who was executed with Pestel, instructed the rest of the family to "obliterate" the memory of their brother. "To a dog—a dog's death," he proclaimed, tearing the portrait of his young, handsome son to pieces.

Count Gustav Olizar, Maria's old friend from Kiev, writing

about the "beautiful role and sacrifices of the women in this terrible political tragedy," notes how repulsive—in the face of their devotion—was the meanness of the men. "Many of the brothers and relatives of the victims deported to external exile tried to show their devotion to the tsar by seeking additional honors in his service. I knew a father who had lost three sons in this affair . . . As a senator from Moscow, he traveled for a long time in Italy at Nicholas's expense. To what depths of moral decline are people brought by the golden enslavement of autocracy!"

Jean Ancelot, the Frenchman who had previously criticized the old Princess Volkonsky, writes more sharply in his *Six mois en Russie* (Paris, 1827): "We all thought that this bloody catastrophe, which had preceded by so few days the coronation ceremony, would sadden the festivities that were supposed to follow it, because there are hardly any families in court circles which would not have had victims to weep over. What was my surprise, my friend, when I saw the relatives, the brothers, the sisters, the mothers of the condemned take active part in these brilliant balls, magnificent repasts, sumptuous parties! In the case of many of these nobles, an ambitious egoism and the habit of slavery have stifled the sweetest feelings of nature. Others, continually on their knees before power, were visibly afraid that their grief might be mistaken for sedition . . . In a despotic state, one could perhaps explain this unnatural behavior in a man mad with ambition and a desire for honors and wealth, but what can one say of a woman, a mother, a sister, or worse an old mother in the last days of her life who, bent by her years toward the tomb, comes every day, covered with diamonds, to take part in the boisterous expressions of public gaiety while her son nears painful exile and perhaps death? Well, my friend, this sorry spectacle has offended our eyes all through the festivities . . . Let us add, though, that not all women here have followed this example." And he goes on to extol the courage of the "lovely young" Maria Volkonsky, Katyusha Trubetskoy, and Alexandrine Muraviev.

To men brought up in a tradition of Christian culture, this sudden, almost overnight change in the mood of a society, and the lack of personal dignity on the part of the majority of Russian aristocrats, was of course a sad and degrading spectacle. It was also a vivid reminder of how thin and impermanent was the veneer of Western civilization imposed on the Russian boyars since the days of Peter the Great. As for the contemporary men of letters, the poets and intellectuals, unlike the poets of the latter part of the nineteenth century, who created an aura of martyrdom and heroism around the Decembrists, certain of their contemporaries, such as Zhukovsky, the poet laureate, anxious to remain in the tsar's favor, condemned them. "What scoundrels they were," proclaimed Zhukovsky at a meeting of the Literary Society of Moscow. But others, such as Prince Vyazemsky, spoke fearlessly in their favor and openly criticized the "savagely short memory" of the Russian people.

Pushkin, of course, knew them all; they were the friends of his youth when he longed to be taken into their confidence—a temptation they wisely resisted. He had always had enormous sympathy for the movement, though he disagreed with the timing of the actual rebellion (cf. *Onegin*, chapter X). He must have congratulated himself on his luck in being away from the capital on the fatal day and not having been more closely involved. He felt a strong poetic compassion for all the Decembrists "deep in the Siberian mines," and wished "their prison walls would crumble and glorious freedom greet them." "My first and best friend," he wrote when Jeannot Pushchin, his childhood companion, was sent into exile:

That providence may let my voice
Bring solace to your soul.

He never saw Jeannot again. His romantic poems addressed to
the Volkonskys in Siberia were of course motivated by the depth
of his feeling for Maria.

Pushkin's biographers have pointed out that when he was
asked by the tsar to write a *Memorandum on Public Education*
which dealt with the uprising, he expressed "an ambiguous feeling about the Decembrists." This is not to his credit, and can
perhaps be explained by the fact that he was entirely dependent
on Nicholas I's goodwill for his existence. Though not an intui-
tive man, Nicholas I must have realized the immensity of Pushkin's genius; one of the few decent acts of his dark reign was the
way he protected the poet from his own secret police.

One of the most moving tributes to the Decembrists came
from the pen of Adam Mickiewicz, the Polish poet, friend of
Ryleev and Pushkin, in his poem "To My Russian Friends":

Now to the world I pour this poisoned chalice,
A bitter tale sucked forth from burning veins.
My country's blood and tears compound its malice;
Let it corrode—not you, friends, but your chains!

But, sadly, the vast majority of the Russian people, the peasants,
the soldiers, the millions of serfs on whose behalf the Decembrists had risen, were unable to appreciate the disinterested
heroism of a handful of idealistic young spirits. The Russian tsar,
no matter how tyrannical his rule, had always enjoyed an
extraordinary degree of reverential love. Over the years, sub-
mission had been deeply ingrained in the whole nation, and had
remained in its bloodstream. The young idealists of 1825 had
never wanted to involve the masses, but without the masses'
participation their uprising was doomed. No wonder they were

misunderstood and condemned. In their faraway exile, the Decembrists never learned of the widespread feeling of indifference
back home. They would have been particularly distressed to
know that in the months following their attempted coup most of
the "simple people" thought that the gentry had risen in revolt
against the tsar because *he* wished to free them from bondage. It
was a twist of supreme irony that as a result Nicholas had to
issue a manifesto denying rumors of the coming emancipation of
the serfs.

In July, the Decembrists were advised of the arrival of an
important visitor from St. Petersburg. On the tsar's orders, he
had been inspecting the entire mine area around Nerchinsk to
find a site for a communal prison-fortress for the political detainees. He was General Stanislav Romanovich Leparsky, a
seventy-two-year-old cavalry officer, a kindhearted disciplinarian
who was to become a central figure in the prisoners' lives there-
after. In arranging for General Leparsky to be their jailer, Providence had stepped in to alleviate their misfortunes.

Nicholas I had of course no intention of bringing succour to
the men whose treason would remain an obsession with him
throughout his life. (He had all the Decembrists' pretrial deposi-
tions bound in leather tomes and kept on a separate table in his
study, and he never discarded the uniform he wore on the day he
rode out to meet the rebels on the Senate Square.) With his
inexhaustible capacity for work, Nicholas insisted on personally
reviewing the minutest details connected with the detainees in
Siberia: their transport, horses, sleds, wagons, allocation of
food, selection of guards, correspondence, etc.—matters that
could easily have been entrusted to his chancery. Now he
wanted to be involved in selecting the ideal prison site for the
"villainous traitors." But Siberia was vast and the tsar had never

visited it. He had to rely on the advice of General Lavinsky, Governor of eastern Siberia, who happened to be on leave in St. Petersburg. "One group of prisoners is more easily guarded than ten," said Lavinsky. Some remote spot should be found in Transbaikalia where they could all be held together. This would reduce the possibility of their "poisoning the minds of other Russians with their liberal heresies." It was a tidy plan that appealed to Nicholas's orderly, soldierly mind and inadvertently became the ameliorating factor in the lives of the Decembrists. Being together made their exile bearable, preserved intact their ideals, and enabled the wives who joined them to act as a powerful force in their favor.

Throughout the summer and autumn of 1826, as the troikas shuttled back and forth between the capital's Peter and Paul Fortress and Siberia, bearing their distinguished human cargo and their armed escorts, the search went on for a suitable commander for the prison-fortress in Transbaikalia. General Leparsky was the personal choice of the tsar. The two men had known each other for years. As a young officer serving in Lithuania, Nicholas I had often stayed at Leparsky's house and knew him as an absolutely loyal servant. But the quality that mattered most in the circumstances was the general's well-known tact. In the sixteen years during which he was in command of the crack Seversky Regiment, Leparsky had never had a soldier or an officer court-martialed. In fact, many an insubordinate guardsman, who for some misconduct or other had been demoted to a regular army unit, profited from a tour of duty under Leparsky. The supervision of the large group of aristocratic and well-educated "state prisoners" posed special problems. Above all, the Decembrists must not be turned into martyrs. "For the wives," Tsar Nicholas remarked, "would see to it that they were enshrined into legend." Leparsky, in spite of his advanced age, appeared to be the perfect man for the job.

Descent into Hell

A Russified Pole and a Catholic, and educated by the Jesuits in western Poland, he was a product of the eighteenth century (he was forty-five years old when the nineteenth century began). He spoke perfect French, German, Polish, and of course Russian; he read the classics; his manners were courtly; he was an exacting but fair commander. As the Decembrists happily discovered, he was kind by nature. With his bandy legs, ruddy complexion, flabby cheeks, smoothly pomaded side whiskers, and a wide assortment of wigs, he looked like an old-fashioned relic of a former era. Recently retired, he lived in Kursk in somewhat strained financial circumstances. When the call came, he unhesitatingly accepted the post, not only because of the financial rewards (he was offered a salary as high as that of the Governor of Siberia), but because of his personal devotion to the emperor.

Nicholas received him in Moscow while dressing for a ball. In his biography of Leparsky, Kuchaev describes how the tsar, "holding a glass of champagne in his hand, stood leaning against the red velvet curtains of his dressing room," discussing the regulations for the new prison and the detainees' food rations, while a valet held the superbly embroidered imperial white evening tunic, with its row of huge diamond buttons, "whose brilliance outshone the flames in the fireplace." Leparsky spent over an hour with the monarch. "Go to Siberia, Stanislav Romanovich. Forget your age—you are just the man I need; God bless you," said the tsar. He embraced Leparsky and gave him an initialed snuffbox as a gift.

Leparsky was to choose his own assistants, all of whom would receive four times the standard rate of pay for their rank. He enlisted his nephew Osip Adamovich, also of the Seversky Chasseurs, and two junior cavalry officers, Captains Rozenberg and Kulomzin, to serve as adjutants. He also found a surgeon named Ilinsky, son of a Siberian priest, whose knowledge of

Siberia was unfortunately greater than his knowledge of medicine. Finally, Father Peter Gromov, whom Maria had met in Irkutsk, was delegated by the Archbishop of Siberia "as chaplain to the political detainees." When all the arrangements were concluded, Leparsky, accompanied by his nephew, crossed the Urals and set off to look for a site for the new prison-fort.

The silver mines of Nerchinsk were scattered over a wild mountainous region more than a thousand square miles, running from the border of Mongolia to the Amur River in the northeast. The existence of silver and lead ore in the area was known even to the prehistoric aborigines of Siberia, and traces of their primitive mining operations were found by the first Russian explorers of the country. In the early eighteenth century, Greek mining engineers in the employ of the Russian government founded the Nerchinsky Zavod near the Mongolian frontier, which Maria used to visit on horseback to go over her accounts with Burnashev. As Leparsky set off on his search, he was told that General Benckendorff's police department had planned to build a special prison for the Decembrists at Akatui, a silver-mining center, which was known for its terrible climate and the lead poisoning in the atmosphere. "Even birds do not survive Akatui" was an old saying of the Buriats. Armed with his superior authority, the general countermanded the order and suggested a small out-of-the-way settlement called Chita in the valley of the Ingoda, known for its bracing climate and picturesque surroundings. An old abandoned Cossack fort was to serve as temporary jail while work proceeded on the new prison, being built to Leparsky's specifications. In the summer of 1827, Decembrists started arriving at Chita from the various pits of the Nerchinsk range.

"We received good news this morning," Maria noted in her diary. "At long last we heard from Alexandrine [Muraviev]. She is living in a place called Chitinsky Ostrog [Chita Fort], a picturesque village where her husband and several other of our friends have been sent. They all arrived in ox-pulled peasant carts, escorted by an entire platoon of gendarmes. Alexandrine informs us that we are all going to be transferred there shortly. What joy, this prospect of our being together, away from the commandant of the Nerchinsk mines!"

Their departure was delayed by a few weeks because of a rebellion in a camp housing criminals near Verkhneudinsk. "The poor devils," remarked Maria, "they are so badly treated that they simply *have* to mutiny. Burnashev is not a bit worried about our safety, he is afraid they might kill *him* if our convoy falls into their clutches." But finally they were on the way. On General Leparsky's orders, Maria and Katyusha were to be escorted by two non-commissioned officers and five peasants, mounted on Cossack horses and well armed to protect them from bandits.

The eight political prisoners were to leave two days later under a guard of fourteen Cossacks. Sergei Volkonsky's health at the time must have been a cause for concern; a note in the archives stipulates that "as of all the eight detainees, Volkonsky appears to be in the most debilitated condition—and there are no medical facilities on the way—the officer in charge is authorized to receive two bottles of madeira wine and one of fruit brandy from the Princess Volkonsky and administer two small glasses a day to the prisoner before meals." Underneath the dry, bureaucratic tone, one detects the new commandant's humanity.

"Katyusha and I purchased two peasant carts—one for ourselves and one for our belongings. We followed the same road on which I had traveled to Nerchinsk in January, but this time in the opposite direction—west, toward Lake Baikal. In the beautiful autumn weather, the forests looked magnificent—there was a profusion of flowers and the air was steeped in the aroma of fragrant herbs, exhilarating to breathe. We stopped for the night at the house of the same kindly merchant who had entertained me on the way to the mines; he arranged for a wonderful bath and a great supper. Katyusha and I shed all our worries for a time—we felt revived. We went from those kind people laden with gifts: warm clothes, food, madeira wine, and pouches of tobacco for our husbands, as well as a large packet of needles and thread, more valuable than gold in these regions." Next day, in the late afternoon, the valley of Chita came into view sitting peaceful and remote between the little river of the same name and the fast-flowing Ingoda. It was to be the setting for a new chapter in Maria's life in exile.

Maria Volkonsky, before her voluntary exile, with her first-born
child, Nikolenka, in St. Petersburg, 1826. Painting by Sokolov

The scene at Senate Square on December 14, 1825, as a painter
rendered it some years later. At right, the Bronze Horseman immortalized by Pushkin

Prince Sergei Volkonsky, in 1837, at Petrovsky Zavod, drawn by his fellow Decembrist Nikolai Bestuzhev

Bestuzhev's drawing of Maria in 1837. Prison stockade and guard-house can be seen outside, and the portrait of General Raevsky, her father, on the wall

This album cover, made by Bestuzhev with inlaid wood, shows the jail at Chita in 1829. Courtesy of the Volkonsky family in Rome

Panoramic view in summertime of the compound at Chita, drawn by Bestuzhev, who is shown with sketch pad under canopy at left

Sergei and Maria Volkonsky, drawn by Bestuzhev in 1832, in their room at Petrovsky Zavod. Maria's piano, transported by sleigh, at right

Bestuzhev's drawing of Dr. Wolff in his quarters at Petrovsky, 1832, with an open volume on his lap, contemplating the skull on the table

View of encampment set up during the 450-mile journey from Chita to Petrovsky Zavod in August 1830. The drawing by Bestuzhev shows two figures wearing Buriat hats

Prince Sergei Trubetskoy and his wife, Katyushka, drawn by Bestuzhev around 1828

[*Opposite*] Nikita and Alexandrine Muraviev, with their daughter, Nonushka, who was born in exile

Alexander Poggio, drawn by Bestuzhev in 1837

Maria's daughter, Elena, with her second husband, Prince
Kochubey. Daguerreotype from the Volkonsky collection in Rome

Daguerreotype of Maria's son, Mikhail, in Moscow in 1858

[*Opposite*] Painting of Princess Elizabeth Volkonsky, Mikhail's wife. Daguerreotype of their sons, Sergei and Grigory, in their traveling costumes

Daguerreotype of Maria Volkonsky and her son made at St. Petersburg at Christmas 1862. She was suffering from kidney disease and died a year later

10

The Ladies of Chita

THE SETTLEMENT OF CHITA lay in a picturesque valley on the great road between Lake Baikal and Nerchinsk, on a plateau surrounded on two sides by high mountains. A few miles to the north was Lake Onon, on the shores of which Genghis Khan had once held a court of justice and drowned criminals in the seething waters of the lake. His nomadic descendants, the Mongols, the Buriats, and the Tungus, still wandered through the countryside with their felt tents and their flocks of horses and cattle. The climate was healthy, and though frosts continued until early June, summers were beautiful, with a profusion of flowers and vegetation of all sorts. Travelers on the way to Mongolia called Chita the garden of Siberia because of the luxuriance of its vegetation. Wheat, barley, fruit, and everything that grew reached amazing proportions, as Volkonsky and other amateur horticulturists among the Decembrists were soon to discover to their pleasure. It was a clement spot, almost an oasis in the surrounding cold waste. Even the winters, though long, were dry and sunny. "We all grew healthier in Chita," wrote Baron Andrei Rozen in his memoirs. "The climate is not nearly as harsh as in the northern parts of my native Finland or in Sweden."

In 1827, Chita was a small *sloboda*, a frontier settlement of about six hundred people, with a rickety old wooden church and a few dozen clapboard houses and cabins. The new jail, built under Leparsky's direction next to a seventeenth-century Cossack fort, consisted of four large, light, well-heated rooms, an entrance hall, and quarters for the guards. It was surrounded by a garden and a tall picket fence. The eight original Blagodatsk veterans settled in one of the rooms; two other rooms housed the Moscow Decembrists and were called "Moscow." Another was christened "Vyatka" after the name of Pestel's regiment. Throughout the time the Decembrists spent in Chita, it was made to house seventy-six people, and became very crowded, but it was an enormous improvement on Nerchinsk. The greatest advantage of the new jail, as far as the Decembrists were concerned, was that they were there together. As Nicholas Bestuzhev remarked: "To have been scattered throughout Siberia and isolated would have crushed our spirits. Instead, we were here reunited in one place, drawing strength from each other, and were able to exist politically beyond political death." This was not at all what Tsar Nicholas had intended when he accepted the unintentionally humane advice of General Lavinsky, but mercifully he never quite realized it.

"From the top of the hill we could see the little village of Chita and the jail, and the tall picket fence," runs an entry in Maria's diary. "The fence was so tall that from the distance it looked like a collection of ships' masts on the ocean. Katyusha and I went straight to Alexandrine Muraviev's house. She had come to Chita two weeks before us, and had rented the dwelling of a local Cossack near the jail. Her house had a large attic window through which she could see her husband and his fellow prisoners as they came out to work in the vegetable garden every day. The moment we arrived, Alexandrine dragged me to the attic to look. I saw Belyaev and the Frolov brothers, and several other new faces. Many of the newly arrived were young—could not have been more than nineteen or twenty-two. They seemed calm, even cheerful, and I was impressed at how clean and tidy they looked. Some walked about with a shovel, others smoked a pipe, or went around holding books under their arms.

"I would have liked to have been able to share a house with Alexandrine, but Madame Naryshkin was there already, so Katyusha and I took two rooms in the house of the local deacon —a jolly, stout, bearded fellow. We later invited Madame Entaltsev to join us and gave her the small separate room in the house. This dear woman was nearly forty-four years old and, it seemed, would not be able to survive the hardships of our life. (She survived it all better than we did.) Madame Entaltsev had brought cases of books from Russia, which we all shared; they were a godsend. I thought it strange that this fine, educated woman was so devoted to her gruff and unattractive husband, an ex-colonel in some unknown artillery regiment. I could not understand it!

"Katyusha, on the other hand, never ceased to amaze me. She adjusted to everything, she who had been brought up in the greatest of luxury in the splendid Laval house in St. Petersburg. The marble floors in that house came from Emperor Nero's forum in Rome, and had been much admired by the tsar. And here she was sweeping the dirty mud floors in our dwelling without ever a word of protest. She always seemed to be in a pleasant mood, loved people, and had a charming, sweet sense of humor. Of all our present and future companions, however, it was Alexandrine Muraviev that I loved most."

The beautiful Annie, born Chernyshev, was the same age as Maria; the two had been friends for years. Daughter of fabulously rich parents who spoiled and pampered their "little goddess," she married Nikita Muraviev when she was only eighteen, and worshipped him. She had no hesitation at leaving her life of luxury and her two young children to follow the man she called "my genius." Nikita was probably a genius, but he was not outwardly as attractive as his wife. To Maria, he seemed "cold and remote, a philosopher and a dreamer, but not a man of action. Alexandrine expected us all to venerate him, but none of us shared her feelings."

Alexandrine was truly beautiful, of fragile build, with a rich mass of auburn hair and blue-green eyes. She was warm, spontaneous, and artistic; she could paint and sing beautifully, a great life-enhancer. Her presence brought comfort and pleasure to everyone around her. She missed her children acutely but was careful to present a happy, contented face to her husband.

Madame Naryshkin was small, fat, and "a bit pretentious, but a good sort." Soon after their arrival at Chita, Madame von Wiesen arrived, who, despite her German name (she was married to an officer of the Finland Regiment), was one hundred percent Russian; she had a round face, milky-white skin, and corn-blue eyes with long lashes. She, too, had had to leave her young children behind and as a result suffered from terrible nightmares: her cries of anguish could be heard down the street. She was eventually soothed and cured by a shaman, a local witch doctor. Madame von Wiesen's husband died in Siberia; she returned to Russia after the amnesty and at the age of fifty-three married Pushkin's childhood friend Jeannot Pushchin.

"Here I am in Chita, my tenderly loved Maman," wrote Maria on September 26, 1827, to her mother the day after her arrival in the village. "How exhausting it is to travel without a maid! The cold in the mountains caused me and Katyusha great suffering, as we had not anticipated it and were not dressed for it. Sergei and his companions are still on the road, and I am awaiting him with anxiety; he was spitting blood on the day of my departure and I fear that travel may have exhausted him and badly affected his poor lungs.

"I found Madame Naryshkin, Entaltsev, and Annie Muraviev subjected to the identical regulations which were prescribed to us in Blagodatsk. It means that we will be able to see our husbands only twice a week. My Lord, when will the trials end for me and my poor Sergei, whose health demands all my attention? How many times did I beg my mother-in-law to intercede for him so that I might obtain permission to see him daily!

"We women have formed here a kind of family and we accept each other with open arms; how misfortune brings people together! Madame Entaltsev brought me the toys of my darling little boy, who I hear is now able to pronounce my name and the name of his father. I was touched by the attention of this kind woman. She and I share a house and she is my 'economist,' who teaches me frugality. My quarters are far more comfortable here than in Blagodatsk; at least I have space for a table to write on, an embroidery frame, and my beloved clavichord.

"Yesterday I received a letter from my father, which did me much good. Dear Maman, I kiss your and Father's hands and feet a million times. I am not writing any more, as I am in a state of total exhaustion. I don't even understand what I am writing, for the women around me make so much noise. Again goodbye from the depths of my heart. Please do not forget to send me my *katsaveika* [fur-trimmed jacket] and the dress I asked for; they are both in my room at Boltyshka. Your loving daughter, Maria."

Gradually the ladies found themselves better accommodations. It was easy to build a home in Siberia. The local markets had logs of different thickness and size ready for sale. All the buyer had to do was specify the size and number of rooms desired. Almost overnight, the timbers would be assembled and carried to the site, the logs put together, chinked with moss, a roof of thin planks laid on top, and the new owner could move in. The only remaining problem was to install a chimney with a proper draft; it required expert attention from a local craftsman. The new houses were all grouped together near the prison, along Chita's main street, which became known as Damskaya Ulitsa, the Ladies' Street.

Prison regulations still allowed visits only twice a week, but the difference was that they could now take place in the privacy of the houses; husbands came accompanied by a guard, who was looked after in the kitchen by the cook (Leparsky allowed the ladies to hire local servants). "The distant jingling of chains became a welcome sound for us, as it heralded the arrival of one's husband," wrote Maria. "For the rest of the time, conversations took place across the little carved-out openings in the palisade which surrounded the prison. We were not officially allowed to talk to the prisoners through the fence, but old Leparsky tactfully kept out of the way during the afternoon hours, and the guard, whom we bribed, always warned us of the approach of one of the non-commissioned officers. We used to group ourselves around Katyusha, who usually brought a folding chair to support her heavy frame, and talked to our men through the small apertures in the fence. For all of us, it was the highlight of the day, and kept the romantic tension alive. But I admit it must have been tough on the men who were not married and had no woman to talk to on those days."

Work in Chita was light compared with the Nerchinsk mines. Though Leparsky was obliged to follow the verdict of the tribunal that had condemned the exiles to hard labor, the interpretation of what the work would consist of was left to his judgment. "In the summer, when there are no public works to be carried out, I make them do soil excavations," he reported to St. Petersburg. "During the winter months, they will be made to mill flour for their own use and for the bakery of the district."

The formidable-sounding soil excavation was a kind of Sisyphus work, invented to keep the prisoners busy. It consisted of filling with earth and sand a large ditch that the Decembrists called the "Devil's Grave." The hollow was supposed to undermine the road, but as mountain torrents spilled constantly over it, it took only a few days to wash away the work of an entire summer, and digging had to start all over again.

Andrei Rozen, who came to Chita directly from the Peter and Paul Fortress, recalls: "Every day except on Sundays and feast days the sergeant on duty would enter the prison early in the morning and call: 'Gentlemen, to work.' In general we were eager to get out, and left with songs on our lips and energy in our hearts. No force was ever used on us. Our column would then amble forth toward the Devil's Grave. Peasants enlisted by the guards carried our picks and shovels and pushed the wheelbarrows, while we ourselves fastened our chains to our belts and jingled our foot fetters to the rhythm of some stirring revolutionary tune." Often, their song would be the subversive *Marseillaise*, a great favorite with the guards, who, to the amusement of the prisoners, thought it a wonderful marching song. They, of course, did not realize that it was on the tsar's proscribed list.

Occasionally, the wives were permitted to go along. The guards then carried the ladies' folding chairs, rugs, samovars, hampers with food, newspapers, chessboards, and reading material. A shady spot would be found on the edge of the forest near the big ditch. The ladies settled comfortably under the trees, sewing or reading, while the prisoners would dig for a couple of hours, and then everyone would have lunch and relax. Some played chess; Davydov, Borisov, and Bestuzhev sketched; some soldiers played cards, others stacked their muskets and went to sleep. Thanks to the sketching skill of Nikolai Bestuzhev, who had trained at the Imperial Academy of Arts and was a painter of stature, we have many aquarelles of Chita as it appeared in the late 1820s when the Decembrists were living there; the valley ringed by larch-covered hills, the ten-foot stockade of sharpened stakes, and the fast-flowing Ingoda River, in which the Decembrists would bathe in the summer.

The men relaxing by the Devil's Grave must have presented an odd-looking sight. Political internees, once outside the walls of the Peter and Paul Fortress, were not issued prison attire. They had to make do as best they could with whatever bits of wearing apparel they could lay their hands on. The tall, immensely thin Prince Trubetskoy, whose long nose seemed to dominate the rest of his bird-like, emaciated face, walked about dressed in a long, fashionably cut redingote from the best St. Petersburg tailor, coupled with a pair of dirty old linen trousers, worn at the knees. "In spite of his untidy haircut and leg chains, he still looked like a born gentleman," wrote Basargin.

Nikita Muraviev sported a pair of felt boots, a reindeer shirt acquired from a local peasant, and a once-elegant felt hat bought in London. Volkonsky was dressed in knee breeches, heavy boots, and a blue linen shirt made in Chita from material Maria had purchased from a passing caravan. Others sported a variety of Chinese quilted jackets, short capes, peasant blouses, and a whole assortment of footwear, most of it held together by bits of string. Alessandro Poggio, Chita's foremost expert on gardening, wore a pair of black velvet trousers, and a shirt fashioned out of Chinese silk, under a tattered guardsman's jacket. "We all looked as if we had been masquerading as gypsies," recalled Obolensky in his memoirs. Indeed, it would have been impossible to recognize in this collection of beggars the immaculately turned-out guards officers, proud courtiers, and pampered sons of some of Russia's first families. The ladies in their voluminous skirts and large-brimmed hats, and the picnic baskets, assorted sewing boxes, knitting needles, books and magazines completed the incongruous quasi-Victorian picture.

In the winter, from the end of September until May, the prisoners worked in the hand mills. Each had a quota of eighty pounds of rye a day. Unlike the easy work of the summer, this was hard labor, and at first they found it difficult to fulfill the day's norm. But slowly they developed muscles in their arms; the strongest and healthiest helped the weaker ones to finish their assigned work. Most of them welcomed the physical labor, which kept them fit.

Mutual help extended to all aspects of the Decembrists' lives in Chita, and the most important feature of it was the artel, the cooperative, "that blessed institution," as they referred to it in their memoirs. Each prisoner was granted the paltry sum of 114 rubles 23 kopecks a year from the state, but the right to receive money from relations was strictly regulated by the governor. Officially, they were permitted no more than a thousand rubles a year, paid out in installments by Leparsky's nephew, Osip Adamovich. But as always in Russia, rules were there to be broken. Several of the prisoners such as Nikita Muraviev and Trubetskoy, who were very well off, received considerably more through official and unofficial channels, and through their wives. In addition, they had countless food and clothing parcels, books, reading material, and so on. On the other hand, thirty-two of their companions had nothing at all, either because they were poor or because they were neglected by their relatives. To rectify this situation and assure everyone a minimum level of subsistence, Leparsky authorized the prisoners to organize an artel, a cooperative, to which everyone with money contributed. It acted as a self-help institution and handled most of the practical problems of everyday life. Under the artel's charter, married prisoners, who were the wealthiest, made the largest contributions. Trubetskoy gave two thousand to three thousand rubles a year, and Volkonsky two thousand rubles. Nikita Muraviev received more than three thousand rubles yearly from family estates, and so did Ivashev, Naryshkin, and von Wiesen. Bachelors who received more than five hundred rubles a year were asked to contribute half of it. This way, even the poorest had a certain amount of goods and services. It placed everyone on an equal footing, and relieved the unpleasant feeling of being dependent on somebody else's bounty.* Baron Andrei Rozen, the supremely efficient and punctilious Baltic landowner, was asked to administer the artel. "Every three months, a paper was sent around on which each man wrote down his contribution in proportion to our common expenses. The sum collected would be spent by me on tea, sugar, meats, and various household necessities. Clothes and linen we all had to obtain for ourselves. The rich bought the necessities and shared them with their poorer brethren. Everything was divided in a truly brotherly way, money as well as suffering. So as not to spend funds lavishly, our clothes were cut and made by some of our comrades. The best tailors were Prince Evgeni Obolensky, Pavel Mozgan, and Anton Arbuzov. Hats and shoes were made by Nikolai and Mikhail Bestuzhev and Peter Fallenberg . . ."

These monies arrived irregularly, however, and for a time the Volkonskys were deeply affected by it. Maria's correspondence from Chita is filled with requests for funds to the point of bitterness. "I must inform you, dear Maman," she wrote on November 14, 1827, "that from the time of my departure from Petersburg I had only the money I took with me [eight hundred

---

* During the ten years they spent as convicts, the Decembrists received from home in cash (besides food and clothing parcels) 354,758 rubles; their wives an additional 778,135 rubles; and this through official channels only. They also received other sums secretly through the administration. In Chita and later in Petrovsky Zavod, where goods and services were cheap, these were considerable sums.

rubles], and the thousand rubles I received from my father. Travel, the sending back of the servants, and the journey from Blagodatsk led to unforeseen expenses, as a result of which I find myself in a difficult situation. I long ago warned my brother Repnin [Sergei's brother] about this, but either my letter has not reached him or he thinks that I took advantage of the letter of credit which Feodor the cook was supposed to bring me; but as he died on the way, I never got it. Since you are, dear Maman, so kind as to send me the proceeds from the sale of the goods at the Makariev fair, I am going to ask you now only for food supplies; but Sergei also needs woolen clothes, new linen, and lots of tobacco. All these things are unavailable here or are too expensive, considering the sums they issue us. Your obedient daughter, Maria Volkonsky."

The difficulty lay in the animosity between the two families and the lack of clear-cut arrangements about the property that Sergei had settled on Maria and their son. Before leaving home, Maria had asked her father to look after her financial affairs and act as trustee for her son, Nikolenka. But it is obvious from the tone of the letters in the Raevsky Archives that the general had no patience with the "mean and greedy Volkonskys"; and he quite rightly suspected that Sergei's sister Sophia had seized a chunk of her brother's property. Though the old princess dutifully fulfilled all the various requests for clothes, books, wine, and medicine, she was oddly reluctant to send cash. It prompted an angry letter from Maria's mother, who complained about the old princess's meanness. "If I had the misfortune to have a son in Siberia," wrote Madame Raevsky, "and my unfortunate, innocent daughter-in-law had followed him, I would have sold my newest dress to send her money." The vexing problem of money was only resolved after General Raevsky's death, when Maria came into her own inheritance, and the Volkonskys, after Prince Repnin's intervention, felt obliged to match it.

Winter passed, and suddenly, within a week, came the explosion of spring. Just as her life in Chita was settling down and Sergei's health showed improvement came the tragic news of little Nikolenka's death. The fair, beguiling boy whom she last saw happily playing with the red seal on the tsar's letter died at the Volkonsky Palace in St. Petersburg at the end of February 1828, barely aged two. The news did not reach Maria until late spring, nor was she told any details. How did it happen? Who was to blame? Was it really whooping cough, or lack of attention? Did his grandmother neglect him? A torrent of guilt swept over her. She blamed herself for "condemning" her innocent child to death by leaving him with his unfeeling grandmother. In reality, however, the old princess loved Nikolenka as much as she was capable of loving anybody. It was never quite clear what caused the boy's death. It appears to have been some kind of pulmonary infection, probably brought on by the drafts and dampness of the Volkonsky Palace.

Pushkin sent a long letter, and the poem which was engraved over the child's tomb at Boltyshka:

> Bathed in light and heavenly rest
> By the throne of our almighty God
> He looks at the land of your exile,
> Blesses his mother and prays for his father.

Nikolenka's death was a heavy blow for Maria. For the first time in her life, her indomitable spirit was shaken. She spent hours alone in her house staring at her little boy's picture as a baby, the picture she had brought from Russia with her. Annie Muraviev, the only woman in whom she confided, remarked that "Nikolenka took Maria's laughter with him." She was deeply hurt by what seemed to her her family's coolness over the death of her child. "Your observations on Nikolenka were very, very cold, but I am not angry with you, since they are only a reflection of St. Petersburg salon talk," she wrote to her sister Sophia. "But I did not expect Mother to remain silent over my grief for such a very long time. What does her contempt of the Volkonskys have to do with my poor son?" She told Ekaterina a few months later that "time did not seem to help her grief"; she felt neglected by her family and was deeply worried at the prospect of old age without support for herself and for Sergei, who "has no one in the world to take an interest in him."

Maria's letters from that period reflect her growing depression; the novelty of Siberia had worn off, she still saw her husband only twice a week, and there seemed to be little hope for the future. She wanted to obtain permission for Sergei to move into the new house she had built on the outskirts of Chita, and wrote to her father asking him to petition the tsar on her behalf. She argued that the death of her son had left her weak and in need of her husband's support. She had, a few months before, asked the old princess to intercede also, but received no reply.

But the old general remained obdurate. "Not knowing the exact state of affairs, I cannot permit myself to approach the tsar on this matter; do as your heart and mind dictate, but I do not want to have any part in this business." The letter sounds heartless, but the old warrior himself was unhappy. The death of his grandson had distressed him deeply. He, too, of course, blamed it on the uncaring old princess and the "perishing cold in that damp pile of masonry on the Moika."

Above all, he was angry with that "stuffed fool, my son-in-law, the cause of everybody's misfortunes." With Maria's departure, Boltyshka had sunk into misery; the hero of 1812 felt isolated from his friends and forgotten by the emperor. He sensed that, with the death of Nikolenka, Maria's ties with Russia were now broken, and that he would be unlikely ever to see his favorite daughter again. Legal wrangles with Sergei's family over property did not help matters. The details of the financial dispute are uncertain, but it appears that the Volkonskys had also implied that the old general did not know much about finances, and told him "that Sergei agreed with their views."

"Mashenka sees everything and makes judgments through Volkonsky eyes," Raevsky complained to his son Nikolai. "She has nothing of the Raevsky left in her . . ." In a brief letter to Maria dictated to her sister Sophia, he gave vent to his feelings of frustration. "If your husband does not know me well enough to believe that I hold my daughter's interests closer to heart than his own mother does, or his brother Prince Repnin for that matter, then you at least should have pointed out to him that I, your father, am not likely to do anything prejudicial to your interests." He asked to be excused from managing her affairs on the grounds of ill health, and assured her and Sergei of his good wishes "in spite of everything."

Much upset, Maria wrote back immediately to ask what she had done to merit his displeasure, but by the time her letter reached Boltyshka the old warrior was dead.

What happened? It appears that Raevsky, far from putting aside his daughter's request to petition the tsar on her behalf, had in fact been waiting for a propitious moment to approach the emperor. He hoped to obtain permission for Sergei to be moved to the Caucasus, which for Maria would be so much nearer to home. In late summer, Nicholas I was on maneuvers in the area, staying at the Fortress of Elizavetgrad, about twenty-five miles from Boltyshka. It had been raining heavily for days; the roads were torrents of mud. Worried about not being able to get to his appointment on time, Raevsky decided to abandon his carriage halfway there and proceed the rest of the way on horseback. The audience was not much of a success. Emperor Nicholas would not be moved. He expressed great pleasure at seeing his old friend, the veteran soldier, but said, "Listen to me, Nikolai Nikolaevich. I will not discuss that traitor Volkonsky, either now or at any time in the future." There was nothing for Raevsky to do but withdraw. In deep gloom and in spite of a raging summer storm, he rode all the way back to Boltyshka, where his wife waited anxiously for news. A week later, he was dead of pneumonia. Facing the bed in his study was a portrait of Maria as a young girl, painted by Sokolov at the time of her engagement to Volkonsky. "That is the most remarkable woman I have ever known in my life," he murmured as life was slipping away. He was buried holding the image of a Raphael Madonna that Maria had embroidered for him in Chinese beads at Blagodatsk.

The death of her father was another terrible blow for Maria. She had always had a strong sense of filial duty, and like the rest of the family idolized her legendary father. Grief and remorse were now combined with a feeling of utter hopelessness. She had not yet recovered from the death of Nikolenka, and this new blow brought on a violent liver attack. "I felt as if the sky had collapsed over my head—desperately ill and for days unable to retain any food." It was lucky that Commandant Leparsky allowed Sergei's brilliant colleague Dr. Wolff (the former surgeon general of the Second Army) to visit her. He was brought to Maria's bedside under a military escort, dragging his chains; but his herbal medications helped her to get over her illness.

Alarmed by Maria's state of health, Commandant Leparsky authorized Sergei to absent himself three days a week from the prison and temporarily move into his wife's house to look after her. It was a brave and humane gesture on his part, for even six thousand miles from the capital there were many of Benckendorff's police spies around ready to denounce him for going counter to the tsar's wishes. To Maria, the move brought the resumption of married life and welcome masculine companionship. She had found the biweekly visits nerve-racking and most depressing. She pleaded that other wives be allowed the same privileges, and gradually, as individual cases came up, the rules became more relaxed. "Our life in Chita has really become quite tolerable," she wrote to Zenaida Volkonsky. "The women see much of each other and get on amazingly well together. We explore the lovely countryside around us; we have even managed to engage local servants, who though raw and untrained help to shift the burden of domesticity from our shoulders. I lead an active and occupied life. I find that there is nothing better than working with one's hands; such labor lulls your mind and there is no time for tormenting thoughts, whereas reading leads you to memories of the past. I am thankful for the provisions you have sent me; I was particularly happy to find bouillon, which enables me to make soups for Sergei, though they are not always successful, since I am unable to find the ingredients. Katyusha is more skillful at cooking than I am, but, on the other hand, not a single one of my friends can repair or sew underwear as I do."

Cooking skills were the most sought-after, and here Madame Annenkov, the former Pauline Guèble, a recent arrival, was supreme. Her story is so remarkable that it deserves to be told. Daughter of a French army officer killed in Spain, Pauline Guèble was a handsome thirty-year-old woman from Nancy who had come to St. Petersburg as a representative of a French couture house. Gay, bursting with vitality, she found life in the Russian capital captivating, and decided to start her own dressmaking business there, at which she was very successful. She met and fell in love with the brother of one of her customers, Ivan A. Annenkov, an attractive, high-living, socially prominent young lieutenant in the Preobrazhensky Guards, and heir to an enormous fortune. In spite of Pauline's ardent hopes, aristocratic conventions were such that there was no question of marriage.

Ivan was totally dependent financially on his fabulously rich widowed mother, who wanted a brilliant career for her remaining son (Ivan's brother had been killed in a duel), and would have been quite capable of disinheriting him had he as much as suggested marrying Pauline, his sister's dressmaker. Madame Annenkov occupied a palatial residence on Moscow's Tverskoy Boulevard, where a special wing had been built to house her wearing apparel. She was reputed to own over five thousand dresses, nearly one hundred furs, and three huge sacks of jewelry. She enjoyed unlimited credit both in Moscow and in St. Petersburg, as well as in London and Paris, and ordered her clothes by post from specially sent books of design from the Paris or London couture houses. Self-centered, capricious, and very temperamental, Mme Annenkov had made up her mind never to listen to bad news. Her terrorized staff waited almost a year before they dared to inform her that her eldest son had been killed in a duel. She adored the army and its trappings; whenever Ivan came to see her, he was made to appear in his gala uniform even at breakfast.

The news of the uprising against the tsar and of her son's part in it outraged her. She refused to go to St. Petersburg to visit Ivan in the Fortress, or even to send him money for shoes and fresh linen and tobacco, as he requested. "My son is a fugitive from justice," she announced. "I want to forget him." Such was the woman Pauline Guèble had to face when she decided to follow her lover to Siberia. She was in a difficult situation, for she had just given birth to Ivan's daughter, and had no money. Pauline, of course, had had no idea that Ivan had belonged to a secret society. It would not have mattered to her. Immediately after his arrest, she mortgaged her jewelry and sold her collection of Turkish shawls to travel to St. Petersburg and see her lover in the Fortress. The permission was hard to obtain, as she had no official status, as a wife would, and was a foreigner. The guards asked as much as two hundred to three hundred rubles in bribes, a huge sum for a self-supporting young woman. But she managed to get in and see him. Ivan, who by now had been suitably chastened and deeply touched by her devotion, sent her a note from the Fortress: "We must be together or die."

Pauline Annenkov's lively memoirs describe her interview with the dowager: "I told her that she had just become a grand-mother and that I intended to follow her son to Siberia and marry him. Mme Annenkov listened in dead silence. She then looked me over carefully and announced that I was throwing myself away on a rascal. 'He deserves the punishment. Let him suffer.' I replied, 'Madame, your attitude is that of a Roman matron, but times have changed.'" They got on well together; the old lady invited Pauline to stay, and to make her home with her in Moscow with the baby, but she refused to help with money. In the meantime, however, various members of the French colony in Moscow, and Annenkov's two sisters, touched by Pauline's devotion, collected enough funds for her journey. The dowager was persuaded to sell a farm and put the proceeds in trust for the little girl, who would be looked after by one of the relatives. There remained the problem of getting the necessary permissions, and here the situation was complicated by the fact that Pauline was a French citizen. "How can we assume responsibility for a foreigner and a woman, and one who hardly speaks any Russian?" said General Dibich, head of General Benckendorff's police section. "After all, the uprising was exclusively a Russian affair," he added. "*Ce n'est pas votre patrie, madame*, you had better return to France and forget." But Pauline kept trying. "Dare and you will succeed," she told herself. She was also buoyed up by a prophecy from Mme Lenormand, the famous French clairvoyant her mother went to see at her request in Alsace. Mme Lenormand told Pauline's mother that after twenty years of hard life Pauline would end up "living happily ever after," respected and loved by everyone around her and surrounded by an adoring family and several children—a prophecy that came true.

Prince Lobanov-Rostovsky, one of the tsar's aides, who had had a brief liaison with Pauline at one time and remained a good friend, hinted that she would have no difficulty in finding a rich protector in St. Petersburg. Realizing how determined she was to follow Ivan, he agreed to help arrange an interview with the tsar, "but it would have to take place away from the gossipy court circles in St. Petersburg." The emperor received her while on an inspection tour of the small provincial town of Vyazma. "Sire, I have no legal rights—but my love . . ." said Pauline. Nicholas reminded her acidly that Siberia was not the kind of country where she was likely to find happiness, and suggested that before even thinking of embarking on such a journey she had better start learning Russian. But he was impressed by her gallantry, and he probably also hoped to enhance his reputation as a humane monarch in France, where Pauline's case was being followed with great interest.

Permission was granted, and Pauline left Moscow on December 23, 1827 (a year later than Maria), at eleven o'clock in the evening, "as the theaters were emptying," accompanied by the good wishes of the entire French colony in Moscow. She traveled with two menservants from Mme Annenkov's household, and had several thousand rubles sewn into the folds of her traveling costume, "extremely well hidden in deep seams, as befitted the head of the leading couture house in Moscow." Her fare to Irkutsk was four hundred rubles eighty kopecks (about two hundred dollars). She arrived in Irkutsk with a severe case of frostbite. Surprised by the arrival of a French citizen, Governor Zeidler refused to allow her to proceed any farther until he could obtain confirmation from St. Petersburg. The letter from General Lavinsky, Governor of eastern Siberia and Zeidler's superior, to the head of the police section in St. Petersburg, written in French, shows imperial bureaucracy at its most typical: "Your Excellency, A seamstress has recently arrived in Irkutsk, a French subject accompanied by two serfs who belong to the household of the lady-in-waiting Annenkov . . . The seamstress tells me that she intends to marry the state criminal Annenkov, and insists that the marriage was authorized by your department. However, she has not presented enough evidence, as the letters from the Moscow chief of police are not certified by the Governor of Moscow."

He went on to ask for instructions as to "what to do with this foreign lady who has so unexpectedly appeared in our town." As a result, Pauline was forced to remain in Irkutsk for over a month; it turned out to be an annoying but materially rewarding stay. The arrival of a young, fashionably dressed Frenchwoman reputed to be a dress designer caused an absolute sensation among the wives of the local merchants, who were bored with their provincial existence and intent on impressing one another with their toilettes. Though there had always been plenty of fine materials about, brought by caravans from Peking, it took a long time to get a book of designs from St. Petersburg, and there were no dressmakers in Siberia. Pauline, being a practical Gallic woman, decided that she might as well set up shop while awaiting clearance to proceed beyond Lake Baikal. She became much-sought-after in Irkutsk, as rich merchants and their wives vied to entertain her in their houses. "Their food was absolutely delicious," she recalled, "a splendid mixture of the best Russian fish, French imports, and Chinese delicacies delivered fresh from Peking, but the standards of cleanliness were appalling. Their table linen and cutlery were very crude." After a banquet organized by Yuri Nekrasov, the leading tea merchant, she sternly admonished his wife: "You are all filthy rich here but you live like pigs . . . *svinya* you are." Luckily for Pauline, Mme

Nekrasov was not only very good-natured but also eager to learn. Ten years later, when Pauline revisited Irkutsk with her husband, the same Mme Nekrasov, her daughters, and all her friends praised Pauline for the "civilizing influence she had had over their households." When she left, Nekrasov himself accompanied her for fifteen miles out of town to the customs barrier to make sure that the Lake Baikal police would not unnecessarily molest her. Just as well, for in her luggage was a strictly forbidden item, a rifle, purchased illegally in town, and enough household goods to equip several kitchens for years, plus scissors, thread, twine, and other vital necessities. She also had plenty of money, a lot of it made in Irkutsk; "her dowry," as she referred to it, was hidden under her fur bonnet in her hair.

The ladies on the Damskaya Ulitsa were told of Pauline's arrival by Commandant Leparsky, and immediately set about preparing accommodations for her at the house of the local baker. It overlooked a stream and had a small balcony with a view over the mountains. Pauline said it was "perfect" and, forgetting about the rigors of the journey, instantly set about unpacking her kitchen supplies. Next day, after paying a call on Leparsky, she invited the ladies to supper.

Two days later, in the presence of the assembled prisoners, Ivan and Pauline were married, with Commandant Leparsky as best man. Maria observed that "the clanging of chains drowned the sounds of the organ as our men filed into the little wooden church. When he came to the altar, Annenkov's leg fetters were removed, as our Orthodox religion demands. Leparsky, being a Catholic, was unfamiliar with our rites; Pauline, who does not speak Russian, could not understand the questions asked by the priest; she laughed a lot and kept whispering to the best man, Alexander Muraviev, for advice. But underneath it all one could feel the depths of her great love for Annenkov, for whom she had given up her little daughter and her country.

"After the ceremony, Ivan's chains were clamped on again. He said goodbye to his bride and returned to the prison. He would have to wait two days before his turn to visit her came round—hard for them both. We all implored Leparsky to be generous, but he refused. He explained it was a relatively minor matter and not worth annoying St. Petersburg. So we all gathered in Annie Muraviev's house and tried to console the poor bride with a feast consisting of smoked fish, sweet biscuits, and wine."

Pauline brought with her a multitude of practical skills which she happily shared with her companions. She taught them to pluck chickens, skin hare, clean fish, make preserves, dress wounds, treat a toothache. Above all, she taught them to expand their culinary skills. Her little house by the stream was neat and tidy. She always seemed to be at home, ready for the unexpected visitor with a glass of tea or a newly baked loaf of black bread and homemade jam.

While in Moscow, Pauline had designed clothes for Princess Zenaida, Maria's cousin. Through her talks with Princess Zenaida and members of her household, she acquired a profound admiration for Maria; her example spurred her on, and she called Maria "my inspiration." She brought Maria sheets of Italian music, a present from Princess Zenaida, a most welcome gift in the wilderness of Chita. As time went on, the two women, in spite of their very different backgrounds, became close friends. Pauline's practical outlook on life and sense of humor were a good foil for Maria's high-strung romantic nature. Alone among the women, the two shared a desire to learn about their surroundings and developed a keen interest in the customs of the local tribes. The fearless and indefatigable Pauline, with her Latin exuberance, energy, merry laughter, and the amusing mistakes she made when talking Russian, cheered everybody around her.

Another addition to the ladies' contingent was Sashenka Davydov, the shy young wife of Maria's Uncle Vasya from Kamenka. She brought with her Masha, a young serf woman who had been Maria's maid at Boltyshka and had waited for three years to get the necessary permit to join her mistress. Masha remained with Maria, and later with her children in exile, and returned with them to European Russia twenty-five years later.

As life on the Damskaya Ulitsa settled into an even if monotonous pattern highlighted by the biweekly visits from the husbands and by occasional arguments with Leparsky about improvements in the prisoners' routine (from which the good-natured commandant usually emerged the loser), the men, as their prison chaplain described it, led a life "reminiscent of the Apostles" of old. Bound together in the smoothly functioning cooperative, they organized a joinery and carpentry shop, put up a shed for the tailor and the cobbler, and laid out a huge kitchen garden. "We salted down in cedar casks sixty thousand cucumbers from our own garden this year," recorded Baron Rozen. The dining room was supervised by an elected "elder," who planned the menu and ordered supplies, which in turn were paid for by the commandant's office if they came from the prison storeroom, or by the artel if they came from packages received from home. The prison senior enjoyed the privilege of being able to come and go freely (though under escort), for both the kitchen and the storeroom were outside the prison compound. The fare was simple, "biblical": yogurt, black bread, cabbage soup, kasha (gruel made of buckwheat), fish, and root vegetables; in summer they had fresh fruit, and vegetables from their own garden. "After Andrei Rozen was elected prison senior, kitchen standards improved to an unbelievable extent," writes

Obolensky. Rozen, a punctilious, efficient Baltic baron, got on particularly well with Leparsky. They were both professional and tactful men; each understood the other's position. He became the official intermediary between the commandant and the prisoners, to the advantage of all concerned.

In his memoirs, Rozen recalls his conversations with the commandant, who apparently worried about his "image for posterity." "What will be written about me everywhere in Europe?" he would remark to Rozen. "They will call me a hardhearted jailer, executioner, oppressor, while the truth is that I only retain my present post in order to protect you men from the persecutions and injustices of unscrupulous officials." He needn't have worried; the Decembrists saw to it that history, like themselves, would remember Commandant Leparsky as a just and very kind man.

It was entirely due to the commandant that in spite of much physical hardship, the detainees were able to lead an intellectually stimulating life in Chita, further their own education, and make a lasting contribution to the general knowledge about Siberia. Leparsky knew that his charges were a very unusual collection of men, with a very high level of intelligence. There were specialists among them in various fields of science and the liberal arts, military historians, agriculturalists, travelers, linguists, and superb craftsmen. Most of them had been suffering from intellectual starvation after their long confinement in the Fortress and in faraway outposts throughout the Nerchinsk mine area. Now that they found themselves together in one place, they were eager to profit from each other's knowledge. A program of informal lectures was arranged; each man studied a subject he knew little or nothing about, and in return gave talks on his own specialty to his colleagues. With Leparsky's permission, books were ordered, and magazines and newspapers in French, German, Italian, subscribed to by the wives, started to arrive from

European capitals. During the prisoners' three years in Chita and later in Petrovsky Zavod, a substantial library was built up (it was moved to Petrovsky Zavod) and expanded into a unique collection.

In reading the Decembrists' memoirs, one is struck by the unusual talent confined within the walls of the Chita prison. How different the next hundred years of Russian history might have been if Nicholas I had listened to the Decembrists' advice and begun to implement their reforms.

"Nikita Muraviev, who possessed beautiful maps and plans, expounded military strategy and tactics to us," recalled Baron Rozen. "Ferdinand Wolff, the brilliant staff surgeon and physician of the Second Army of the Ukraine, gave us lectures on anatomy and chemistry. Pushchin explained the higher branches of mathematics, Alexander Kornilovich and Peter Mukhanov were eminent historians, Obolensky and the young Prince Alexander Odoevsky both lectured on Russian literature (and taught Russian to those of us, like myself, who spoke it poorly). At nine o'clock in the evening our doors were shut and every light had to be extinguished. As we could not fall asleep so early, we would talk for a long time or listen to the colorful accounts of Mikhail Kuchelbecker, who had traveled all over the globe. Several of us studied foreign languages; Zavalishin was our greatest linguist; he knew not only Latin and Greek but eight modern languages as well, and he managed to find a teacher for each one of these languages among our comrades."

There were others: Torson lectured on political economy and state finance; Nikolai Bestuzhev, the gifted painter, was also an expert lexicographer and while in Chita started compiling a Buriat–Russian dictionary. Agricultural matters were in the hands of Sergei Volkonsky and the charming, fun-loving Italian, Alessandro Poggio; they were advised by Andrei Rozen. The three of them introduced barley, melons, and cauliflowers to

Transbaikalia, all grown from seeds sent from European Russia. Later, their cultivation spread to most of Siberia.

They called their self-styled university the Academy of Chita. "Within a year," writes Basargin, "the little settlement had been transformed into an important intellectual center. Our lectures were attended by local officials, merchants, school-children; even Buriat princes came to study in our shed." The less erudite, or those who were simply in need of the relaxation afforded by manual crafts, worked in the adjoining carpentry tent, which was fitted with benches for carpentry, smithy work, and bookbinding. The other shed became the much attended music room. Alexander Yushnevsky excelled at the piano; others played the violin, the guitar, and the flute. During their second year in Chita, a string quartet was formed which became immensely popular throughout the countryside and attracted hundreds of listeners. When in 1885 George Kennan visited Chita on his survey of detention camps throughout Russia, he found that latter-day exiles still gathered in the same wooden building which had once been the Decembrists' carpentry and joinery shop. It had been slightly expanded, but the original benches were still there.

What made Chita so different from the later phases of their exile was the fact that most of the Decembrists were still young and full of hope. They did not yet have the feeling that their lives were irrevocably ruined. "In view of what came later, Chita was our poem to youth," wrote Jeannot Pushchin. Surrounded by the lovely countryside, many of them lived moments of carefree optimism, even joy. When news came of the great Russian victory over the Turks in 1829, they sincerely believed that amnesty was around the corner; there was the same heady anticipation after the 1830 Polish insurrection was suppressed. But each time they were disappointed.

There were of course other aspects of their imprisonment

which, quite apart from the absence of freedom, made life hard to bear. When strongly individualistic men of different temperaments and backgrounds are cooped together in a restricted space, it is inevitable that various personality conflicts, jealousies, and petty irritations should arise. "The blessed artel" went a long way to solve what might have become the most aggravating factor in community life. But even so, certain of the men saw "aristocratic privilege" in the way the rooms in prison had been allocated, which of course was not so. There was envy toward those who received more mail than the others; and there were individuals who, when in the throes of depression, blamed the leaders of the uprising for having bungled "their revolution," and for having landed them in the hell of Siberia. Trubetskoy was twice attacked by younger men for his "double-faced turn-around on the 14th of December." But these were isolated outbursts, quickly smoothed over by wise Dr. Wolff and Baron Rozen, the two men who never lost their tempers or their common sense. But the most enduring objects of envy were the married men, the lucky ones whose wives enabled them to lead normal lives. The majority of the prisoners were young and unmarried, in their early twenties or younger. They found their enforced celibacy hard to bear, especially when compared to their fortunate married colleagues. There were moments when the fetters were more than they could stand.

One small improvement occurred in the autumn of 1828. As they were coming out of church on a frosty Sunday morning in late September, the prisoners were summoned to a meeting in the commandant's house. They marched down the road in a phalanx of jingling chains and animated chatter, while the wives, curious and somewhat apprehensive, took up stations by General Leparsky's garden gate. Leparsky came out of his house looking festive and extremely pleased with himself. He had on his full-dress uniform, decorations, and a new wig. His cavalry boots shone like mirrors. "It has pleased His Imperial Majesty," he announced, "to command that the prisoners' leg irons be removed." Leparsky had applied for this favor some time before, first for the sick and for those with old wounds. Now, "in his infinite kindness," the tsar was extending it to all those "whose behavior warranted it." Leparsky took it upon himself to advise St. Petersburg that this would apply to everybody. At a signal from the commandant, soldiers went down the serried ranks of the prisoners unlocking the fetters which most of them had now worn for over twenty-six months. It was good to be able to flex one's ankles again, and a colossal relief to sleep without their all-encumbering presence. But the Decembrists were not Byronic heroes for nothing. To many, the chains had become a sort of status symbol, a token of their fight for liberty. There were those who felt sorry to be parting with them. The majority, however, welcomed what they hoped would be the first step toward their eventual freedom. "The only thing I shall miss," remarked young Odoevsky, the poet, "is that they jingled so pleasantly to the tune of our songs." The ladies, of course, were delighted, particularly as the men were given the day off to celebrate the occasion. In a charming short speech in French, Maria expressed their collective appreciation to Leparsky. Pauline Annenkov asked that she be permitted to keep her husband's leg fetters, as "such nice bracelets could be fashioned out of them." In time, Bestuzhev and Yakubovich, the two craftsmen, made them up into bracelets in the smithy shop. They were so handsome that all the Decembrists' wives proudly wore them on their wrists. In the years after the amnesty, they became the rage in St. Petersburg, and every fashionable woman aspired to a copy of a Dekabristi bracelet.

Throughout 1829, Maria's health showed considerable improvement. Dr. Wolff's medical potions, made from herbs collected (under military escort) on the shores of Lake Onon and on the banks of the Ingoda River, improved her digestion, which had been impaired by the dietary regime and her cooking experiments in Blagodatsk. Chita's excellent climate and high elevation suited her. At twenty-four, she still showed great resilience amid hardship. Baron Rozen, who had never met her before Chita, described her as "lithe of figure, with beautiful eyes, smooth, olive complexion, and aristocratic bearing. She was unmistakably a princess," he wrote. "I admire her, though my preference always goes to blond, blue-eyed, Baltic women." She developed a fondness for gardening, and spent long hours tending the plot between her house and Pauline's. Her only regret was that she was not allowed to work in the prisoners' garden, where Sergei and Alessandro Poggio achieved miracles of cultivation. By now, the prisoners' primitive vegetable patch had become a splendidly varied market and flower garden, with colorful flower borders in between old bits of stone, beds of asparagus, watermelons, tomatoes, cauliflowers, and colored cabbage, hitherto unknown in this part of the world. (Until then, the natives of Transbaikalia only knew how to grow cabbages, potatoes, and onions.)

In 1829, spring was unusually mild and pleasant and autumn frosts did not start until late September. Sergei and Poggio's market garden yielded such an abundant harvest of fruit and vegetables that they gave a large part of their produce to the guards and shared the rest with the entire population of Chita, much to everyone's pleasure and surprise. Maria noted that "Sergei is patient and meticulous—that's what makes him such a good gardener. As long as he has a little plot of soil to work on, he is content. Alessandro, on the other hand, is not patient, but he has great imagination and a sense of beauty." Alessandro had the two qualities Maria most admired in a man.

She had known him for years, for he was distantly related to the Raevskys through his brother, who married a second cousin of Maria's. He used to visit Kamenka during Maria's childhood, but as he was seven years older and already a guards officer and she was barely thirteen, it was in Chita that the two met as adults. Annie Muraviev—a close and observant friend—was the first to notice that Maria "tended to regain all of her former sparkle the moment Alessandro was around."

Maria's letters from Chita to her family in the Ukraine are full of gardening requests, for cuttings, for textbooks on how to put in beds of asparagus, and enthusiastic reports on Sergei's horticultural achievements. On March 2, 1829, she wrote to her sister Elena: "Soon Sergei will be putting glass in the frame to build a small orangery. I hope he will succeed, for it would give him great pleasure." A month later, she adds in a note to her mother: "The box of vegetable seeds that you sent me from Kiev, chère Maman, has been received." She proudly describes an experiment Sergei had carried out recently on how to grow tobacco from the seeds sent from Danvers, the fashionable seed store in St. Petersburg. He must have done very well, for he was told by a visiting botanist that the height of the stems and the spread of the leaves on his tobacco plants were as good as those grown on American plantations.

"According to the local calendar, our summer is supposed to be over," Maria writes later that year, in September. "But so far we have not had one morning of frost; this is excellent for our garden. I have got red cabbage, artichokes, beautiful melons, watermelons, and a whole lot of various vegetables for the winter. At the moment, the nights here are wonderful, brightly lit by the moon; Nikolai Bestuzhev is painting our flower borders and the vegetable garden by moonlight." Painted on midnight-blue paper, Bestuzhev's sketch done in sepia shows Sergei's small orangery, the flower beds with the prison buildings on the left, the tall picket fence, and the mountains towering in the background.

In November of that year, Maria realized that she was pregnant. Since the death of Nikolenka, she had been reluctant even to think of having children, the unhappiness of his loss had been too great. But now she was delighted.

The wives had been busy in Chita that spring, for during the first fortnight in March three of them produced babies: Alexandrine Muraviev had a daughter, Nonushka; Sonya Davydov a son, Vadka; and the irrepressible Pauline Guèble a daughter, whom she named Anna, in honor of Ivan's tyrannical mother. The delicate, small-boned Alexandrine almost died during labor, and was only saved by the attention of Dr. Wolff, whom Leparsky allowed out of prison to keep watch at her bedside until the crisis was over.

Leparsky was greatly perturbed when he learned from reading the women's correspondence to their relatives that babies were to be born here. His book of rules did not foresee such an eventuality. He confronted Pauline and Annie Muraviev with their letters, looking extremely embarrassed. "Permit me to say that you have no right to be pregnant," he stated in some confusion. "When the births begin—well, then it is another matter." "Why does it seem to him that after the babies are born everything will become legal, but not before?" Pauline said, laughing.

And now it was Maria's turn. During the long winter months, letters crossed back and forth between Chita, Moscow, St. Petersburg, and Boltyshka, announcing the happy event and asking for knitting wool, medicine, and above all, "small woolly clothes." Ekaterina was the one who responded most generously; and so did Princess Zenaida, who, before leaving Moscow for Rome, where she was to remain for the rest of her life, sent sable-lined quilted jackets of various sizes, wrapped in sheets of Italian music.

On July 1, 1830, Maria gave birth to a daughter, Sonyushka; she was born with a defective heart valve and lived only two days. Nikolai Bestuzhev helped Sergei to make the tiny wooden coffin in which baby Sonyushka was carried to her grave on a hill overlooking the river Ingoda. Weeks passed before Maria was able to communicate the sad news to her family. When she finally wrote, her grief was so overwhelming that even her tough brother, Alexander, was moved to tears: "In the entire surrounding landscape I can see only one thing, the new cross on the grave of my child. How will I ever find enough courage to live here and continue to look after Sergei, whose health has again taken a turn for the worse? Sonyushka would have given me strength to continue. I am very lonely these days."

The last sentence implies that perhaps Sergei was failing her. He himself was affected by the child's death and felt ill most of the time. He was unable to give Maria the masculine comfort she craved.

To take her mind off her sad loss, Pauline Annenkov suggested Maria accompany her on a visit to a Buriat encampment a few miles out of Chita. She wanted to meet the tribe's shaman, the witch doctor who had cured Mme von Wiesen of her nightmares by administering an herbal potion and uttering incantations over her. No one ever discovered whether the cure had been the result of mild hypnosis or the shaman's knowledge of herbal medicine. But since the day of her visit, Madame von Wiesen had slept soundly like a child.

For the last two years, Nikolai Bestuzhev had been busy compiling a Buriat–Russian dictionary, and Maria had taken pride in learning the basic elements of the language. "As they are all around us and were here long before any Russian set foot in this country, we might as well learn to address them in their own tongue," she told the other women, but only Pauline had been willing to try. The nomadic Buriats constantly passed through the village, driving sheep and riding their blunt-nosed, fast little horses. In summer, small Buriat boys with shaven heads and not a stitch of clothing on their bodies ran through the Damskaya Ulitsa to bathe in the Ingoda.

To Maria, the children were a welcome distraction, and it amused her to see their astonishment when she addressed them in their tribal dialect. A Buriat prince regularly called on her whenever he happened to be passing by: tall, clean-shaven like an old print idea of a Chinese, he dressed in a blue caftan with silver beads. He would appear suddenly, unannounced, bow gravely, and request the pleasure of offering her a packet of tea from Peking. Each time, he paid her the same homage, delivered in a slow, resonant tone of voice: "I respect you deeply, Princess, and wish you much happiness in this world." She came to regard him as a friend. When Pauline suggested they visit the shaman, Maria sent a message to her Buriat prince, asking him to escort them to the "sacred island" on the Ingoda where the shaman was in residence. She later described the experience:

"I walked up to Pauline's cabin at the edge of the forest; one could see the lake and the river from the window—lovely view. I found her cooking something delicious on her charcoal stove. We often would arrive unexpectedly at her house, bring our provisions with us, and call: 'Pauline, please cook something.' She served wonderful game, which her Siberian servant was adept at trapping.

"When we saw our friend the Buriat chieftain riding down the Damskaya Ulitsa, Pauline and I got into the peasant cart we had hired and drove down to the river's edge. From there, we were ferried out to the island in a small boat. The shaman was a young man with a haughty manner—a sign of the great importance he attached to himself. He was a member of the local tribe, and we were told that his father had been killed by lightning, 'thus passing to his son contacts with the supernatural world.' This young man's ability to communicate with the spirits had been recognized at an early age. We were told that he could heal, divine the future, assist the dead on their journey to the other world. His second sight had important practical applications, for he could, we were told by the chief, usually see where lost horses or cattle could be found and summon distant flocks of reindeer to his tribe's hunting grounds.

"Our shaman was dressed in his sacred shamanistic coat made of reindeer skin with hair outside, with a fringe around the neck and the sleeves; besides the fringe, there were slits ornamented with cured leather; these slits and fringes were supposed to represent the curves and zigzags of the Milky Way. His shamanistic cap also had fringes, with a tassel on top and another, double tassel on the left side. The Buriat chief told us that the tassels were made of alternating pieces of white and black rabbit fur and were a remedy against headaches! . . . The strange coat had a red apron adorned with iron thongs and numerous amulets and pendants made of beads which are supposed to serve a magical purpose . . . On his feet were red felt Chinese boots, and he wore stockings made of some kind of brown fur. His drum, the most important object for a shaman, stood by him; it was very large and oval in shape. Next to it lay his other paraphernalia—his whip, and the rattle with which he wards off evil spirits. We were told that he was about to perform the bird dance."

Maria and Pauline were being accorded the privilege, rare for outsiders and particularly women, of an introduction to the Buriat shamanistic rites. Shamanism, which still exists in certain parts of Siberia, is a primitive form of religion or religio-magic, an expression of the desire, commonly felt among aboriginal tribes, of establishing contact with the supernatural world through a priestly inspired intermediary, the shaman. During his ecstatic trance, the shaman's soul is supposed to leave his body and, depending on circumstances, travel either to the sky or to the evil underworld. The Buriats believe in a mythical river of the universe—a world stream, linking the upper world inhabited by humans with the lower world inhabited by evil spirits; the shaman travels on this river. He is a priest, a medicine man, and a prophet. What is thought to be a supernatural gift is a necessary qualification, and the office can be hereditary if a descendant shows a disposition for the calling. The shaman's trance, induced by the beating of the drum, is often combined with hysteria and arrived at through dreams, visions, and fasting. His healing powers, which can be very effective, are probably a combination of cunning, psychology, and the application of folk medicine. According to nineteenth-century travelers, the shamans were particularly good at curing various forms of mental illness prevalent among the northern tribes, which are deprived of the light of the sun during a large part of the year. In the case of a mentally disturbed person, the shaman would "summon the spirits and order them to withdraw the intruding agent from the patient's body." The Tungus and Buriat shaman were reputed to have particularly strong healing powers and were famous for their "second sight."

Maria described the shaman's performance as strange and very frightening: "We all retired inside the yurt, where a white mare's skin had been spread on the floor for the shaman to dance on. At first, everything was silent; a handful of white horsehair was thrown on the fire, putting it out; in the faint gleam of the red coals we could see the black figure of the shaman, silent and motionless, with drooping head, big drum on breast, and face turned toward the south, as is also the head of the mare's skin on which he is sitting. He gradually began to play the drum—first softly, then rising to a crescendo like an oncoming storm with peals of thunder and squawking of wild birds. When the music swelled to its highest pitch, the shaman began to leap and dance, at first on the skin and then, becoming more rapid, gliding all over the floor of the yurt, beating the drum furiously, jumping about, turning his face to the south, then to the west, then to the east; his eyes were closed, his hair tumbled, his mouth strangely twisted, saliva streaming down his chin . . . His fury rose and ebbed like a wave now smooth, now frantic and frenzied . . . After what seemed to us quite a long time, he finally slowed down. We were told that the ceremony was now over. With a final leap, the shaman collapsed onto the white mare's skin and was carried out of the tent by two assistants.

"Pauline and I felt exhausted. We turned down the prince's offer to have the shaman prophesy our future for us. We remained silent on the way home, thinking about the mysteries of that ancient faith of which so very little is known to us."

It had been rumored in Chita for some time now that a new prison was being constructed about 450 miles away, to which the prisoners were going to be moved. It was said that the tsar himself had designed its shape and accommodations. Early in June, Commandant Leparsky left for Irkutsk, and when he returned at the end of the month, though he answered all questions with a cryptic "No comment," one did not need a shaman's prophetic powers to realize that the prisoners' stay in Chita was drawing to a close. The announcement came early in July: "Next month we will be leaving for Petrovsky Zavod; the commandant orders everyone to be ready for the big move." The women wept, now that the rumor they had dreaded was confirmed; the future seemed full of foreboding again.

11

Petrovsky Zavod

NEWS OF THEIR IMPENDING DEPARTURE for a permanent
prison far away created general consternation. Life in
Chita had been peaceful; conditions were by no means perfect,
but considering that they were all serving severe penal sentences,
their lot was quite tolerable. A permanent prison sounded
ominous. Prospects of an amnesty seemed to be receding. There
were rumors that the new prison had been badly built, that it
was in unhealthy surroundings next to a swamp, that it looked
"like a stable with a row of stalls," and worst of all that it had no
windows.

There was one redeeming factor: each prisoner would have
his own fairly spacious cell, and a separate wing would be allocated to the married men. The wives would be permitted to
move in with their husbands, and those with children were encouraged to build separate houses near the prison, in which their
men would be allowed to visit them. For the unmarried, the lack
of community life would be made up by the advantages of
greater privacy. Not everyone appreciated this, and all felt that

it was a pity the new prison could not have been built in Chita.

Once the date of departure was announced, preparations had to be made quickly. Personal belongings were assembled and loaded onto carts; the "Academy's" by now extensive library was packed in cases. The convoy was divided into two marching groups: one under the command of Leparsky's nephew Osip Adamovich, the fat and good-humored Platz-Major. The second, which included all the married men and their wives, was led by Leparsky himself. The ladies traveled in telegas, local carts, with their belongings carefully packed around them. Each group was escorted by a detachment of soldiers, and mounted Cossacks provided an outer screen for further protection. Buriat tribesmen were employed to transport the prison equipment, build fires, put up tents, carry water. It was the beginning of the Siberian autumn and the weather turned out to be unexpectedly fine.

Leparsky set a sensible routine which allowed them to cover about ten miles a day. The convoy would start off, as a rule, at 3 a.m., so as to avoid the hottest hours of the day. Camp was pitched about 9 a.m., and a short rest followed after lunch. Andrei Rozen's task was to ride ahead at dawn each day with the servants and some of the guards to prepare an encampment for the night, preferably in a picturesque location, and have supper ready when the main parties arrived. The nights were spent in yurts, cone-shaped felt tents, capable of holding four men each.

One of Nikolai Bestuzhev's drawings made during the journey shows a line of yurts spread along a mountain stream, like a small military encampment, and a group of Decembrist wives in wide skirts and straw hats reclining under a tree after what must have been a pre-dinner walk. All cooking was done in the open air; in rainy weather, the Buriats would build protective shelters of sticks and brambles. On warm days, the prisoners were allowed to bathe in the rivers or lakes along the way, while the ladies set off to find wild blackberries and Siberian bilberries.

The Decembrist Baron Schteingel describes the relaxed atmosphere which prevailed: "Lunch was always followed by a siesta; even the guards slept by their stacked muskets. Then, when the heat had somewhat abated, the prisoners would go for a walk, after which they would lie down for a cup of tea, chatting until nightfall. There was communal singing by the campfires under the stars, and performances of native dancing by the Buriats. Then the sentries strung along the outer rim would start hailing one another at regular intervals, the native Buriat guides would huddle in their picturesque robes around the campfires, silence fell, and we all went to sleep . . ."

The autumnal weather was lovely, hot by day and going down to almost freezing at night. The road led over hills and dales and wooded valleys; there was not a single village on the way; only occasional Buriat encampments provided signs of human habitation; the spectacular banks of the broad and powerful Selenga River offered the grandest scenery in the whole of Siberia. Amid the magnificent natural surroundings, the convoy must have looked somewhat incongruous. At the head rode Leparsky, mounted on a white horse, with his soldiers strung out on the flanks. Then came the prisoners, dressed in an odd assortment of clothes. Some wore plain men's overcoats, others—like Poggio—wrapped themselves in Spanish-style cloaks. Still others had on what looked like former guards' uniforms, supplemented by home-sewn fur-trimmed jackets, which must have once belonged to their wives. Zavalishin, the great traveler and linguist, strode along with a stick in one hand, an open book in the other, a broad black hat on his head, the picture of a Quaker preacher. For most of them, the enforced daily march turned out to be a most invigorating exercise. Later they would always recollect it with pleasure as an attractive interlude in a long succession of gray years.

One may wonder why none of them tried to escape while discipline and surveillance were temporarily relaxed. The likely answer is that chances of survival in the surrounding wilderness would have been very slight. Buriat tribesmen, though outwardly friendly to the prisoners, lived in fear of the military authorities, and many would track down a fugitive and bring him back to Leparsky in exchange for a handsome reward. And so would the Chinese frontier guards, if a foolhardy prisoner succeeded in penetrating into Mongolia. Only a handful of men ever managed to escape into China, and they were all tough criminals strong enough to survive for weeks below the subsistence level. But the most powerful reason of all was that escape for some would cause others to be badly treated. "There was nothing to do," Baron Schteingel recalled, "but to yield to the law of necessity."

They regularly came upon camps of nomadic Buriats grazing their diminutive horses on the steppe. Andrei Rozen thought that the descendants of Genghis Khan were semi-savage and dirty: "Their heads are shaved except for one tuft, which crowns the top. They all have got tiny little eyes, low and flat foreheads, with broad, prominent cheekbones and pale yellow complexions . . . They spend their time tearing and cutting the skins of animals with their bare teeth, or shaping arrows, while their naked children tumble among their elders. They all have a passion for tobacco, which they smoke in little copper pipes, inhaling all the smoke." The Buriats who escorted the convoy did not carry bread or provisions with them. Twice a day they left the camp to gorge themselves on bilberries; it seemed to be their only food, though they supplemented it now and then with birds and wild game brought down with their arrows. The sight of a galloping

Buriat tribesman with his bow and a handful of arrows in his belt particularly delighted Pauline. "Here comes the brown Cupid with his arrows—come and watch him; he is going to shoot down a wild pheasant for our supper," she called to her companions.

On one occasion, much to the women's delight, they were visited by a local Buriat chieftain, a *taisha,* who brought with him two shamans, whom he persuaded to perform the bird dance in their honor. Afterwards the *taisha* asked to play chess and was pitted against Basargin and von Wiesen, the two Decembrist chess champions. He beat them both easily. Chess was a passion with the Buriats, inherited from the Chinese. They often came and watched the prisoners playing after supper, loudly express-ing their approval or displeasure. Baron Schteingel recalls that the Buriats were fascinated by the prisoners, the "enemies of the Great Khan of Russia." They clustered around Lunin, who as a wounded war veteran was permitted to ride in a cart. "Why have you been deported?" they asked him. With an eloquent gesture across his throat, Lunin told them that he wanted to *chik* ("cut") the Great Khan. The Buriats gasped and edged away, awed, back to their yurts.

Halfway to their destination, they were met by Anna Rozen, wife of Andrei Rozen, the Baltic baron, who had waited three years to join her husband. She heard at the last posting station that the prisoners' convoy was approaching. Leaving her car-riage and her possessions behind in the care of her servants, she set off under military escort to meet them, riding horseback, dressed in a black riding habit and a flowing green veil. She galloped straight into her husband's arms as he walked ahead of the convoy with his kettles to prepare accommodations for the night. Mme Rozen had driven from Irkutsk and brought the news of the July Revolution in France. That night from the campfires on the banks of the Selenga rose the magic tune of the

Marseillaise; it echoed from the red granite and porphyry rocks, carrying the message of hope over the Buriat steppes.

Maria's first sight of the Petrovsky prison filled her with foreboding. "As we approached Petrovsk, I saw an immense building with a red roof in the form of a horseshoe. There was not a window to be seen.

"Alexandrine Muraviev, who received quite a lot of money from her mother-in-law through secret channels, had written to a contractor in Petrovsk and had had a house built for herself near the prison. I left most of my belongings with her and moved into cell 54 with Sergei. It was pitch-dark; we had to have candles on at all times, which was very tiring for the eyes and a great fire hazard. But the worst of all was to hear the guards going around every night and putting on those heavy locks. 'Here I am,' I kept repeating to myself. 'I now live in a real prison.' I hated it."

The gloomy building was divided into twelve sections. Each section consisted of a corridor and five separate rooms with exits into the passage, which was kept warm by a wood-burning stove that had to be stoked all the time. The builders had obviously lined their own pockets by providing unseasoned timber; as a result, the entire structure soon began to warp and bulge and large openings appeared between the boards, letting in the cold and the drafts. Logs had been placed in the walls so badly that one could draw them out by hand. Even the stoves had been poorly built, and repeatedly cracked, constantly causing minor fires, to the great horror of the commandant. None of these problems had existed in Chita, where the contractor had been honest and the proximity of the river ensured that a fire could easily be dealt with. In Petrovsk, there was only the marsh.

The worst problem, however, was the absence of windows, for the only light in the rooms came from the corridor, filtered through a grated opening over the doors. It was so dark that even on summer days it was impossible to read or make out the hands of a watch. "By day we were allowed to leave the doors open and in warm weather to work in corridors," recalls Zavalishin, "but how long does the Siberian sunshine last? Even in September, we had to make our choice of burning candles or sitting in the gloom. We certainly had not imagined that, having spent four years in the small but tolerable prison of Chita, we should now be punished—for no reason—by removal to a far worse place and be deprived of natural light." Why, indeed? Only the tsar in his "infinite wisdom" could have answered that question. He would undoubtedly have pointed out that they were being granted a big favor by being allowed to live in single cells, the married prisoners sharing quarters with their wives.

The indomitable wives set to work without losing any time on recriminations. Maria, who by now was the acknowledged leader of the group, composed an urgent letter to General Benckendorff demanding that windows be put in the cells. Her request was reluctantly seconded by Leparsky. Strange as it may seem, the powerful General Benckendorff, chief of police, did not have the authority to act on what, on the face of it, was a trivial administrative detail. The tsar's obsession with the Decembrists made it a matter requiring the personal approval of His Majesty. The report took a long time to be acted on. As a result, the winter of 1831 was a somber one for the inhabitants of the Petrovsky prison. They spent it crouched over candles or beside open doors, heavily bundled because of the freezing weather. Large openings were constantly appearing in the outer walls, letting in the damp and the cold; there were frequent disturbances—small fires, alarms, false moves, and workmen coming in to plaster walls. Finally, in April 1831, permission was received from St. Petersburg to make "small windows" in the cells. But Leparsky, who suddenly, according to Maria, "had lost his nerve," ordered that these be only one foot square and so near the ceiling that even the tallest among them could see nothing but a bit of the sky. Nikolai Bestuzhev had to build a platform of planks in his room three or four feet from the floor to be able to paint or draw. In spite of these difficulties, his output remained remarkable.

It is thanks to Nikolai Bestuzhev's aquarelles that we can form an idea of what the interior of the prisoners' rooms looked like in Petrovsky. Unlike ordinary prison cells, they were fairly spacious, some with rugs on the floor, pictures on the walls, and soft furniture, and personal objects on tables. "We each fixed our *komnatas* [rooms] to the best of our ability," wrote Maria, describing her living quarters to Ekaterina. "I covered mine with blue silk from the curtains in Zenaida's bedroom in Moscow that she so very kindly sent me, installed my clavichord, which had survived all the moves and miraculously had kept its tune, our bookcases, two sofas, family portraits . . . It is quite an elegant room. I only wish the windows could have been bigger and not so very high up. Our men are forced to climb on chairs and tables to be able to read." A few months later, she sent Ekaterina Bestuzhev's aquarelle of the room, with herself sitting at the desk, looking older than her twenty-six years; she asked for copies to be made and dispatched to her mother-in-law and Prince Repnin. "Now you will be getting a true idea of how we live," she wrote. "The room is still somewhat dark, for the window is three arshins [seven feet] from the floor. Do you see Father's portrait over the desk, and can you recognize yourself in the one over the piano? You are all there: Maman, yourself, Sophia, Nikolai, and Alexander. I only lack a portrait of Elena." Bestuzhev's aquarelles, at which he was so prolific, filled the place of modern-day photographs; they were promptly copied by professional copyists, who were usually present in great houses, and sent around to members of the family. Later that year, Maria dispatched a portrait of herself and Sergei to Princess Zenaida, "to accompany her in her new life." (Princess Zenaida, disgusted with Nicholas I's regime, was moving to Rome.)

Shortly after her arrival at Petrovsk, Maria had a small house built next to Annie Muraviev's imposing dwelling; she installed in it her maid, Masha, and her cook. It was a welcome relief to get away from the gloomy prison walls. "I went there every day to have a bath, fix my clothes, write letters, but returned to Sergei to sleep in our heavily padlocked cell," she described to the family. This was not entirely accurate, for after a few months the visits to the padlocked cell became fewer and fewer and she began to spend most nights in her own house.

Another Frenchwoman arrived to join the ladies' contingent at Petrovsk. She was Camilla Le-Dantu, the fiancée of young Vasily Ivashev. Camilla was the daughter of a Mme Jeanne Le-Dantu, a governess in the Ivashev household in Moscow. She grew up together with young Ivan, her employer's son, and, predictably, fell in love with him. But she kept her feelings secret, for there was no hope of her marrying the socially prominent officer of the guards. In 1820, Vasily became a member of the secret society in the south, working closely with Pestel and Sergei Volkonsky. Following the arrest of Pestel, he was sent to the Peter and Paul Fortress. Camilla was unable to visit him there, and the young man had no idea that the rather plain and shy girl was in love with him. When Camilla heard of Pauline Guèble's marriage to Annenkov in Siberia, she decided to follow her example. Ivashev's mother thought it "an excellent idea, as who else would ever marry her son after his disgrace?" The only snag was that they were not sure Vasily would welcome the idea, but the old lady decided to get the documents prepared, "just in case." There followed the usual delay, which lasted over a year.

In the meantime, out in Chita, young Vasily, who had never been a convinced revolutionary, was bitter and resentful in exile; he dreamed of teaming up with the convicts and escaping into China. Volkonsky and Bestuzhev, to whom he confided his plans, tried to dissuade him from the mad venture, which was bound to end in disaster. But Vasily remained unconvinced. He was deeply enmeshed in his plotting when he was summoned into Commandant Leparsky's presence and asked in the most formal tone of voice "whether he would be willing for Mademoiselle Camilla Le-Dantu to join him in Siberia for the purpose of marriage."

It was a difficult decision. The young man had not seen Camilla for over six years, and as he confided to Maria, "so much had happened in the meantime that I only had a vague recollection of her." He remembered that she was two to three years older than he and not a beauty; nor, as he could recall, did she have Pauline Guèble's vivacity and her charm. Still, the prospect of having someone he had known all his life share his dismal existence in Petrovsk was appealing, and he fully recognized the sacrifices Camilla would have to make if she married a "state criminal." After much hesitation and soul-searching, he finally reported back to Leparsky that he was ready to receive Mlle Le-Dantu and marry her. The Volkonskys and all of Ivashev's friends were delighted, for as he was now formally committed, he would have to abandon his plans of escaping to China.

Camilla reached Petrovsk late in 1831, a year after Vasily had learned of her wish to marry him. Much had changed in the three years since Pauline Guèble had married Annenkov, who had to walk up the aisle in chains and leave his bride immediately after the ceremony. This time the benign commandant allowed the newlyweds to spend their first three days in his own quarters, while he tactfully set off on an inspection tour of the countryside. A few weeks later, Camilla moved into her own house, hastily assembled out of red timber.

Maria recalled that the Ivashevs' wedding was a cause for celebration in their little group. "I was asked to be matron of honor; all the ladies were present, of course. We had tea with the young couple afterwards, and next night I gave a dinner for them in my house. We were gradually resuming a semblance of civilized life."

The Ivashevs' marriage was happy in spite of the bridegroom's forebodings, but they were plagued with misfortunes: one of their children died at the age of two, and three years later Camilla, who was eight months pregnant, caught a severe chill while driving in an open sledge and died. She needn't have, but there was no medical attention in the remote village near Turinsk where the Ivashevs had been sent after leaving Petrovsk. Her husband—sad and lonely—succumbed to a heart attack, leaving a five-year-old girl behind who had to be taken care of by a family of local tribesmen until Ivashev's mother arrived and took her back to Russia with her.

The year 1832 was a momentous one for Maria, for on March 10, in her house overlooking the swampy river in Petrovsk, she was safely delivered of a son. She named him Mikhail. "My adored little Misha," she wrote when recalling the happy event. "I shall always bless the year when you appeared among us, to the infinite joy of your parents. Thank God I was able to nurse you myself. I became your devoted nanny and later your teacher, and when two years later God gave me Nelly, your sister, my happiness was complete. From then on, I thought only of you; I hardly visited my women companions anymore. My love for the two of you was all-absorbing..."

Misha's birth was indeed a godsend. Life in Petrovsk had by

now settled into an even and monotonous pattern, and it looked as if they were going to be there for many years. The prisoners, each in his separate cell, reverted to their own individual occupations and hobbies. The women were busy with their children. Under General Leparsky's kind rule, the need for a strong leadership of the feminine clan became less pressing. Maria had time to brood over her own big personal problem: the disintegration of her marriage.

One of the main difficulties encountered by a biographer in trying to reconstruct the latter part of Maria's life in Siberia is the fact that, because of increased censorship in that period, her letters home became bland. Tsar Nicholas decided that Leparsky's control was not enough and superimposed additional layers of censorship in Irkutsk and St. Petersburg. Quite understandably, Maria, like the rest of the wives, refrained from revealing her inner thoughts to an array of unknown officials. After the birth of the children, her diary changed from a reflection of herself to a chronicle of events recorded for the benefit of the new generation. She was not by nature a confiding person. Annie Muraviev was the only woman in Petrovsk that she was on intimate terms with, and her early death two years later affected Maria deeply. Essentially, she was an extaordinarily proud being with a strong sense of duty, very conscious of living up to the image of a Decembrist's wife. She was determined to keep her problems to herself. But it is difficult not to notice, after her sentimental outpourings and expressions of love for her husband in the early stages of his imprisonment and during their stay at Blagodatsk, that the adulation of her early letters had been replaced by a certain detachment, irony, and weariness at the lack of mutual understanding.

Theirs was not the solid, unshakable relationship that existed between Katyusha and her husband. Prince Trubetskoy had behaved badly during the uprising, worse still under the tsar's questioning, when he broke down and gave out much harmful information; but Katyusha adored him. His presence alone made her happy. Their marriage was founded on the rock of deep love and perfect mutual understanding and would have survived any trial. This was not the case with Maria and Sergei.

What happened to the Byronic romance? The most likely answer is that it had existed solely in Maria's imagination. She certainly was not in love with her husband when she married him; afterwards, her passionate temperament, combined with her lack of experience, confused physical satisfaction with love. Her imagination, which for years had been fed on the romantic poets of the period, took over the moment she heard the news of her husband's arrest. From then on, there was no stopping her. She was in love and Sergei was her idol. It was only natural that somewhere along the way she would take on herself most of the Decembrists' ideals, of which she knew nothing before but which she came genuinely to believe in and would champion for the rest of her life. Elation was all very well; reality, as it presented itself in everyday life with Sergei, was something else.

Volkonsky was not a strong personality. In fact, one of the reasons he initially fell in love with Maria was "that bit of tempered steel" he sensed in her which was there in spite of her very young age. He behaved magnificently during the hearings, refusing to reveal the name of a single plotter; it drew the imperial wrath on his head. But somehow, during the first year of exile, the convict's chains broke his spirit.

Sergei was now forty-three, ten to fifteen years older than the majority of his comrades. His health, always delicate, had been affected by the wounds he had received during the Napoleonic campaign. All this must have contributed to his misery; it is hard to define the exact cause, but by the time the Decembrists left Blagodatsk, Volkonsky had become a tired, prematurely aged man, silent and extraordinarily moody. During their three years in Chita, Maria made heroic efforts to distract him, to promote his interest in gardening and in nature studies. She occasionally succeeded—often with Alessandro Poggio's help—but most of the time Sergei remained gloomy and aloof. She had hoped that their efforts to resume married life would be successful, but after the sad death of the infant Sonyushka, they began to drift apart.

None of this was ever reflected in Maria's correspondence with her family or her in-laws, though it was inevitably remarked by other Decembrists. As in any close community, it was impossible to disguise certain facts and personal relationships, and comments on the "Volkonsky marital difficulties" appear in a number of contemporary memoirs.

To what extent was the estrangement due to Maria's growing affection for Poggio? According to present-day Russian historians, all references to Maria's involvement with Poggio and to their long-lasting love affair have been deliberately excised from the Raevsky and Volkonsky family archives, except for a few letters from Poggio to Volkonsky after they all returned to European Russia; for, in spite of what may have happened, the two men remained good friends. The story of Maria and Alessandro's relationship has to be pieced together from the accounts of other Decembrists.

Alessandro Poggio, by all descriptions, was a wonderful-looking man with an attractive personality. N. A. Belogolovoy, who was his pupil in Siberia and remained under his spell all his life, describes him as of medium height and graceful proportions, with shoulder-length black hair falling in thick locks around his face, a beautiful forehead, expressive black eyes, aquiline nose, and a sensitive mouth. He had an "innate grace of movement and a liveliness which bespoke clearly his southern descent." He seems to have had all the characteristics of a romantic hero, and he so appears in Nikolai Bestuzhev's aquarelle.

According to his pupil, Poggio was a man of only "average intellect," but he was well educated and an outstandingly good teacher, gentle, patient, and clear. He was immensely popular with his prison colleagues in Chita and in Petrovsky Zavod and later as a settler in Urik; he was loved and respected by all who came in contact with him. Yakushkin, a fellow plotter from their days at Kamenka who came across him twenty years later in Irkutsk, said that Poggio was a miracle, "for he has retained all the Italian fire and all the convictions of his youth, in spite of hard labor and prison life."

What was this Italian knight errant doing in a Decembrist prison in Siberia? It appears that in 1775 Alessandro's father, Vittorio Poggio, a well-to-do nobleman from Piedmont, for reasons that have never been fully established (it was rumored that he had killed a man in a duel), had to flee his native Novara, and was persuaded by a friend—a Spanish adventurer, Don José de Ribas—to seek his fortune in Russia. At that time, Odessa was Russia's new frontier, a bustling, cosmopolitan settlement, where Russians, Greeks, Armenians, Turks, Jews, and Tartars worked together in building a new maritime city. With the French Revolution came an influx of distinguished French refugees, headed by the famous Duc de Richelieu, who became governor of the province and built Gurzuf, Maria's childhood home in the Crimea. It was not long before Vittorio Poggio and his wife established themselves in Odessa in opulent style. On the Duc de Richelieu's recommendation, Poggio was appointed adviser on administration. His house became a center for social gatherings. Two sons were born, Giuseppe in 1792 and Alessandro six years later; though the family always spoke Italian at home, the boys were educated in Russian schools and both joined smart guards regiments; Giuseppe was just old enough to take part in the last stages of the Napoleonic campaign. He then married one of the numerous Raevsky cousins and bought a country estate. Alessandro, who remained a bachelor, joined the Preobrazhensky Guards and while in Kiev with his regiment came into contact with Volkonsky, who was busy recruiting new members for the Southern Society. The inevitable followed. Alessandro, an admirer of the Italian Carbonari (revolutionaries), came under the influence of Pavel Pestel and joined the conspiracy. When it failed, he was arrested a few days after Volkonsky; he was sentenced to hard labor and exiled to Siberia, and in spite of his Italian blood was punished as a Russian subject; he was thirty-two years old when he found himself sharing a prison with Maria five cells away.

We will never know when the romance began and how much time the two were able to spend together in Petrovsky Zavod. A few years later, when several of the Decembrists were moved to Urik and then to Irkutsk, their closeness became a matter of common knowledge and wide comment. On the other hand, as they were vaguely related, many people took their friendship for granted, including Maria's children and her husband. Yakushkin, a friend and admirer of Poggio, wrote to his wife from Irkutsk: "Everyone here is convinced that Alessandro has fathered both Volkonsky's son and the daughter." M. S. Dobrynin, a small merchant who lived in Petrovsky Zavod in the 1830s and was then very poor, recalled with gratitude how Maria tended the sick in the town and how she helped him get over a severe illness. "Her husband," he adds, "had grown prematurely old and had become miserly, for which the princess had to chide him. She was still young and pretty, with wonderful sparkling eyes and a proud bearing, but Volkonsky had let himself go. He was always on his guard—almost like an ordinary criminal—looking around to see whether Leparsky or his adjutants were there and scurrying along to wherever he had to go. How it upset the poor princess! She had had little happiness in her life. No wonder she fell in love with Alessandro Vittorovich."

Whatever the truth may be, Sergei was devoted to the children, but it was Maria who had charge of their upbringing. They and Poggio seemed to be the center of her universe, and from the time of their birth her personality appears to have undergone a complete change. Poggio is seldom mentioned in any of her letters home, which are mostly filled with news about the children. "You would not recognize me," she wrote to her sister Ekaterina shortly after Nelly's birth. "I am like a hen with my chicks, running from one to another. When I am with Misha, I worry about the baby, Nellinka. When I am with her, I worry about Misha picking up filthy habits from those around him." A few weeks later she informed her mother: "I no longer have quicksilver in my veins. I must now have infinite patience to deal with the little ones in these very difficult circumstances. I don't care about anything as long as my children are healthy." Her husband's name has almost vanished from her letters. He is mentioned only rarely and in minor matters.

Nelly's birth had been long and difficult, but from the start she was a beguiling child, with Maria's huge eyes, a mass of dark curls, and lovely long limbs. She became the darling of all the Decembrists, she and her brother running freely between the prison yard and Maria's house down the road, happily unaware of the circumstances they were in.

There were by now quite a few little ones about. Annie Muraviev had one daughter, the Annenkovs had two, the Davydovs three boys, the Trubetskoys managed to have four and another one was expected. The von Wiesens had two boys, and so it went. The arrival of the children made a tremendous difference to the Decembrists. All Russians love children, and to have a crowd of exuberant little people running happily around playing games, notwithstanding their dismal surroundings, brought joy to the prisoners' monotonous existence; even the guards were known occasionally to let down their reserve and join in the merriment.

A more liberal pattern had now been established. The wives could live outside the jail if they wished, and visit their husbands in their cells. In time, Leparsky became even more accommodating. All the men, not only those whose wives lived in Petrovsk, were allowed out several times a week, either to visit houses of friends or on personal errands in the town, and not always under police supervision. If one of the wives or children fell ill, the husband would be allowed to stay overnight. Leparsky's generosity paid off. Never once in almost ten years as a commandant did he have to punish a prisoner. Naturally, whenever an inspector came from St. Petersburg, the guards were ordered to look fierce and the prisoners cooperated by appearing cowed and unhappy; it made an excellent impression and usually resulted in high praise for the old general for the excellent discipline he maintained.

Only once did an unpleasant incident occur, which indirectly had grave consequences. The lovely Alexandrine Muraviev was talking with her husband in slow, careful Russian, which was still an uneasy language for her, but now and then she instinctively interjected French sentences. A half-drunk Cossack officer lounging in the doorway to the prison took objection. "Don't you dare speak French," he shouted. *"Qu'est-ce qu'il veut dire, mon ami?"* she asked her husband. The guard, imagining she had said something derogatory about him, rushed toward her, gun in hand. Terrified, Annie jumped up and ran out of the room, with the guard in pursuit. Her husband, Nikita Muraviev, and Vadkovsky, a fellow prisoner, pinioned him by the arms. Furious, he called out to the soldiers to load their muskets and come to his rescue, that "mutiny had broken out." Luckily, one of the men had the presence of mind to alert Leparsky's deputy, the Platz-Major Adamovich, who arrived posthaste, released the officer, and succeeded in calming him down. But the episode had a fatal effect on Annie Muraviev's high-strung, nervous constitution. Two weeks later she developed influenza, with chest complications, and despite Dr. Wolff's excellent care, she died. Maria kept a vigil at her bedside. "When Annie realized she was dying, she asked me to write farewell letters to her parents, and not wanting to awaken her four-year-old daughter, Nono, she had the maid bring her the child's doll and kissed it instead. She received the last rites like a saint, and afterwards comforted her husband as well as she could. Alexandrine died at her post, and her death plunged us all into mourning. How I will miss her . . . Since then I have been obsessed by a great fear: What would become of my children if I died?"

And so began a period of years in Petrovsk without any appreciable change in the lot of the detainees. Those like the Annenkovs whose term of imprisonment had come to an end left for the settlements, permanent places of exile, in different parts of Siberia. Pauline and Ivan were sent to Kurgan, six hundred miles away; the jolly, practical Pauline and her husband would be greatly missed by everyone in the prison. Von Wiesen, Naryshkin, Ivashev, and their wives were also among the first to go; the Rozens and Yushnevsky followed a few years later. Life went on in the dark building, divided between hours of compulsory outside work and free time, which the prisoners spent in the pursuit of individual interests. Some of the rooms had been transformed into studies, others into workshops, with machinery and lathes; others were just sitting rooms, such as Volkonsky's and Trubetskoy's. Unlike the rules in Chita, there were no constraints on personal hobbies: smokers could smoke, since tobacco was obtainable at reasonable prices; and chess was a popular pastime between work and sleep. "Cards might have been obtained through the warden," recalls Rozen, "but we agreed among ourselves not to allow card playing in order to avoid any cause of unpleasantness or dissension."

As in Chita, music was a great solace. They played the guitar, flute, and flageolet (at which Rozen was particularly adept), and the fine string quartet infinitely brightened prison life. "Talent was plentiful," recalls Belyaev. "Vadkovsky played the violin beautifully, Svistunov played the cello, Yushnevsky was a very fine pianist, Naryshkin and Lunin played the guitar." Concerts and musical soirees were given, Odoevsky's verses were set to music. One of the most popular of his poems was in praise of the ladies—"those goddesses of the northern dawn," who came to the land of "tears and endless horizons" and brought "laughter, joy, and hope to the prisoners." One of his poems was dedicated to Maria; it described how each day "the tall, proud princess" would walk to the wooden palisade and sit there, "under the vast Siberian sky," waiting to collect the prisoners' letters for home. As they were not allowed to communicate directly with their families, the men would compose brief notes to their relatives, which Maria enlarged on to give the families news they so longed to receive; on some "post days," she wrote as many as thirty letters at a time. She of course had help from the other women, who tried to share the burden, but as Maria was the quickest and the most articulate, her services were in constant demand.

The "Academy," started in Chita, was flourishing, with a full program of lectures. Many found new interests that would sustain them in their lonely years of banishment. I. I. Gorbachevsky developed an interest in shamanism, Yakushkin in meteorology; Nikita Muraviev, desperately sad after the death of his wife, tried to prepare himself for a career of teaching. His own daughter and the children of other Decembrists owed their skill in reading and their wonderful vocabulary to his efforts. The library of books in several languages was constantly being expanded; there were also an astonishing number of magazines and periodicals from France, Germany, Italy, and even England. "We would plunge with delight into the waves of an intellectual ocean that all but choked us," wrote Bestuzhev. "We received the whole range—then limited, of course—of Russian weekly and monthly journals, and among the foreign ones—as I remember—*La Revue Britannique, Revue de Paris, Revue des Deux Mondes, Revue Industrielle, L'Illustration Française, Journal des Débats, L'Indépendence Belge*, also *The Times, Quarterly Review, The Edinburgh Review, Morning Post, Punch, Frankfurter Zeitung, Preussische Zeitung*, and several Polish and Italian papers." So that everyone could read the papers and the journals in good time, they elected a "director of reading," who received the mail, compiled lists of readers, and glued them to each issue of a journal or a book. When the allotted time elapsed, the item had to be handed on to the next person on the list. "This system did more than a little to weaken our eyesight," says Bestuzhev.

There was also a continuing interest in horticulture. The dampness of the climate, and Petrovsk's position in an extensive depression surrounded by low hills, was not conducive to gardening or growing crops. Though wheat grew several miles to the southeast, it was hard to cultivate potatoes, beets, or cabbage. But adverse climatic conditions could not deter an enthusiast like Poggio, for whom growing vegetables and flowers was part of his Italian heritage. There was no large expanse of garden to cultivate as in Chita, but allotments could be started in the individual courtyards which connected the horseshoe prison. Within a year, Alessandro had beds of flowers, cucumbers, melons, even asparagus growing in between the various sections

[2 4 3

of the building. "The moment the weather got warmer, we engrossed ourselves in cultivating fruit—a wonderfuly therapeutic exercise," he recalled in his memoirs.

Poggio was one of the handful of men at Petrovsk whose physical fitness and mental health remained unaffected by prison life. From the first day of his confinement in Chita, he had set for himself a daily program of physical exercise, which he religiously observed. His interest in botany led him to a study of local herbs, and he enjoyed nothing better than to set off on a long day's expedition in search of medicinal plants for Dr. Wolff's ever-growing homeopathic pharmacy. He returned from his treks beaming with boyish excitement, triumphantly bearing an armful of herbal trophies for the physician's approval.

Gradually, the prison was emptying. One after another, the Decembrists were being released from hard labor and dispatched to various settlements and hamlets throughout Siberia, where they were expected to live for the rest of their lives. When Nikita Muraviev and his daughter, Nonushka (Sophia), were preparing to leave Petrovsk for their place of exile, they went to say a last goodbye at Annie Muraviev's grave. Maria recalled that Nikita's farewell to his wife was heartrending: "You could say he relived his loss all over again . . . Poor little Nonushka, she kept kneeling on the flagstones and running back and forth to the carriage; at one moment she disappeared for a while and returned with a bouquet of wild flowers, which she handed to me, and asked that I put it on 'Mommy's knees' . . ."

A few of the Decembrists received permission to enlist as simple soldiers in the Caucasus; the tsar said it was to serve as a purgatory for them. Several took advantage of this, such as Odoevsky, the young poet, for whom fighting in the ranks was infinitely preferable to "vegetating alone in some godforsaken frozen spot." (He died in a skirmish with the Circassian rebels a year later.)

Alexander Raevsky, the older of Maria's two brothers, on whom Pushkin had modeled his "Demon," renewed the petition previously submitted by his father, asking the tsar for a change of residence for Volkonsky to the Caucasus. The family believed that Sergei would prefer to fight even as an ordinary soldier rather than eke out his days in Siberia. For Maria and for their children, it would have meant a return home. Alexander's petition coincided with the unveiling of a monument at Borodino to commemorate the heroism of the famous Raevsky redoubt—a sector of the battlefield commanded by General Raevsky. But in spite of this, Tsar Nicholas turned down the request. Even if the emperor had agreed, it is doubtful that Volkonsky would have been strong enough to take advantage of this favor. For by now his health was seriously undermined. He suffered from an inflammation of the bladder, arthritis, and he was rapidly losing his teeth. Even Dr. Wolff's medications had little effect.

For months now, Maria had been haunted by a nightmare: the prospect of ending up somewhere on the eastern shore of Lake Baikal in a remote Buriat village alone with an ailing husband and two young children. Her letters home reflect her intense preoccupation with being sent "within striking distance of civilization," and to be "near our friend the eminent surgeon Dr. Wolff, so he could continue to look after Sergei's and the children's health." She begged her mother-in-law to intercede on their behalf with the Dowager Empress. As Maria's letter arrived, the old princess had only one more month to live. She died in November 1835, and her emotional petition reached the emperor after her death. He could hardly refuse the last request of someone who for more than fifty years had been almost a member of the imperial family.

The order came for the Volkonskys to go to Urik, a village on the Angara River twenty miles from Irkutsk. Dr. Wolff and Mikhail Lunin had been residing there since earlier that year; Giuseppe Poggio, Alessandro's brother, was in Kuda, five miles away, and Alessandro had been promised by Leparsky that he would be allowed to join his brother when his term at Petrovsk came to an end. "God took pity on me," Maria confided to her diary. "My children will have medical attention, and there are schools in the district. Nothing else matters." She did not mention her fervent hope that Alessandro would come to Urik too.

Before leaving Petrovsk, Maria asked Bestuzhev to paint the portrait of her two children. (Bestuzhev was much in her debt, for she had arranged with her cousin Zenaida, who was now living in Rome, to send him regular supplies of color pigments, canvas, and brushes. He continued to receive them long after he left Petrovsk, even when he was living alone at Selenginsk; it enabled him to go on painting and kept him sane and busy in his exile.) "Misha will not sit still, even for five minutes," she complained to her sister-in-law, Alexander's wife, in a letter. "I wonder what you will make of his portrait. Nellinka, on the other hand, is an angel. This child is so attentive and good; she never asks for anything without saying please. Everyone here says she looks exactly like me. What do you think?"

When Bestuzhev's portrait reached the family at Boltyshka, they were delighted with the likenesses of the children but saddened by the look of suffering on Maria's face. "I couldn't look at the sorrowful expression of your features without feeling my heart ache," writes Sophia. "I cried, and only the sight of your darling children calmed me a little. These good angels must be a great comfort to you. I looked with lively interest at the tender little face of Nellinka and the clever face of Misha, both of them endowed with their mother's magnificent eyes. Your mother, as you know, is in Italy with Zenaida, and I shall have the portrait copied before she returns home."

Their departure "for the colonies," as they called it, was delayed for almost a year because of Sergei's health; his arthritis kept him almost continually bedridden. Thanks to Leparsky's intervention, he was allowed to spend two months taking the cure at the mineral baths of Turinsk, renowned for their beneficial effect on arthritis. After two months Sergei, much improved, was delivered back to Petrovsk, under military escort, as usual. Walking toward his wife's house along the wooden planks between the prison and the street, he ran into a sad-faced Nikolai Bestuzhev, who told him that their old friend Alexander Pushkin was dead. He had been killed in a duel on February 2, a month before. News had just come to Leparsky, and he immediately told Maria about it.

Sergei found his wife reminiscing about the past. The poet's death was almost impossible for her to believe. For Maria, Pushkin was a life-force, a genius who had only just begun to spread his wings. In the last years she had had only brief messages from him—one in Chita, after the publication of *Poltava*, which he said was dedicated to her; another was the poem which came after Nikolenka's death. Many of his recent works, which Ekaterina faithfully sent on, had been stopped by the censors. Lately, Maria had almost given up trying to follow his expanding career. The harshness of everyday life at Petrovsk had nothing in common with the glittering existence in the midst of which Pushkin and the beautiful Natalia shone so brightly. "On hearing the news, Gurzuf came to my mind," she recalled. "The lovely house and the crescent beach on the Black Sea, the orange groves, and my sisters and I reading Byron to an exuberant, black-curled youth who claimed to be in love with all four of us." She wondered how the tsar could have allowed the man who was Russia's national genius to be killed in a duel, of all things.

Thoughts of Pushkin overshadowed Maria's last days at

Petrovsky Zavod. In mid-March 1837, the Volkonskys and their two children, in a convoy of five tightly packed sledges, crossed Lake Baikal and took up residence in Urik. Their status had changed from "state criminals" condemned to hard labor to that of settlers destined to eternal residence in Siberia.

12

Misha and Elena

I T HAD BEEN MORE THAN ELEVEN YEARS since Maria had last experienced the intoxicating speed of a sleigh-troika as it flew across the vast snowy expanse of nothingness. She had forgotten how exhilarating it was. She recalled it again on that bright sunny morning in early March as she and her family, tightly wrapped in their bear-lined shubas (overcoats worn over furs), with the children snug in their little furry cocoons from which only eyes could be seen, galloped toward Lake Baikal. The "sacred sea," the huge, mysterious body of water steeped in legend, worshipped by Siberian aborigines since the beginning of time, was frozen solid. The ice was mirror-clear and transparent, the visibility so perfect that one could clearly see the snowy peaks of the mountains on the opposite shore, forty miles away. *"Poidi!"* shouted the driver. *"Poidi!"* repeated Misha after him, his eyes shining with excitement. The horses launched themselves onto the ice at tremendous speed, skillfully jumping over the minor fissures that occasionally appeared on the surface. Maria addressed a fervent prayer to God for her family's safety.

On her previous journey across the lake, headed in the opposite direction, toward the east, she had had only one thought—to join Sergei at all costs. In the intervening years, the exalted young girl full of romantic elation had been replaced by a mature woman tempered by hardship, proud, still beautiful, still desirable, but above all a mother, passionately devoted to her children. Here they were next to her in a traveling sleigh, a Siberian *povozka,* strapped to their seats among pillows and cushions of various sizes which filled the space between the luggage and helped to break the force of the jolts on rough ice. "Huddled together, the four of us flew across a sunny white universe—our breaths coming out in bursts of steam, our eyes shut against the blinding reflection of the sun on the myriads of broken ice crystals on the lake. Our driver told me that we had crossed the lake in three hours, which, going west, was supposed to be record time. I did not care how long it took. Here we were safe on the western shore, all in one piece and nearly four hundred miles closer to Europe than before." They drove along the Angara River on a road that seemed to be suspended in misty mid-air through which could be seen the dark, craggy heights of the opposite shore. The Angara is an unusual river; it is the only stream that flows out of the Baikal, unlike the 437 rivers that empty into it. At its source, it is more than a mile wide, with a powerful current. Because of the existence of hot mineral springs under its bed, it is also the last river in Siberia to freeze. But on that frosty March morning its surface was solid and glistening like the lake.

They came to Urik by nightfall. It was more of a settlement than a village, not much bigger than Chita, spread along the precipitous northern bank of the river. The countryside was like a gigantic quilt of dark forests crisscrossed by streams, all flowing into the Angara. To their joy, they saw Dr. Wolff, immaculate as usual, his reddish-brown sideburns neatly trimmed, a fresh clean shirt under a much-darned woolen jacket, standing in front of his own tiny cabin. They also found Artamon and Nikita Muraviev and Nonushka camping in a large wooden house at the edge of the settlement, making a valiant attempt to cultivate their allotted acreage. Tsar Nicholas had ordered that each settler be granted free fifteen dessiatines (forty-two acres) for cultivation, from which they were expected to gain a livelihood. Dr. Wolff was busy looking after the local sick and cataloguing his ever-increasing herbal pharmacy. He had reserved rooms for them with Osip Poggio, as there was not a spare isba in the village and the Muravievs' house, though quite spacious, was not yet finished. The Volkonskys stayed the night with Nonushka and her father. After selecting logs for their new home, they drove three miles further to Uda, where Osip Poggio, Alessandro's brother, was ready to house them in the meantime. Osip, or Giuseppe, Alessandro's older brother, had come to Uda from the Schlusselburg Fortress, where he had been kept in solitary confinement. As an experienced staff officer, who "ought to have known better," he had received a much harsher sentence than Alessandro. For eight years he saw no one except his jailer, who was forbidden to talk to him. He was not allowed out for exercise, and whenever he ventured to ask the time of day, the guard invariably answered, "I don't know." The humidity in his prison was such that his clothes were constantly mildewed, and so was his pathetically small tobacco ration. World events passed him by. He had no idea that there had been a revolution in France or an uprising in Poland; that wars with Persia and Turkey had been fought, or even that there had been a massive cholera outbreak throughout Russia. His New Testament in Italian saved his sanity. As he was not allowed pencil and paper, he "mentally" translated the Scriptures—first into Russian, then into French. By the time of his release, he had literally forgotten how to talk, and his letters were nearly incoherent. Gradually, his faculties returned. When she saw him, Maria was struck by the extraordinary serenity he radiated, his "Olympian calm." Even his wife's desertion while he was in prison, and her subsequent remarriage to his best friend, failed to move him.

Giuseppe was delighted to see them; he was starved for company. Like Maria, he too was eagerly awaiting Alessandro's release from Petrovsky Zavod. The Volkonskys stayed with him for a month, until their house in Urik was completed. Like other Decembrists' wives, Maria had managed to sell her house in Petrovsk to a local merchant, and used the money to construct a new dwelling. Urik, being an insignificant village off the main track, was less expensive than Petrovsk; it had a much better choice of timber, so they could afford a bigger house. With Sergei and Giuseppe's help, Maria chose an attractive spot on a bluff overlooking the Angara, facing south. The house, which was built in little over a month, was a roomy if somewhat primitive wooden dacha, two stories, with a front porch, glass windows, and six bedrooms; it had separate quarters for the servants in the courtyard and was reached by two flights of wooden steps. They called it the Kamchatnik, because the man who supervised the construction came from Kamchatka. The Volkonskys lived in it until they moved to Irkutsk seven years later, but even then the Kamchatnik remained in the family as a summer house to which they frequently repaired.

Once they were settled, the education of the children became Maria's most pressing concern. Misha, a bright, mischievous little boy brimming with life, was now almost six, his sister Nelly (Elena) was four. The progeny of "state criminals," those "victims of unrestrained passion," as the police department in St. Petersburg called them, were classified as illegitimate by the state and officially were not allowed to use their family names. Thus, Mikhail and Elena were registered at birth as "Mikhail

Sergeevich and Elena Sergeevna." They had been too young to suffer from this at Petrovsky Zavod, unlike the slightly older Trubetskoy boys, who had been hailed in the streets with catcalls and abuse as "convict brats" by the children of the local factory employees. When news of this reached the Trubetskoys in St. Petersburg, they felt that centuries of proud family history had been defiled by the jeers and taunts of the street urchins of Petrovsk. But here in the remote Urik countryside, no one cared. Misha and Nelly happily found companions among the local peasant children; they learned to capture butterflies, look for birds' nests, set rabbit traps, explore the wilderness for wild blackberry bushes, and net the small brown trout in the streams. There was only one problem: "Nelly is growing up a Sibiryachka," Maria complained to Ekaterina. "She talks only in the local dialect and there is no way to stop her doing so. As for Misha, I have to allow him to go camping in the woods with the wild boys from the village. He loves adventure; he wept uncontrollably the other day because he had slept through an alarm caused by the appearance of a wolf on our doorstep. My children are growing up *à la Rousseau* like two little savages, and there is very little I can do about it except to insist that they talk French with us when at home . . . but I must say that this existence suits their health."

Some of young Misha's French must have permanently rubbed off on his playmates, for N. A. Belogolovoy, the Siberian merchant, pupil of Alessandro Poggio, recalls his surprise when years later he came across a middle-aged farmer from Urik and heard him throw in occasional French words when discoursing in his native dialect. It turned out that as a boy he was a companion at games of Misha Volkonsky.

Maria's fears for her children's education were unfounded. They were both very bright and learned to read and write at an early age, not only in Russian but also in French and English.

As more and more Decembrists came to settle nearby, Misha and Elena acquired a set of distinguished private tutors that no ordinary school could have provided. Peter Mukhanov taught them mathematics; Mikhail Lunin, the brilliant intellectual, gave them lessons in history and Greek (which he called "the language of the angels"). Nikita Muraviev organized a course in literature, and Maria herself taught them English. When a year later Alessandro Poggio was released from Petrovsky Zavod and came to Urik, he devised a program of formal education, with regular schedules and homework. Thus, they were well prepared when the time came to enroll them in the Irkutsk secondary school.

The Volkonskys were lucky to have been sent as settlers to a place like Urik, where several of their companions were already settled, and which was within striking distance of Irkutsk, the "Siberian metropolis." Many of their comrades were not so fortunate. For the most part, assignments to particular locations were made in a capricious, haphazard way, either by the head of the police department in St. Petersburg or by the military governor of Siberia. Few of the St. Petersburg officials had ever been to Siberia; one small dot on the map, denoting a settlement, was as good as another. Some of the prisoners ended up in remote places, with only a handful of Buriat or Tungus tribesmen and their wives for company. Some went mad, a few drank themselves to death. Colonel Entaltsev and his wife were exiled to Yalutorovsk, a dismal little place near Tobolsk. Within a year, Entaltsev began to show signs of mental illness. To live with a mentally disturbed man alone in a Siberian village was a terrifying prospect. Madame Entaltsev began to plead they be granted permission to return to European Russia, but her appeals were denied. She coped with her husband for eight years, and when he finally died in 1845, she was not even then allowed to return; she remained alone in that distant land for another ten years. When Colonel von Wiesen died in Eniseisk, his wife had to remain alone in the village with her small children for an additional eight years, until rescued by the amnesty; she heard of it only by chance several months after its promulgation, through an itinerant merchant. Even the postman had forgotten about her. Mikhail Kuchelbecker, of the Northern Society, after spending eight years in solitary confinement in the Fortress, was exiled to Barguzin, a hamlet in eastern Siberia, where he eventually married the daughter of the local postmaster, a coarse and unattractive girl who treated him badly. Plagued by ill health, he died long before the amnesty.

Prince Obolensky, the "wonderful Evgeni," scion of a great family and the darling of St. Petersburg salons, ended up marrying a simple servant girl in western Siberia. Even the local Russian administrator was against the misalliance, and so was the bride-to-be. "If Evgeni Petrovich really wishes me well, why doesn't he provide me with a dowry and help me marry someone from my own world?" she kept asking. In spite of this, their marriage was not unhappy; she turned out to be a good wife and a proud housekeeper. In his enforced solitude, Obolensky developed a pre-Tolstoyan craving for the "simple life." His wife, with whom he had so little in common, failed to notice his growing depression and lassitude. He died at about the time of the amnesty, without returning to European Russia. Several other Decembrists married Siberian girls of humble origin, daughters of Cossacks, village priests, or simple peasants, not just out of desperation, but by choice. Many of them were kind, good girls who brought these men peace and a measure of domestic happiness. Curiously, in spite of their material insecurity and the restrictions on their freedom, the exiles were generally considered "a good match" because of the glamour of their former titles and the respect with which they were regarded in the community; in their brides' eyes, that made up for their lack of freedom, relative poverty, and in some cases for their advanced age.

What all of them missed the most was companionship. To many of these well-educated, highly sophisticated men, even chains were preferable to a dreary existence in some small provincial town in Siberia. "My thoughts go back to that first Easter at Chita," wrote Baron Rozen from his exile at Kurgan in western Siberia, "when the priest came to our prison to celebrate the Divine Service. I remember how at daybreak there resounded from all sides the shout of 'Christ is risen' and the chains of all of us prisoners clanked loudly as we threw ourselves into each other's arms in fraternal affection."

Gathered in Urik were some of the best brains from among the exiles. Not only was the school a magnet for the neighborhood, but Dr. Wolff had become a cult figure for miles around. People journeyed from far distances to seek his advice. In those days, there was only one doctor to about forty thousand people in Siberia (roughly 250 miles apart), and Dr. Wolff was not only one of the outstanding surgeons and all-round practitioners of his day but, contrary to general custom, he charged nothing for his services. Another man who attracted respectful attention was Mikhail Lunin, a brilliant eccentric and a loner. Educated as a Catholic by the Jesuits, Lunin was an intensely religious man and a distinguished scholar; the Decembrists' children were lucky to profit from his knowledge. Lunin came to Urik from Petrovsky Zavod a year ahead of the Volkonskys. He built himself a small cabin at the edge of a stream, where he lived with his seventy-year-old servant and six hounds. His devoted sister in Moscow, Madame Uvarov, supplied him with many of the necessities of life. Lunin was a one-man university; not only the local peasants but people from all over the province would constantly drop in to ask his advice. Children loved him for his inexhaustible font of stories; he was particularly devoted to Misha and Nelly, and had great affection and respect for Maria. "There is about her a wonderful quality, fine, indomitable, and strong, which creates a bond of understanding between us . . . She will never confide in me, but she knows that I am like a brother to her in this exile," he wrote in a letter to his sister.

One can be reasonably certain that Maria did not discuss her marital problems with Lunin; she was far too private a person. But the observant Lunin, who had been with them in Chita and Petrovsky Zavod, must have drawn his own conclusions. For the gulf between Sergei and Maria was growing wider. While she looked after her young, cared for the sick in the village, busied herself with the administration of the school, and taught Russian to illiterate Buriat children, the prince devoted all his time to supervising the clearing of the forty-two acres he had been allocated by the government, which he planned to farm. His arthritis had improved slightly, but physically he had let himself go; he wore old peasant clothes, rarely washed, grew a beard, and was now almost toothless; he looked old enough to be Maria's father. Relations between the two appeared amiable but distant.

On December 18, 1838, a week before Christmas, Alessandro Poggio arrived from Petrovsky Zavod. He brought with him news of Commandant Leparsky's death, in Moscow, where he had gone on leave and had died of a stroke in his carriage before reaching the capital. At eighty-one, he still felt strong enough to plan to return to his post. Kind Leparsky was greatly mourned by the handful of prisoners remaining in Petrovsk. But shortly after, the last batch of offenders were "freed," dispatched to settlements all over Siberia, and the prison was closed. "Madame la prison de Petrovsk, after a confinement of thirteen years, was successfully delivered of twenty-three children today," joked Vadkovsky, one of the last inmates to go. "The newly born seem in good health, though prematurely aged; many suffer from asthma, a few have rheumatism, others are weak, and the remainder are gray."

Alessandro Poggio was neither rheumatic nor gray. Bestuzhev's aquarelle painted about that time shows a man at the height of his powers, brimming with life. His thick black hair falls down to his shoulders, his eyes are clear, the expression is one of kindness and strength. Alessandro first stayed with his brother in Uda; later, when he took charge of the administration of the school, he had a house built at the edge of the village in Urik; he and Maria saw each other every day. Sergei was probably aware of the situation, but it does not seem to have weakened his bonds of affection and loyalty to an old comrade. Deep down, he must have realized that Maria's triumphant vitality needed an outlet he himself was too worn out to provide; he may have been secretly relieved that, when the inevitable happened, the man in question turned out to be his old friend Alessandro, whom he had known for so long and admired. Judging by one of his rare letters addressed to his friend Jeannot Pushchin, he was thoroughly depressed about his own life. "I vegetate *po malenko* [little by little], farming. It is not easy, but the worst thing at my age is to be still *pod opiekoi* [under custody of the authorities] . . . The governor keeps us all on a leash."

To Misha and Elena, Alessandro was part of the family and their beloved teacher. The Poggio brothers were called uncles by the children because of Giuseppe's marriage to one of the Raevsky cousins. With their father absent for most of the day, farming his acres, Misha and Elena became accustomed to Uncle Sandro's continuous presence at their mother's side. It did not seem unusual to them. It did seem so, however, to the nosy Vadkovsky, who in January 1841 wrote to Svistunov, another of the Chita Decembrists: "Poor old Volkonsky seems to be excluded from his own family's life; he farms all day, while his wife runs the household and spends morning to night in the company of the Poggio brothers." And he adds, on a sententious note: "I hope there is not going to be a scandal." Their friend Yakushkin, who spent a week with the Volkonskys on his way to western Siberia, described Misha and Elena as wonderful, highly intelligent, splendid children who adored their mother. "She watches over them with such vigilance that the old man [Sergei] seems to have little influence, but it is obvious that he loves them very much."

Upon their release from prison, the "free settlers" still were subject to police supervision, but within those limitations they could do more or less what they pleased, as long as they did not change their place of residence. Shooting game was one pastime that the men at Urik enjoyed more than anything else. Handling guns (which on paper was not allowed) restored to them the long-lost feeling of freedom. The countryside teemed with wild duck, snipe, geese, wild swans, pheasants, and hare. What was more, Urik lay on the migration path for birds returning from India and southern China to their hatching grounds in the north. Here is Maria's description of a walk alone along the Angara River in late May: "As May advances, night entirely disappears, and as the twilight draws near, swans, geese, and duck appear in clouds and the air resounds with the flapping of their wings; their numbers surpass anything that can be imagined, and must be seen to be believed. Each species of bird has its own particular note, and it struck me as a chant, marvelously solemn, a hymn raised by so many millions of creatures in tones which the Creator himself had taught them. Around me, as far as the eye could reach, were countless chains of duck, geese, and graceful Siberian cranes traversing the sky without any interruption, like so many streams all in the same northerly direction; there wasn't a clear space in the air, and all the expanse of water below, the river and the islands, was completely covered with them, as thickly as the stars stud the firmament on a clear night."

The place was obviously a sportsman's paradise, and both Poggio brothers and Lunin were enthusiastic game shots. N. A. Belogolovoy, who was only ten when his rich merchant father brought him to Urik to be tutored in French and Italian by Alessandro Poggio (he later became a famous doctor in Moscow), never forgot what he described as "our magical expeditions to the islands," looking for wild duck, pheasant, and geese, and hunting hare in the autumn. "We used to meet at the Volkonsky dacha, the Kamchatnik, the night before," he recalled, "and spend the entire evening making cartridges while the ladies fixed the food for the next day . . . Early next morning, we boarded boats across the Angara, landing on one of the islands where hare were known to be numerous. Osip [Giuseppe] told everyone where to go; I remained close to Alessandro, carrying his gun. The peasants whom we took with us acted as beaters and formed a ring, driving the hare into a trap. Lunin, transformed by his passion for hunting, shot with great accuracy, and so did Giuseppe and Alessandro. In late morning, we returned to our designated picnic spot, where the princess and the Volkonsky children would be waiting, and triumphantly compared our bags . . . Then in the evening twilight we often set off again to shoot duck among the marshes hidden in the forest of birches, with Basnya [Fable], Poggio's white-and-black retriever, in tow."

Belogolovoy remained in touch with Alessandro and the Volkonskys throughout his life; years after the amnesty, he and Alessandro ran into each other in Lucerne in Switzerland, where Poggio had stopped on his way to Italy. Sitting in a café overlooking the lake of the Quatre Cantons, the by-then-famous doctor and the now elderly former exile recalled those luminous Siberian mornings on the Angara, satisfying interludes in a long series of dark years.

All of a sudden, the even tenor of life was shattered by an unexpected command from General Rupert, the Governor of eastern Siberia, summoning the married Decembrists of the district to report to his office in Irkutsk. Volkonsky, Nikita Muraviev, and Trubetskoy, who after his release from Petrovsky Zavod had been resettled with his wife and five children thirty-five miles away in a village on Lake Baikal, were sent for and brought into the governor's presence. "I instinctively knew that this summons had something to do with our children," recalled Maria. "I could not possibly describe what I went through during those four days of waiting. My anxiety was such that I was literally paralyzed, unable to talk or move. I recalled the tsar's warning years ago: 'Your children will become the property of the state.' What had been a chilling memory now turned into a dreadful nightmare . . . After what seemed an eternity, the men returned from Irkutsk, and as he got out of the carriage Sergei said: 'You were right—it *did* concern the children; but don't worry—the decision has been left up to the parents.' That was all I wanted to hear. I rushed out to where Misha and Elena were playing, hugged and kissed them, and vowed that I would never allow them to be taken from me."

What transpired was that on the occasion of the marriage of the Grand Duke Alexander, heir to the throne, General Benckendorff, the chief of police, had been asked to review the situation of all children born in exile to Decembrists "of noble lineage" who were married *before* they were sent to Siberia. At the instigation of his son (the future Tsar Alexander II, who had never forgotten his visit to western Siberia, during which he came into contact with some of the exiled men), Tsar Nicholas was proposing to have the children sent back to European Russia and educated at his own expense; the boys at the Imperial College of Tsarskoe Selo, the girls at the Smolny Institute, the fashionable school for young ladies founded by the Empress Catherine. It was a sign of imperial favor, for which the condemned men were supposed to be duly grateful. However, there was one stipulation which showed that the tsar's vindictiveness had not abated. The children would still be required to renounce their family names, which in fact would make them legally illegitimate. The tsar graciously let it be known that "it was up to the mothers to decide whether they wanted to avail themselves of the favor." Tempting as the thought of a brighter future for their children might have been, most of the exiles declined the imperial offer. It was felt that the children might one day reproach them for having signed away their family names without their consent. Several parents saw in it an attempt to destroy the link between past generations and the future. They also felt that the implied illegitimacy was an affront to their heroic wives. "Fully recognizing the kindness of heart of His Imperial Majesty and the thoughtful memory of the Heir Apparent," wrote Muraviev, "I must in the name of my young daughter decline the favor. Accepting it would cast an aspersion on the memory of a wonderful mother and devoted wife."* Trubetskoy, declining the offer, wrote: "My

* When Nikita Muraviev died in 1843, his fourteen-year-old daughter Sophia (Nonushka) was sent for by her grandmother, who decided that the tsar's offer to have her educated at the Smolny Institute was infinitely preferable to having her grow up as a "Sibiryachka" in Urik. Nonushka went to St. Petersburg, where she was officially known as Sophia Nikitin, though everyone was aware that she bore the proud name of Muraviev. Her arresting beauty won her many admirers, and she became a favorite with the empress, who took a special interest in the girls of the Smolny

excellent wife does not deserve to be sullied with the taint of illegitimacy, and I cannot be responsible for depriving my children of their centuries' old heritage."

Volkonsky stressed the extreme youth of his children (Misha
was barely seven, Elena five) and "the torture the separation
would cause to their mother." He went on to say that it would be
wrong to purchase what perhaps might be a better future for his
children with the "terrible suffering of their mother." He begged
to be excused for not accepting the imperial favor. The replies
were forwarded to St. Petersburg with General Rupert's caustic
remarks about the exiles' "stubbornness and lack of appreciation
for the Emperor's goodwill."

Only one of the Decembrists decided to go along with the
emperor's suggestion. Vasya Davydov, Maria's uncle, settled in
Krasnoyarsk, had four children he had left behind in St. Petersburg. Five more were born in Siberia. Their education posed an
impossible problem. Much to Maria's indignation, he decided
that the future of his children would be better served if they were
educated at the Cadet Corps in St. Petersburg, under the common name of Vasilev, than if they remained in Siberia. Only
years later, after the amnesty, were they allowed to resume the
illustrious name of Davydov of Kamenka.

One of Maria's preoccupations at Urik was to keep in touch
with her husband's former fellow prisoners, now scattered
throughout Siberia, and to ascertain which of them needed financial help. Before their arrest, most of the Decembrists had

---

Institute. "I want you to think of me as your mother," Empress Alexandra
is reputed to have said to her on one occasion. "I am sorry, I only have one
mother," answered Nonushka, "and she is buried by the prison stockade
in Siberia."

been comfortably off or quite rich, and certainly free-spending young men. While in prison they were kept insulated from money worries, thanks to the "blessed artel," the cooperative which saw to it that they did not lack anything. But now in their distant settlements, with only a miserly allowance from the government, they had to struggle for their everyday existence. They found it tough. Those who took up farming and had some previous knowledge of it, like Baron Rozen, did modestly well; others tried to scrape a living in building, contracting, flour milling, or teaching. The Borisov brothers, Peter and the "mad" Andrei, earned money drawing reproductions of Siberian butterflies and flowers for museums and scientific publications in Russia and Germany. They developed a system of entomological classification which was later adopted by the French Academy of Sciences. But in most cases the income was not sufficient to meet the men's needs. "So many of our friends are crying out of sheer poverty," wrote Volkonsky to Jeannot Pushchin. "The Muravievs and the Trubetskoys are well off, we have no debts, but there are others who haven't got a kopeck . . . We help as much as we can." It was Maria's task to act as link between the dispersed exiles; she did this superbly well, earning for herself immense gratitude to the end of her life. For, apart from occasional contributions from relatives back home, the most reliable source of help for the needy settlers was the regular donations from their wealthier comrades, mainly the Muravievs, Trubetskoys, and Volkonskys, channeled through Maria's one-woman assistance society. She was aided in this task by the Dowager Countess Muraviev, Nikita's and Artamon's mother, back in Russia, who over the years spent the better part of her fortune to help her two sons and their friends.

During their first year in Urik, because of some administrative mix-up, the Volkonskys themselves were short of money. At one point, Maria appealed to the tsar, asking that their previous remittance from home be reinstated and stressed the high cost of the children's education. The tsar replied, "In Siberia there are no teachers, so you shouldn't have any expenses." Nevertheless, due to the intervention of Prince Repnin, Sergei's brother, their remittance was not only reinstated but increased by the addition of the legacy left by the old princess. (Sergei's personal fortune had been taken over by his sister Sophia, which was a cause of constant friction.) But from the time of Prince Repnin's intervention, the Volkonskys had few money problems. They could live in a relative degree of comfort and increase their assistance to their less fortunate comrades.

There was also plenty to do closer to home. Several local children were taken in by Maria to be brought up and educated together with Misha and Elena. Fascinated as she always was by the aboriginal tribes of Siberia, Maria adopted a young Chukchi girl of the reindeer-riding people, whose ancestors roamed the forests of northeastern Siberia. The girl, who must have been about ten years old, was found by the Poggio brothers half starving in the woods one spring day, obviously abandoned by her tribe. At first she could only communicate in the tribal dialect, but she turned out to be incredibly bright; within a few months she learned to speak Russian and even some French, started to read and write, and could do sums, much to everyone's delight. Maria named her Liutik (Buttercup) because she had been found in a field of buttercups. Liutik was devoted to her princess; she followed the family to Irkutsk, where she later married the son of a local merchant.

Mikhail Lunin in his memoirs describes how one day he came upon Maria and her "Chukchi shadow" helping an old woman to gather medicinal herbs for a poultice. "The princess showed the woman how to apply it, gave her food, and accompanied her back to her dwelling. She is greatly loved by everyone around here," he noted.

No sooner did the danger of a separation from the children recede from Maria's horizon than news came of the death of her brother-in-law Mikhail Orlov. The "magnificent Orlov," husband of the good and generous Ekaterina, who had so luckily escaped punishment for his involvement in the December uprising, died of pneumonia suddenly in March 1842 in Moscow. "I am too upset at the moment to write to Ekaterina directly," said Maria in a letter to her brother Alexander Raevsky. "Having just suffered a terrible anxiety on account of my children, I realize how shattering it must be to face eternal separation from a dear one. Ekaterina will be looked after by her children, but how I wish I could be with her . . . It is at moments like this that I feel my separation from you all most acutely."

Maria was now nearly forty; she had spent over eighteen years of her life in exile. She knew that as long as Tsar Nicholas was alive there was no hope of going back. But there is no indication in her letters that she felt that her life was being wasted. "My motherland is where my children are," she wrote to Zenaida in Rome. "Life is full, though the thought that I might never see you all again saddens me." Alessandro undoubtedly contributed to her equilibrium; they were alike in their zest for life and their genuine affection for their fellow men. "Alessandro is one of the most humane people I know," Giuseppe used to say of his younger brother. His gaiety and Latin humor balanced Maria's occasional bouts of Slavic depression. She admired his deep attachment to Russia despite the way the government had treated him. "What a luxury this country is," Poggio would tell her. "When I was a boy in Odessa, my dream was to go to the United States because of all the wonderful space out there. But how could I wish for more than these endless horizons?"

Pride was another vital strand in her personality—it was

pride connected with what she called her duty to the Decembrist legend; she knew they were all part of one of history's unforgettable chapters and she was determined to sustain it. It is doubtful whether throughout the years of her unhappy marriage she even for a moment considered leaving Sergei; nor did she neglect his welfare. "Pride is faith in the image that God had of us when he brought us into this world," she once told her daughter, Elena. "You must be conscious of it and always be proud of who you are; it will help you to fulfill your destiny."

As the children were growing, the matter of their education became more and more pressing. Though tutored by a team of distinguished people, they were obviously in need of more formal schooling, as well as the companionship of children their own age. Mikhail Lunin, a great teacher, had just been deported to Akatui, the deadly place where "even a bird could not survive." His departure greatly upset Mikhail and Elena. Lunin was always an irrepressible individualist, determined not to relinquish his convictions. But once released from prison, he became even more outspoken and critical of the government. "In Russia," he would say, "I am known as a resettled state criminal. In England, they would refer to me as Lunin, a member of the Opposition. For that in fact is my political status. [Lunin did not take part in the December uprising.] My weapon is my ability to think."

In letters to his sister, Countess Uvarov, his only channel of communication with the outside world, he became more and more virulent in his criticism of the government and even the tsar. His communications turned into political pamphlets. "The whip of sarcasm cuts as deeply as a headman's ax," he wrote, for the benefit of the censors. General Benckendorff, who had known Lunin in his youth and was fond of him, was finally forced to impound his letters and ordered that, for his own good, he be forbidden to correspond with his sister for a year. But when the year was over, Lunin, by now bored and resentful, resumed his "seditious propaganda," or "teasing the White Bear," as he called it. He attacked the government's entire handling of the Decembrists' trial, now almost twenty years past. No action could have been more calculated to infuriate Tsar Nicholas. As a result, late one evening a posse of gendarmes rode into Urik, surrounded the cabin, and arrested Lunin. According to a contemporary account by G. Lvov of Governor Rupert's staff, who had driven into Urik with the police, it happened on the Thursday before Easter, when the local inhabitants were returning from Vespers. They all loved Lunin and they collected in front of his house to see him off. "Farewell, Mikhail Sergeevich!" they called out. "May God will it that we meet again!" They promised to pray for him and to look after his house in his absence. He was allowed to say goodbye to the Volkonskys and left Maria his gun and his two dogs, asking that the other four be put down.

Lunin did not survive the prison in Akatui, built by an architect who, as he said, "must have inherited Dante's imagination." His cell was tiny, the walls covered with mold, the food unspeakable. Worst of all, he was not allowed any books, which for him was torture. He died after three and a half years, his spirit unbroken. Another brilliant mind was lost to Russia, a victim of the tsar's revenge.

Lunin was impossible to replace as a teacher, but luck brought the Volkonskys a Pole, Julian Sabinsky, who had been deported after the 1830 uprising and was now living in the neighboring village of Granovskoe. Sabinsky had been brought up in Paris and his French was idiomatically perfect. He devoted himself to teaching both the French language and French literature to the children and insisted on doing it without compensation. Years later, when Elena was complimented at court by the Empress Maria, wife of Alexander II (Nicholas's son), on the excellence of her French, she explained that it had been taught to her in the wilderness of Siberia by a Polish political detainee.

The year 1844 brought many changes. It began with two sad pieces of family news: in January, Maria received a letter from Zenaida telling of her mother's death in Rome. A few weeks later, a distraught Ekaterina advised her of the death in the Caucasus of her favorite brother, Nikolai. Maria was stunned. Quite apart from her sadness at the loss of her mother and Nikolai, she realized that there was no one left in the family to look after her children if anything happened to her. Alexander was too busy, and Ekaterina, now a widow, had too many children of her own to cope with. Maria lived with the fear that, in spite of Sergei's rejection of the emperor's offer, the government might somehow at some point spirit Misha and Elena away. She decided to apply for permission to reside in Irkutsk, so that Misha, now twelve, studious and very bright, could be educated at the local secondary school. She supported her application with a letter from Dr. Wolff which stated that for medical reasons residence in town was to be recommended. Alexander Orlov, Mikhail's brother, had by now replaced Benckendorff as chief of police. On February 25, 1844, she wrote him a private letter in French: "My dear Count: As you are well aware, both of my parents are now dead, so it is to you I am addressing my request, with the hope that you will present it to the Emperor in a favorable light . . ." She went on to say that, being in poor health herself (since the birth of Nellinka, Maria suffered from occasional kidney problems), her main preoccupation was the education of her children, and that is why she pleaded to be permitted to reside in Irkutsk, so that her son could enter the local school. She assured Orlov that "under the auspices of this well-run institution, we will all lead a very private and tranquil life."

To her surprise, General Rupert, the hard-boiled Governor of eastern Siberia, supported the application. "Such education would give the youth a direction that would harmonize with the views of the government," he added in a pompous postscript, forwarding Maria's letter to St. Petersburg. Count Orlov submitted it to the tsar with his own personal comment: "This family has recently suffered many blows at the hands of fate." Nicholas I yielded, but only halfway. Permission was granted for Maria and her children to move to Irkutsk, but not Sergei. For the time being, he would be allowed to come to town only once a month, but as there were no restrictions on Maria's travel in the district, the prohibition did not matter too much. Sergei would continue to live at the Kamchatnik, where the children and Maria planned also to spend the summer and the holidays.

At the end of March, just before Easter, Maria and her two children moved to Irkutsk. The next nine years were to be the high point of Maria's life. This is when the legend of the Princess of Siberia, which had been steadily growing since the mines of Blagodatsk, consolidated and became a moving part of women's contribution to history.

13

The Princess of Siberia

THE AUTUMN OF 1844 found Maria and the children living at Irkutsk in a large two-story house of fine seasoned timber, with attractive hand-painted decorations around the windows and the front door. The rooms were large and well proportioned, with high ceilings and tall porcelain stoves built into the walls; light poured in through the snugly fitted large double windows, which kept out the whipping gales and Arctic cold. The house was set off from the road by a tall white picket fence pierced by a wide arched gate, giving onto a vast courtyard with assorted outhouses, and quarters for numerous servants and stables. Siberian firs and white birches surrounded it on all sides. This imposing residence, purchased from a prosperous fur merchant who was moving to Tobolsk with his family, was quite a change from the Cossack isba at Blagodatsk, the cabin in Chita, the dark prisoners' quarters at Petrovsky Zavod, and even the picturesque but fairly primitive Kamchatnik in Urik. Its acquisition by Maria was a great stroke of luck; it came with the help of Nikolai Belogolovoy, the father of Poggio's pupil, Nikita, and part owner of the Irkutsk bazaar, who persuaded his friend and colleague the fur merchant to "let the Princess have it at a reasonable price." For once, circumstances played into the Volkonskys' hands: after the death of Maria's mother, the vast estates of Maria's great-grandfather M. V. Lomonosov, near Oranienbaum on the Gulf of Finland (which were given to him by the Empress Catherine), passed on to Ekaterina Orlov on condition that she share a substantial part of their revenues with Maria. Ekaterina proposed a lump sum. The outcome of the negotiations between the sisters is not clear—some bitterness resulted from it at a later stage—but it appears that at that particular moment Maria was very glad to have a sum of money at her disposal which enabled her to purchase the kind of house which was nearer in keeping with her former social status. Not that her "official" status had changed much in the move to Irkutsk. As late as 1847, she was still listed in the town police files as "wife of the state criminal Volkonsky." But this description was solely bureaucratic. In town, she was known as "our Princess."

Maria's house is still there. It stands in a quiet backwater in the old part of Irkutsk, where streets of ornate wooden dwellings have not yet been destroyed to make room for cement structures. It survived the great fire that ravaged the town in 1879, and when I was there in 1980 it was part of the Decembrist Museum, of which the city is very proud. (The other part of the museum is in what used to be the Trubetskoys' house.) Several well-preserved pieces of the Volkonsky furniture remain in place, including Maria's clavichord; there is a fine Oriental rug on the floor of Maria's bedroom, and an impressive sideboard, presumably used to display food at her dinner parties, which she had ordered from St. Petersburg in 1853 before the visit of Sergei's sister Sophia. The walls are covered with reproductions of Bestuzhev paintings from Chita and Petrovsky Zavod, and latter-day

photographs of the Decembrists. Maria's bedroom overlooks
what was then presumably a large garden and is now an assortment of ugly tenements, yet there is an atmosphere of authentic-
ity about this room. The natural cedarwood paneling, which
makes it warm and intimate, is the same that Maria looked at
when she woke up in the mornings a hundred and forty years
ago, the blue painted shutters are the ones she had made to keep
out the sound of the wind; her bed is gone, but her desk, a small
French *écritoire* with ormolu drawers, a present from Katyusha
Trubetskoy, stands on the left of the window and is the most
evocative object in the room. Copies of several of Pushkin's
poems and Nekrasov's eulogy of Maria are on the wall above it.
All over the house there are moving relics of their imprisonment: pieces of embroidery by Maria, Pauline Annenkov, and
Katyusha; an iron kettle in which Maria and Katyusha carried
out their cooking experiments at Blagodatsk; herbs collected for
Dr. Wolff's pharmacy by Alessandro Poggio, dried out and un-
recognizable under glass; bracelets made by Bestuzhev out of
the prisoners' fetters; and the famous heavy iron Dekabristi
wedding rings the wives wore until their deaths. Many of the
trees have obviously disappeared, but there is one magnificent
Siberian fir tree by the arched gate which must have been there
in Maria's day, and a clump of silvery birches frames a charming
white belfry of an old church, which I was told has now been
turned into a warehouse. Near the gate leading into the courtyard, where the stables used to be, is a little wooden bench
which looks as if it had been there since time immemorial. One
could imagine Maria sitting on it waiting for the carriage to
emerge from the stable block, to drive on some errand into
town.

By the end of April 1844, Maria, accompanied by her servants, Masha, Liutik, and the children, was installed in the
house. Additional help was hired: a tutor for Misha, who was to

enroll in the secondary school in September, and a French teacher, Mlle Millard, recommended by Alexander Raevsky's wife, who was on the way from Moscow to act as governess for Elena. Pieces of furniture and china were being shipped from St. Petersburg. All this was very different from Maria's visit more than seventeen years before, when on the way to the Blagodatsk mines she had had to stop to sign General Zeidler's cruel ultimatum. It was a mercy to lead a semblance of civilized life again, even though she was still registered as a "state criminal's wife" and her husband continued to be under strict police supervision.

"The exterior of Irkutsk and the mode of life of its inhabitants are most pleasant," wrote Adolf Erman, the German traveler and friend of the explorer Humboldt, who visited there in March 1845 and met Maria briefly. "During my entire stay in this town, the sky may be said to have been without a single cloud and of the deepest blue color. There rarely passed a day after the commencement of March when it did not thaw in the sun. I felt no reluctance to exchange my Ostiak dress, purchased in the far north, for a cloth frock and a mantle lined merely with hare skins. The streets here are well kept; the snow much better swept than in other parts of Siberia; all the wooden foot paths near the houses are clear of it." What delighted the traveler was the extraordinary purity of the air and the brightness of the atmosphere, which lent an unusual clarity to the landscape. "Nowhere else have I heard church bells sound so pure," he recalled. Situated on a high plateau between mountains, and far removed from the sea, the town had a typical dry and sunny continental climate which suited Maria very well. Her health, undermined by years of the all-pervading dampness of Petrovsky Zavod as well as Urik, where the river fog affected her bronchia, improved dramatically; her old vitality returned, and with it her impact on people.

Irkutsk's official "society" consisted of officers on the governor general's staff, a vast number of civilian officials engaged in the administration of the province, and their wives, and a handful of scientists sent out from St. Petersburg to study animal and plant life around Lake Baikal, teachers at the local secondary school, navy personnel who looked after navigation on Lake Baikal and river communications with the northeast, a dozen or so local priests, and about sixty families of rich merchants, who basically despised the officials, though outwardly they cooperated with them. Their wives, however, were very keen to "belong." Much social distinction was made between women of "pure Russian blood" and those whose ancestors "diluted" their blood lines by intermarriage with the Buriats. According to Maria's description, those women were "square and muscular, with swarthy brown complexions and slanting eyes." At the top of the social pyramid stood the governor general and his wife.

In Siberia there was no established upper class as in Russia, and no aristocracy or landed gentry; civilian officials and military personnel, who represented the tsar's authority, were often looked on as a hostile garrison imposed by a victorious enemy; relations between them and the merchants were often strained. Nevertheless, in Irkutsk, as in provincial towns throughout the Russian empire, the rigid caste system, the *chin* (rank), was strictly adhered to. Established by Peter the Great, the *chin* reached its apogee during the reign of Nicholas I, who rejoiced in its exactitude. It enclosed each man in his special grade and uniform, be it a military or a civil servant (*chinovnik*); there were fourteen ranks altogether, and the prevailing hierarchy was strict and immutable, involving ascending degrees of splendor, from a lowly "assistant to the assessor" to "*true* Assessor" or "Assistant Inspector" to "Inspector General," and so forth, as in Gogol's play. Any man who had completed the course of one of the higher educational establishments in Moscow or St. Petersburg automatically qualified for a rank. The same, of course, applied to the army and the nobility, who were graded according to their military rank or title. Artists posed problems, for being an artist was not considered a profession, and as it was absolutely essential to belong to a certain category, painters, musicians, and writers had to be given invented grades and occupations. The composer Borodin, a chemist by profession, was listed as a member of the second guild, rank 8; Musorgsky, as an officer in the Preobrazhensky Guards, had his own military rank; Pushkin was a gentleman-in-waiting, first court rank for any nobleman.

When the American George Kennan, in the course of his tour of Siberia in 1870, paid a call on the Grand Lama in his exotic lamasery on the Selenga River, he was asked by the Russian interpreter who accompanied him to the interview whether "he was a prince or at least a count." When told that he was neither, the official insisted that Kennan must invent a title for himself, "the more high-sounding, the better." Kennan's refusal and his explanation that he was "a free American" traveling privately and at his own expense were rejected; to his amusement, he heard himself introduced to the Lama as "the very high-ranking envoy from the Imperial Great Country over the sea."

The arrival of a real princess bearing an illustrious historical name caused a sensation in town. No matter that she was officially listed as "wife of a state criminal." Women vied with each other to call on her and entertain her and the children, but at first Maria refused to join in the social whirl. Her position was still tenuous; General Rupert, though he had lately appeared favorably disposed to her cause, was an uncertain ally; a false move and Misha's permission to attend the secondary school might be revoked. It was better to tread warily, and in any event, she wanted first to get acquainted with the ordinary people. Like most of her fellow exiles, Maria liked the Siberian people, who were more independent than people in European Russia, and were intelligent and steady. The Siberian children of the Russian and Cossack settlers knew nothing of the landowner's power; the institution of serfdom was unknown in Siberia. The immense distances saved the average peasant from too frequent contact with state officials and made him independent and proud, while the dangers and exigencies of everyday life in the remote villages produced a people that were resourceful, open, ready to help, but at the same time prepared to put up resistance if taken advantage of. Most of them had welcomed the political exiles and respected them for the sacrifices they had suffered in their fight to abolish serfdom.

Followed by her faithful maid Masha and her manservant, and often accompanied by Poggio, who had also moved into town, Maria was seen browsing through the Gostiny Dvor—the ancient Irkutsk bazaar—a massive stone structure dating back to the seventeenth century, when the town was first founded. Its roof was overgrown with grass and weeds, its sides encrusted with endless rows of stalls and booths of retail traders selling a huge variety of articles of Chinese and European manufacture. Around it during the busy hours of the day surged a throng of Russian peasants, Buriat tribesmen, Mongols, Cossacks, and local women, who seemed to be buying and bargaining for every kind of merchandise. It ranged from Chinese tea and silks from Kyakhta to Russian telegas (carts), fine St. Petersburg china, and secondhand boots. Maria loved the Gostiny Dvor; she enjoyed talking to the shopkeepers, inquiring about their travels and the origins of their goods; she and Poggio would return from these forays with valuable additions to the furnishings of her new house. The Buriats were old friends; many of them came down from the mountains every day in the winter, bringing hay in wagons drawn by oxen; others rode down to the city, fur-lined capes draped colorfully over the left shoulder, "which," she noted, "gave an appearance of elegance even to the poorest." Each tribesman carried his smoking apparatus slung from his belt and his tea cup projecting under the breast of his jerkin. She talked to them in their own dialect, much to the astonishment of the bazaar people.

The foundling hospital was a great preoccupation; but here again she did not dare to suggest help as yet. Over 370 children were being reared in a derelict mansion on the bank of the Angara River on the outskirts of Irkutsk. Most of them had been fathered by Russian settlers who had refused to recognize them. No one seemed to know much about governing an institution of this kind. The severity of the climate, the inhumanity and negligence of some mothers, and the incompetence of the nurses were responsible for a horrifying rate of mortality among the babies. All Maria could do for the time being was visit it regularly, make practical suggestions, and offer material help. Even so, the news of her interest (none of the rich merchants' wives had ever visited the hospital) spread around town, aroused wide admiration, and enhanced the esteem in which she was held. This regard on the part of the population was to land her in trouble with the governor.

It happened shortly after Christmas, during the festive carnival season. A distinguished violinist and pianist had been invited by Governor Rupert, who was being recalled to St. Petersburg, to come from Tobolsk to give a concert. As this was to be a special carnival celebration on the eve of the governor's departure, all the local people were invited. Irkutsk had no concert hall and no theater, so the performance was to take place in a section of the Gostiny Dvor, the ancient bazaar, which was being cleared for the occasion.

It had been a long time since Maria had heard classical music, which always gave her infinite pleasure; that day, on the spur of the moment, she decided that she would go to the concert and take Elena with her. She also wanted to be with the local children, with whom she had spent many weeks at the primary schools, teaching them to sing Christmas carols. She was proud of the fact that within a relatively short time she had managed to form a competent young people's choir: for the first time in years, Irkutsk had its own carol singers, youthful revelers going from house to house, dressed in an assortment of fancy, supposedly biblical costumes. Everyone was delighted, and the older people were particularly thankful to "the Princess" for bringing back the customs of old Russia to this raw frontier post.

The massive stone building was filled to capacity when Maria and her young daughter arrived. Every bench and stool was occupied; people were sprawled on bales of hay on the ground as well. Mother and daughter briefly paused at the entrance, their distinctive silhouettes lit up by the flares at the door. According to an eyewitness account, "suddenly an incredible thing happened. In a spontaneous gesture, the entire audience rose to their feet and applauded—not the musicians, who were about to take their seats on the podium, but 'the Princess.' People fell back, a passage opened in the crowd, and the Princess, holding her daughter by the hand, moved forward in her gliding walk; they were led to two seats right behind the governor and his wife."

Maria was deeply moved, and much too surprised to speculate on what the governor would think. He had turned around and seen it all, but he could hardly have ordered her away, short of provoking a riot. She knew that he would be displeased, as indeed he was. She received a curt note the next day forbidding any further public appearances. "Governor Rupert ordered me to disappear from sight for a while," was Maria's caustic comment to Ekaterina. "I wish there were some nice spots around here one could go to for a change of air, but the only place I can think of is the hot baths on the northern shore of Baikal. Unfortunately, at this time of the year their limited accommodations are taken up with merchants and caravan owners busy restoring their health after the excesses of the annual fair at Kyakhta."

For a time she feared that the incident might do harm to Misha's progress at school, but luckily, Governor Rupert was busy preparing for his return to St. Petersburg, and there were more important matters to attend to before his departure. Misha was doing well in his studies; he was to graduate with a gold medal four years later. Elena, popularly called Nellinka, was now fourteen, a beautiful, dark-haired, lively girl adored by everyone around her; she was a great favorite in Decembrist circles. For by now several of the old comrades had managed to get permission to reside in Irkutsk. Katyusha Trubetskoy and her husband bought a house near the Znamenskoe Monastery, a few streets away from the Volkonskys, where they lived with their five children. Two of their boys hoped to enter the Irkutsk secondary school, but permission had not yet been granted (it came after the change of governor). The sweet and friendly Katyusha, devoted mother and Trubetskoy's ever-adoring wife, was not well; she had cancer. Sitting in a deep armchair, wrapped in a shawl and with an old-fashioned lace cap over her graying hair, she showed no sign of the agony she must have suffered at the thought of her children growing up in Siberia without her. Maria walked over to her house every day and spent long hours trying to alleviate her friend's anxiety for the future. To take Katyusha's mind off her troubles, they sometimes drove to Urik together to visit Sergei and spent a few days at the Kamchatnik. Prince Trubetskoy recalls in his memoirs how the local inhabitants would "come forth to greet them with offers of fresh eggs and newly caught fish from the river."

One fine summer day in late June, they drove to a natural mud spa, the famous hot baths on the northern shore of Lake Baikal, from a high point of which the lake could be seen in all its magnificence. The spa was run by the government of the province as a resort for arthritis and rheumatism sufferers and as a hospital for those seeking a cure from that "well-known disease called the plague of Siberia." They stayed in a small hotel and at dawn Maria watched the amazing spectacle of wild animals coming down from the mountains to "take the waters." She was told that, since time immemorial, seals, reindeer, foxes, bears, lynx, and raccoons—the wild creatures of the northern taiga—had been descending from the mountains with the first light of day to wallow delightedly in the curative mud. They appeared to pay scant attention to the presence of humans nearby.

Maria was thrilled by this exotic sight. Wild animals, Buriat tribes, Chukchi tribesmen riding their reindeer in the forests—those were the images of Siberia she would recall with pleasure for the rest of her life. The two women were surprised to see the array of wondrous vegetables grown within a radius of several miles; the local people attributed the miraculous size of their produce to the "beneficial vapors" emanating from the hot springs.

Alexander Muraviev was also living in Irkutsk now. So was Giuseppe Poggio, who had joined his brother in his house a short walk from the Volkonskys. (Alessandro found employment giving lessons in Italian and French to the pupils of the Irkutsk secondary school.) Giuseppe's health was rapidly declining; it was obvious that he had only a short time to live. As it was hard for Alessandro to look after him, Maria had him moved into her own house. She and Nellinka nursed him devotedly, but long years in the Fortress had taken their toll. He died of scurvy, with his brother and the Volkonsky family around him.

"I shall always look kindly on the last eight years of our exile in Irkutsk," wrote Maria in the closing pages of her diary. "For the post of Governor of eastern Siberia was then held, not by General Rupert any more, but by Nikolai Muraviev, the most loyal, kind, and gifted man on this earth. It was he who gave Russia its access to the Pacific Ocean at a time when the French and the English were trying to wrest the Black Sea from us. The governor and his wonderful French wife have been kindness itself; it was he who helped you, my darling Misha, to develop your mental abilities so that you could serve your country with distinction, and it was he who taught you discipline and perseverance, so essential in your career." General Nikolai Nikolaevich Muraviev, known in history as Muraviev-Amursky (one of the numerous Muraviev family, and a cousin of Alexander), was a remarkable person. A liberal and an idealist by conviction, a visionary and a brilliant leader of men, as well as a benevolent despot, he was fashioned in the great tradition of the nineteenth-century British empire-builders, whom he admired. He possessed enormous personal charm, great integrity, and independence of spirit, which made him despise the petty bureaucratic set-up of his predecessors, with its multitude of antiquated rules, which slowed down the development of the province and fostered privilege, theft, and corruption.

Before Muraviev's arrival, Siberia had been badly governed. The choice of governors had been particularly unfortunate. Either they were eccentrics, like the one who had a habit of firing off a cannon in Irkutsk "whenever he felt merry," or another who, when drunk, "insisted on saying Mass in his house in full vestments in the presence of a scandalized bishop"; or they were men in the final years of their service, worried about their pensions, unwilling to disturb the status quo. To them, Siberia was a camp to be plundered or a cellar with great stores of gold, fur, and precious metals to be looted and forgotten. They thought of it as a hostile country, buried in snow, poor, without roads, populated by odd tribes, and the sooner they could leave it, the better. Muraviev was determined to change all that; his policy was more farsighted than his predecessors'. To him, Siberia had a great future, and he wanted to "carry it forward with American rapidity," as he was fond of saying. He visualized the northern part of the Pacific Ocean as "the Mediterranean of the future," and Siberia, reaching out to the Chinese frontier, would become a link between America and Russia.

Muraviev was convinced that in order to consolidate its power in the Far East, Russia must relinquish its possessions on the North American continent, which, since 1848—the year California was admitted to the Union—he believed, had become untenable. His objective was to block British influence in China after the Opium Wars by expanding the Russian frontier to the Amur and annexing the vast uninhabited regions which in the early days of the conquest of Siberia had been ceded to the Manchu empire. This became the governor's ambition and he forcibly argued for prompt action, brushing every obstacle aside. "Muraviev, you are going to lose your head over the Amur question," Tsar Nicholas said to him on one occasion.

As the Crimean War drew nearer and anti-British feelings mounted in St. Petersburg, Muraviev was given the go-ahead. The result of his military expeditions, and the subsequent colonization with Cossack settlers, was the acquisition from China of the huge territory running north of the Amur and Ussuri Rivers to the Pacific seaboard and the founding of the naval base of Vladivostok. A few years later, in 1867, Alaska (called

"Seward's Folly") was sold to the United States for the ridiculous price of $7,200,000.

Shortly after his arrival, the new governor succeeded in getting rid of the old staff of civil-service officials. He gathered around him a brilliant group of young civilian and military administrators, honest and competent, who shared his exciting vision of the future. He ruled Siberia from a splendid white colonnaded mansion overlooking the Angara River—which he called the White House, in honor of the American President. The elegant building, the most attractive in Irkutsk, still exists; these days it is pitted with shell marks and bears the scars of the battles between the Red and White forces during the Revolution; it now houses the city's scientific library and its regional archives. In an adjacent small park stands Muraviev's statue, a commanding bearded figure looking eastward toward his newly conquered domains on the Amur. Before the Revolution, all loyal Siberians removed their hats when they passed it.

The arrival of Muraviev and his entourage ushered in a new era in town. It was a godsend for Maria and her family. Not only was the new governor young (in his late thirties), warm, and friendly, but he was an open admirer of all the Decembrists stood for. Muraviev and his delightful French bride* treated them as close personal friends, with total disregard for what the St. Petersburg authorities might think. One of Mme Muraviev's first calls was on the Volkonskys in their house (she was a personal friend of Princess Zenaida and had seen her in Rome recently); from then on, Sergei, Maria, and her children were

---

* She was born Catherine de Richemont and had met him in Paris in 1845; he proposed to her by letter and they were married in Tula in 1847, just before they left for Siberia.

welcome guests in the White House. It was not in Muraviev's power to return the exiles to their homes, or to remove the offensive classification of "state criminal" from the town's police files, but he did everything possible to better their existence and enhance their standing in the community. For Maria, it meant that she could now freely devote herself to many projects for the common welfare. The foundling hospital was her first interest; helped by Katyusha Trubetskoy, she reorganized the staff, introduced measures of hygiene, and aided by Poggio and Dr. Wolff, she appointed two eminent doctors to look after the wards. She also collected money for a new wing, the opening of which by the governor's wife turned out to be a great occasion. Her next project was the primary schools, and her cherished dream of a theater and concert hall. As her civic activities developed, Maria's social life became more and more active. Invitations to Princess Volkonsky's receptions were eagerly sought after, the more so as one was usually certain to find the governor and his wife there. With Katyusha living in retirement because of her illness, it fell to Maria to assist the Muravievs in their entertaining. She also became a rallying center for the exiles living in and around Irkutsk. With twenty-five servants in the house and two carriages, it seemed at times as if she were back in Kiev or St. Petersburg.

Alessandro Poggio, now well established as a teacher, became a member of Muraviev's advisory circle, the group of clever young men who were planning the development of Siberia. In good weather, Alessandro and Maria would drive out to Urik, with the governor and his wife, to visit Sergei and enjoy fishing or shooting.

Sergei posed a big problem: he had turned into an eccentric old farmer; nothing except his fields interested him any more. In winter, when Maria's house was busy and open to all, and everyone in Irkutsk considered it an honor to be invited there,

Sergei preferred to spend his days in the bazaars, chatting to peasants. The townspeople were shocked to see him sitting on bundles of straw on a cart in some seedy section of the bazaar, eating kasha. He much preferred living at Urik, for the luxury of his wife's house did not suit his taste and his muddy boots were not welcome in the drawing room. Eventually, he built himself a hut in the yard behind the stables, to "carry on with his peasant friends." Young Belogolovoy, the eager diarist, recalls one of his rare appearances in his wife's drawing room, "smeared with tar, with pieces of straw in his long, unkempt beard, and smelling of the cattle shed." It was a strange reversal for a man who was once so at home in the salons of Vienna, Paris, and London. However, in spite of his uncouth appearance, many of Maria's guests soon discovered that, when approached, Sergei spoke perfect French and discoursed knowledgeably on all sorts of topics.

Maria is described in contemporary accounts as a woman looking younger than her forty-five years, tall, shapely, slender, with a small head and beautiful eyes, which "she constantly narrowed"; it was said that she carried herself with aristocratic grace, "had an innate kindness and the charming gift of worldliness which belong to the highest society." All accounts mention her abiding interest in the young; they were impressed by her because she spoke slowly and was always patient with them and anxious to further their education. "She loved her own two children passionately and was very strict in their upbringing, but she did not receive much assistance in this from her husband," adds young Belogolovoy.

It was obvious to all that the Volkonskys were leading separate lives. The diarists of the period may have been unfair to Sergei and misunderstood his genuine belief in farming and honest labor and his desire to "go back to the roots." Like Tolstoy thirty years later, he truly enjoyed the company of simple peasants, loved to gossip with them about farming and their needs;

they, in turn, respected his knowledge of agriculture (most of which he had gathered from books while in prison, and from his association with Andrei Rozen); they liked his frankness and open approach. They thought him eccentric at times and "a trifle strange"—he also was reputed to be mean (a trait that ran in the family), but he was "their Prince" and enjoyed their affection. One of Bestuzhev's last portraits of Sergei, done in the 1850s, shows him with a peaceful and serene gaze, a wide forehead and silvery hair, looking like a distinguished patriarch. But it is not a strong face, and Maria must have come to the reluctant conclusion that most of the burden of life and the responsibility for the future of her children rested on her own shoulders.

Misha and Elena were now at a crucial point in their lives. Having graduated from the Irkutsk secondary school in 1849 with a gold medal, young Misha, now almost eighteen, was ready to begin life. What were his prospects? There was no university in Siberia where he could further his education, and he had no desire to join the army, where as the son of a "state criminal" he could only have served, for the rest of his life, as a private—a dismal prospect. Misha had no interest in politics, which was understandable when he saw what unhappiness it had caused his father. Writing to his uncle Alexander Raevsky shortly after graduation, he explained that he was "simply repelled" by anything to do with philosophy or politics. "I never read political theory and only glance at the newspapers to find out what goes on in the world. Papa does not like my attitude, but I would expect him to understand it." Young Misha longed to "belong," to place himself in a circle that was above suspicion, to live like other young men of his age, to join the mainstream of life. He admired Muraviev-Amursky, and wanted to join the Siberian civil service under his aegis.

Maria decided to talk to the governor and went to see him in his study. The fine room, with its white porcelain stove and lofty windows overlooking the river, has been preserved virtually in its original state; it is now part of the scientific library. On my visit, I saw students working there at long tables, preparing for their exams for the newly opened University of Siberia. One can imagine Muraviev-Amursky, "the governor with the piercing gaze," sitting at his desk in the deep window recess, and Maria opposite him (under the ruby-red and turquoise Bohemian glass chandelier, which I was told has remained in its place throughout the years), engaged in an animated conversation about young Misha's future. Both Muraviev and his wife were devoted to Maria and greatly sympathized with her problems. Misha was an attractive young man of orthodox ideas and with an excellent school record. He made a good impression on all the interviewers. His application to join the civil service in Siberia was supported by the governor, and such was Muraviev-Amursky's influence that it took only a few months to process. "I have joined the civil service," a triumphant Misha wrote to his aunt Sophia Raevsky, Alexander's wife, in the summer of 1850. "Thank God I am out of that inbred circle, though Papa's friends do not love me for this. But I worship Mama more than anything else on this earth . . . I was born for a quiet, hardworking life and the civil service suits me fine. I want to be able to look after Mama and surround the days of her old age with peace and happiness." Admirable words from a son; Maria's devotion to her children was bearing fruit.

Beautiful Elena's future was much more of a worry. She was in her seventeenth year when Misha joined the civil service. From her mother she had inherited a lithe figure and splendid eyes, but unlike Maria's her complexion was of a milky whiteness, which provided a striking contrast to her dark hair. She was both affectionate and lively, attracting love and attention wherever she went. According to her contemporaries, Elena was an extraordinarily "well-loved" person throughout her life. Even in her old age, after three marriages, she was still "raising eyes in wonder at her personality." Here she was at the threshold of her life, a jewel any man would be proud to possess, fit to shine at the capital, but who was there to provide the proper setting? Surely she could not be allowed to remain in Siberia, marry some dull minor *chinovnik* in a remote township of Siberia, bear his children, and slave away in the wilderness until her radiant beauty faded.

Among the several officials who had come with Muraviev to Siberia was a Dmitri Vasilevich Molchanov, a graduate of the University of Kazan, recommended to the governor for his administrative talents. Shortly after his arrival, Molchanov was dispatched up-country to the northeast to check on the shipment of supplies from Okhotsk to the Russian bases in Alaska and on the North American continent. He returned to Irkutsk in February 1850 and fell desperately in love with Elena. Molchanov was in his early thirties, at the mid-point of his civil-service career. He was the son of an impoverished landowner in the province of Kazan, and in normal circumstances would never have been considered a match for the young Princess Volkonsky. But in the Siberian wilderness Maria thought him a suitable candidate: Muraviev-Amursky liked him, his career prospects were excellent, and he was due to go back to St. Petersburg at the end of the year. The thought of her daughter returning to a civilized life and resuming her proper rank in society outweighed the pain of separation and the considerable difference in age between Elena and the bridegroom. Elena, who so far had met very few "civilized young men," was impressed by Molchanov's worldliness and touched by his admiration for her. Throughout the remaining months of the winter, Molchanov called regularly at the Volkonsky house, partnered Elena at dances, masquerades, and sledge parties. In April, he formally requested her hand in marriage.

However, rumors began filtering through from European Russia which held that Molchanov was a man of "dubious integrity, an inveterate gambler at cards, and prone to shady financial transactions." None of this could be substantiated; it was well known that Molchanov had the governor's confidence, but still, the rumors would not disappear; they grew worse. It was said that while on a tour of duty in Okhotsk Molchanov had allowed himself to be bribed by a local contractor. This allegation Molchanov firmly denied, and it was also angrily dismissed by the governor. None of these adverse reports seems to have made any impression on Maria. She saw nothing wrong with Molchanov; what mattered to her was to get Elena out of Siberia. But Sergei was of a different opinion. From the outset, he did not like the looks of the suitor. "His eyes are shifty," he said. Actually, Molchanov was very nearsighted, which accounted for the narrowing of his eyes. Through his Decembrist friends, I. D. Yakushkin and Peter Alexandrovich Mukhanov, who had taught arithmetic to Elena at Urik, Sergei collected a good deal of information about his prospective son-in-law, much of it derogatory. Mukhanov, in particular, urged him not to allow Elena to marry a man "who was not universally respected." Yakushkin seems to have shared his opinion, for in a letter to his wife he deplored the fact that "fate brought Molchanov to Irkutsk, to the misfortune of the Volkonsky family." He described him as a "narrow-minded man, already known for some dishonest acts, but one of a certain charm, with influence on the governor." Yakushkin was surprised that Maria Nikolaevna did not consider him a bad man, and added sarcastically that "she probably imagines that he will be useful to her son in his career." All this strengthened Sergei's opposition. He left Urik, settled down in his shed in the garden, and announced that he would never consent to the marriage. He loved Elena; she was much too good and too beautiful to be wasted on a "potential scoundrel." The absentminded farmer, the patriarch with the tangled beard full of straw, was suddenly transformed into a determined old man, a hereditary prince whose command in dynastic matters was law.

This must have caused havoc in the household. "Imagine Papa looking on with fury, for all to see, whenever Nelly is talking or dancing with Dmitri Vasilevich," Misha complained to his Uncle Alexander back in Russia. "When Mama tells him that she will not tolerate such public scenes, he gets angry and shuts himself in the shed, but then comes into the house in the evenings to torment Dmitri Vasilevich if he is calling on Elena." Misha, for what might have been his own reasons, saw great qualities in Molchanov. He praised him for his genuine love for Elena and "the support he would be for Mama." It is difficult to tell to what extent the prospects for his own career influenced his judgment. "If Papa is going to behave like this to all future suitors of Nelly, my sister will end up an old maid." Misha was concerned about the effect of the domestic tension on his mother's health. "While she was well, Mama could cope somehow with Papa's behavior," he confided to his Uncle Alexander, "but now all this worries and alarms her." Misha was certain that Nelly wanted to marry and told his uncle that his father had "turned on him for taking his mother's side." He pointed out that Molchanov had the governor's confidence, and he asked his uncle to lend his support to the match. (Molchanov himself wrote to Alexander at some point, but the details of the correspondence are unknown.)

I. D. Yakushkin, who was in Irkutsk at the time and took great interest in the affair, reported that Maria was getting so desperate that she told a mutual friend (presumably Katyusha

Trubetskoy) that if Sergei continued to oppose the match she would simply tell him that he had no right to forbid it, because "Elena was not his daughter." Yakushkin was an inveterate gossip, and there is no way to determine the accuracy of his information. It does reflect, however, the rumors that had been circulating among the tightly knit group of veterans of Petrovsky Zavod. Mercifully, Maria never had to resort to such a drastic and unpleasant act. Moreover, her pride would not have allowed her to do so. She was stubborn, but she was much too kind to hurt her poor, pathetic husband and ruin a lifetime of friendship between him and Alessandro. Even if (as is quite possible) Sergei had suspected the fact all along, he certainly never would have admitted it. He adored Elena, he had watched her grow up, she was his child. It was Muraviev-Amursky, the seasoned diplomat, who finally broke the deadlock and persuaded Sergei to agree by "guaranteeing" Molchanov's integrity and extolling the prospects of his future career.

Nelly and Dmitri were married on September 17, 1850, in Irkutsk's Znamenskoe Monastery; the Orthodox golden crowns were held above their heads under the richly mantled Fedorovsky Virgin, which still hangs there on its background of hammered silver, surrounded by small icons, crucifixes, and votive offerings. Present at the wedding ceremonies was Maria's younger sister, Sophia, who had been granted permission for a visit of a few months. It was the first time in nearly a quarter of a century that a relative from western Russia had been permitted to visit the exiles in Siberia. Her arrival was a happy omen, perhaps the end of the interminable exile was in sight.

The wedding reception at the Volkonsky house, attended by the governor and his wife, was the most talked-about event in Irkutsk. A week later, the newlyweds left for Moscow. Maria's dream that her family might return was beginning to be realized.

After a twenty-five-year silence, Sergei wrote to his brother-in-law Peter Volkonsky,* field marshal and court minister, and husband of his sister Sophia, asking for his protection for the young couple. His love for Elena overcame his distaste for Molchanov.

One may wonder where Alessandro Poggio was at the time. He is not mentioned in the voluminous letters to the family written by both Elena and Misha, who loved him, and whose lives he was a part of. It appears that Poggio, who had always been close to Elena, did not approve of Molchanov and said so; this led to a temporary estrangement with Maria, though he certainly attended the wedding. But there were other reasons why the relationship was changing. With his Italian love of home life, Alessandro longed for a family, for children he could bring up as his own, and for a wife who would look after him in his old age. He had loved Maria; she had been the center of his existence for fifteen years; theirs was a friendship for life, but since his brother's death, he had felt progressively more lonely. From the time of Governor Muraviev's arrival, Maria had been fully occupied with her welfare projects, her busy social existence, and preoccupied—almost obsessed—with her children's careers. Poggio, who had no private income, was eking out a modest existence teaching French and Italian to the children of rich Irkutsk merchants. He and his old Decembrist comrade Zavalishin† were spending much time in the company of Muraviev's assistants, lending advice based on their knowledge of Siberia and helping to draw plans for the conquest of territories in the Amur River basin.

* A Volkonsky of a different branch of the family.
† Zavalishin was on Muraviev's staff for a while but opposed his policy; he wanted to retain Russia's possessions on the North American continent; they eventually quarreled and he was sent out to Chita.

Poggio and Maria were still close, but physical intimacy had now given way to profound friendship. In the year following Elena's departure for Moscow, Poggio married Larisa Andreevna Smirnov, a teacher at the town's Agricultural Institute. He was fifty-three and his bride twenty-seven. She gave him a daughter, called Varya. We will never know how Maria reacted to the marriage, but the links between the two families were never broken. Poggio was to remain in the Volkonsky orbit until his death.

The young men who came with Muraviev-Amursky from St. Petersburg to Siberia belonged to a relatively small group of liberals who had grown up in the oppressive post-Decembrist period but somehow managed to develop a concept of democratic thought. Tsar Nicholas was obsessed by the Decembrist rising throughout his life; he saw himself as the ruler appointed by Providence to save his people from the horrors of liberalism and revolution. Ever since that fateful day in December, he did his best to eradicate every form of political opposition. Only the Polish Rebellion of 1830 had disturbed the "dark silence" of Tsar Nicholas's somber country, and that was now almost twenty years in the past. Since then, Poland lay resentful but subdued under the Russian proconsul's ruthless yoke. But Poland's revolt had been an exception. There were no signs of serious internal conspiracy anywhere within Russia, and no apparent danger to the regime. As a result, the ferocious censorship gradually eased, and in the latter part of 1840 several liberal journals made timid ventures and "subversive French doctrines" were again openly discussed in the capital. Alexander Herzen, the earliest of the new liberals, had to leave Russia in 1842, never to return; but the voices of his friends like Belinsky, Gogol, and Dostoevsky were also beginning to be heard. As in the past generation,

France was the model they aspired to. Saltykov-Shchedrin, a typical liberal of the period, vividly describes the prevailing atmosphere: "In Russia everything seemed finished, sealed with five seals, and brought to the post office for delivery to an addressee whom it was beforehand decided not to find. But in France everything was beginning. Our sympathies became particularly intense in 1848 . . . With unconcealed excitement, we watched the drama of the last years of Louis Philippe's reign. With passionate enthusiasm, we discussed the events that followed . . ."

The Revolutions of 1848, the "Spring of Nations" which swept through Europe, overthrowing absolute regimes in their path, bypassed the Russian empire. Tsar Nicholas saw to it. He was stunned by the news of the abdication of Louis Philippe and outraged at the declaration of a republic in France. Believing that his worst fears about the instability of European governments had just been confirmed, he decided to take immediate action. There is a wonderful account in N. K. Shilder's 1903 *Life of Nicholas I* of how, upon hearing the news from Paris, the distraught emperor drove straight to the palace of his son, the future Alexander II, where a ball on the eve of Lent was in progress. Bursting into the ballroom, he stopped the dancers with an imperious gesture and cried: "Gentlemen, saddle your horses, a republic has been proclaimed in France," and swept out, his courtiers following. Even if apocryphal, the story does depict the nearly hysterical atmosphere of the time.

Prince Peter Volkonsky, Sergei's brother-in-law, who was the man closest to the emperor, was convinced that the tsar was bent on declaring a preventive war with France but was held back by a lack of money. Even so, huge reinforcements were sent to Poland to guard Russia's western frontiers, and in the summer of 1849 Russian troops crushed the revolution in Hungary. Although Europe's "Spring of Nations" failed to break through the glaciers surrounding the Russian empire, Tsar Nicholas commanded that all projected reforms be instantly pigeonholed, and censorship of the press was reinstituted with savage severity. Uspensky, a contemporary writer, painted a gloomy picture of the final years of Nicholas's reign: "One could not move, one could not dream; it was dangerous to give any sign of thought; you were required to show that you were scared, trembling even, when there were no real grounds for it. You lived in perpetual fear. 'You are lost,' cried heaven and earth, air and water, man and beast—everything shuddered and fled from disaster into the first available rabbit hole."

It was good to be away from the center of power in those days, and for more than a decade the governor's mansion in Irkutsk was a refuge for talented young men of liberal thought like Kukel, Bakunin, and later Kropotkin, the "revolutionary prince."

An indirect effect of the revolution in France was the postponement of the exiles' return from Siberia. It had been widely reported for some time that an amnesty would be granted in 1850, on the twenty-fifth anniversary of the December uprising. Twenty-five years was an inordinately long sentence for a political crime; and it was known that the heir to the throne had petitioned his father on the exiles' behalf. So had their families, who pointed out that most of the detainees were now older men, racked by illness, and unlikely to pose a threat to the empire. For a time the emperor appeared to be "leaning toward clemency," but the revolution in France and the events of 1849 changed his mind. Nothing more was heard about amnesty. The exiles were to remain forgotten, "presumed dead."

"When I arrived at my aunt's palace in St. Petersburg," wrote Elena to her mother, "I was greeted like a dove sent from the Ark." Sergei's family did not know what to expect and were astounded at the sight of this beautiful woman, poised, with impeccable manners, speaking better French than most of the ladies at court. They were not particularly impressed by Molchanov—"insignificant man of uncertain origins," decreed Prince Peter—but everybody agreed that he worshipped Elena and had given up his drinking and gambling. Unfortunately, his past was to catch up with him.

Elena's arrival at Sophia Volkonsky's house revived the princess's suppressed feelings for her brother; Sophia was getting older, the family meant more to her now than it had in the past when her life was overshadowed by her court duties. She also felt guilty about her past financial dealings, which had deprived her brother of a large part of his inheritance. She wanted to heal the rift between them and decided that she might one day go to Siberia to visit him and Maria. In the meantime, she presented her niece with a sizable sum of money and told her to buy some "nice clothes" and to explore St. Petersburg, which to a girl newly arrived from Siberia was like being asked to partake in magic.

On the Monday before Lent, there was a gala performance at the St. Petersburg opera, and the court minister and his wife asked Elena to accompany them in their box. The seventeen-year-old girl's radiant beauty caught the tsar's attention.

"Who is that charming young creature?" he asked.

"My niece, Sergei's daughter, sire."

"Indeed—the dead prince's child?"

"But my brother-in-law is not dead, Your Majesty—he is in Siberia."

"When I say someone is dead, he *is* dead," was the implacable reply.

Two years later, Prince Peter Volkonsky, the seventy-six-year-old courtier and field marshal, who had served both Tsar

Alexander and Nicholas I, was dying in his palace in St. Petersburg. Elena, who helped to nurse him, sat at his bedside. Suddenly the tsar was announced; he had come to pay a last call on a faithful friend of the Romanovs. Without raising her eyes, Elena swiftly moved out of the room. The emperor came again the next day, unannounced. This time he asked her to stay and talked to her of her brother and of his work with Muraviev in Siberia. Elena's existence was now officially acknowledged.

Meanwhile, in her never-ending exile, Maria was pursuing her dream of building a theater and concert hall for Irkutsk, a town which had shown her so much affection. Through her sister Sophia, who was now back in Kiev, she got in touch with an architect who had once been employed in Odessa by her kinsman, the great Prince Michael Vorontsov, when the city was becoming the cultural center for Russia's southern provinces. Urged by Alexander Raevsky and his wife, he agreed to make the long journey to Siberia, on condition that the project be supported by the governor. After the necessary letters had been exchanged, police and travel permits obtained, and assorted formalities dealt with, Andrei Yakubovich Berezov arrived in Irkutsk in the early winter of 1853. Maria had been highly successful in her fund-raising campaign. The well-to-do merchants vied with each other to display their generosity; many of them, as latecomers to Siberia, treasured a certain cultural heritage from life in Moscow and St. Petersburg. There were donations from modest stall-keepers in the bazaar, and sometimes even an individual Buriat tribesman meeting Maria in the marketplace would pull out a few rubles from under his cloak and hand them to her, "for the music."

It was decided that the building would be of Siberian cedar, wood being more suited to the climate and more easily available than brick; it was to be of a round shape and erected on a small elevation, facing southeast, toward Lake Baikal and the mountains.

Maria often visited the construction site, and it gave her enormous pleasure to see her dream taking shape. Now that she and Sergei were alone and the vexing problem of Molchanov was out of the way, Maria's relations with her husband improved. "Your father is good to me," she wrote to Nelly. "He cares for me as much as his nature allows, and he is tactful . . . All is well as long as that intriguer friend of his, Mukhanov, is not around, for he is the one who always sets him against me." A more difficult problem, however, was how to cope with Sergei's jealousy of the children's affection for their mother. "Sergei is terribly jealous of the children and especially of my authority over them," she complained to her brother Alexander. "He does not understand that it flows from mutual love and trust and that it cannot be created on command." It got to the point where she did not dare to share with Sergei the contents of some of Nelly's or Misha's letters to her, "lest he be upset by their tenderness." She often asked Nelly to write a letter directly to her father and put in a few words in Russian, for "that would make him happy."

To her new son-in-law, who she felt was somewhat intimidated by her, she explained that if "at times I appear haughty," it is because she has to hide "the surfeit of maternal feelings with which I am blessed. My strength of will is equal to my love for my children, particularly when their fortune is at stake. In any other circumstances, I am just a wet hen, frightened by anyone." That comparison was a wild flight of fancy, for Maria's opinion of herself would certainly not have been shared by anybody else in Irkutsk. After the governor's wife, she was the town's first citizen, respected and admired by all. Thanks to her, the foundling hospital had expanded and had become a model for similar institutions in the province; she had done much to improve teaching in the primary schools, and had persuaded the officials to include music lessons as part of the curriculum; the town's hospital owed her much; and now a new theater and concert hall was rising on a site where caravans bound for China used to water their camels.

The much talked-about opening of the new theater was postponed for a month to await the arrival from St. Petersburg of Sergei's famous sister Sophia. She had been planning the trip for some time, since shortly after the funeral of her husband. She was sixty-eight years old, a robust, eccentric *grande dame* who, in spite of her age, was avid for new experiences. As a young married woman she had accompanied her husband to the Congress of Vienna, where her wit had been much remarked on. "I was never beautiful," she noted in her reminiscences, "but I had a *je ne sais quoi*, which attracted men." During a visit to London with her husband, she was presented with a tea service by King George III; according to her, this was not an "official present" but "a gift from a man to a pretty woman." She loved to travel on the Continent between Munich, Vienna, and Berlin and often turned up unexpectedly at the house of some foreign relative, accompanied only by an elderly domestic and dressed in stained traveling clothes, but "with her hair full of diamonds." Her travels came to an abrupt end when, against the known wishes of the tsar, she called on Alexander Herzen in London. After that, she was refused a foreign passport. In the last years before the old prince's death, she developed a passion for the newly constructed railroad between Moscow and St. Petersburg; she purchased a railway carriage of her own, upholstered in bright green and mauve velvet, which she ordered to be attached to the train; she traveled in it back and forth, much to her husband's irritation.

In early 1854, the formidable dowager announced that she was off to visit her brother in Siberia. The tsar reluctantly agreed to grant her a permit, but he reminded her sternly that "no letters must be brought back from the exiled men." Not that the order would have made much difference to the princess, for she reveled in disobeying the tsar, "in *small* matters." She set off from St. Petersburg in the depths of winter, accompanied by two lackeys and her Italian woman companion. Her journey was long and arduous and created much upheaval in its wake. As she understandably despised the dismal wayside *korchmas* (inns) at the relay stations, she would descend on unsuspecting local government officials or town merchants and demand food and lodging for herself and her entourage. Nor was she shy of criticizing her hosts for their alleged shortcomings. Generosity was not one of her virtues; she was known for her stinginess and disliked tipping.

Maria was at her desk writing letters when she heard the jingling of bells and loud shouts from below her window. She saw an angry old woman getting out of a traveling sleigh, arguing with the driver about payment. *"Nyet,"* she heard. "I have been generous enough; *basta!"* Behind her were two other sleighs loaded with luggage; she had brought fifteen trunks, obviously prepared for a long stay, for, as Misha recalled, "there weren't too many presents among them."

Sergei found his sister "very tiresome." Though they had not seen each other for over twenty-eight years and there was much news to communicate, Sophia was so self-centered and eccentric that, as Maria remarked, "she only wanted to talk of herself." She was also afflicted with kleptomania; like a magpie, she carried small objects belonging to Maria or Sergei into her room, from where they had to be painstakingly retrieved by the faithful Masha, the housekeeper. No wonder that she had had no compunction about seizing her brother's properties in the past. Still, she sparkled with occasional witticisms and, when in a good mood, could be excellent company.

The arrival of Prince Peter's widow created a sensation in Irkutsk; she was the highest-ranking personage ever to reach that distant outpost of empire. The governor and his wife gave a reception for her (which she found boring) and she was asked to preside at the formal inauguration of the new theater. Before that, she insisted on "putting her foot into China," much to everyone's consternation, as she might easily have been arrested if she ventured too far over the border. She went off to Kyakhta, the center of the tea trade, saw the yak caravans and the camels, and "the little men in funny hats converging from everywhere with tin-lined boxes full of merchandise," and loved it all.

A company of singers, a distinguished violinist, and a pianist made the arduous journey from Tobolsk, the medieval capital of western Siberia, to perform at the opening of the new theater. Maria does not tell us what the program was, but there must have been music by Glinka, a great favorite at the time; perhaps some Mozart, and very likely a Paganini etude for the violin. The great age of the Russian composers had not yet dawned: Borodin, Musorgsky, Rimsky-Korsakov were still in their teens or just reaching twenty. It was an evening in late June, when in Siberia there is almost continuous daylight.

At the close of the concert, after the players had collected their applause and been duly thanked, the audience turned toward Maria, sitting next to the governor in his box, and gave her a standing ovation. Princess Sophia was astounded.

"I see that you have a kingdom of your own out here in Siberia," she said to her sister-in-law.

"A kingdom I bought with my tears," replied Maria.

14

Going Home

ON FEBRUARY 18, 1855, the Emperor Nicholas I died in his chilly bedroom in the Winter Palace. Spartan in death, as he had been in his habits throughout his life, the Autocrat of All the Russias lay on a thin mattress filled with straw, with one hard pillow under his head and a soldier's dark gray overcoat for a blanket. The immediate cause of death was a pulmonary infection, contracted at a military review, but those around him were convinced that he had died of a broken heart following the disasters of the Crimean War. Everything had suddenly collapsed and disintegrated around him. His glorious army, on which he had bestowed all his care and affection, turned out to be much inferior to the armies of his adversaries, Britain and France, both in organization and in equipment, and had been routed at Balaklava and at Inkerman; his Danube campaign had failed; all that was left to him was surrender. He felt that he had been betrayed by his allies and by the corruption and disorder prevalent throughout his realm. His words to the priest who gave him the last sacraments—"I believe that I have never done evil knowingly"—express perfectly the tragedy of his life. He was incapable of understanding that the thirty years of his reign had been a long, dismal period of darkness for Russia.

"We heard of Tsar Nicholas's death about midday, through some servants who had been to the market," recalled young Prince Kropotkin (*Memoirs of a Revolutionist*). "It was said that the people in the market behaved in a strange way, showing no regret, but indulging in dangerous talk. Full-grown people spoke in whispers among themselves, and our stepmother kept repeating, 'Don't talk before the men,' while the servants whispered among themselves, probably about the 'coming freedom.' In St. Petersburg, men of the educated classes, as they communicated the news to each other, embraced in the streets. Everyone felt that the end of the war and the end of the terrible conditions that had prevailed under the 'iron despot' were near at hand."

Tsar Alexander, the new emperor, was a less tyrannical and much kinder man than his father. He had long been haunted by the memory of those Decembrists he had met when, as the young tsarevich, he had visited Kurgan in western Siberia and saw them praying in church that God and the emperor might grant them freedom. More than twenty years later, he was determined to put an end to the exile of those by now harmless old men. But there were so many matters to attend to after his accession, matters connected with the termination of the Crimean War, the peace treaty, and a host of other problems, that eighteen months passed before the formal proclamation of amnesty. Alexander timed it to coincide with his coronation, on August 26, 1856.

When the news of the tsar's death reached Irkutsk, Maria's reaction was: "God be praised—now we will be going home"; but Sergei appeared to be grief-stricken. He shut himself in his shed in the garden and cried like a child. "Your father is crying

... this is the third day, I don't know what to do with him," she wrote to Elena.

Why was Volkonsky in tears? Over his "broken oath" of long ago, or fear for the future of Russia, now that the cruel but steady pilot was not at the helm any more? Or was it that, like the majority of his countrymen, he confused oppression with the strength of the state? To Sergei, as to all Russians of his generation, there was something mystical about the tsar-emperor, whether benevolent ruler or despot. They had wanted Nicholas out of the way only if he opposed the much-needed reforms; but during the countless days of their exile, when past events were dissected in minutest details, they may have wondered where the truth lay; how could the tsar be an enemy? Reverence for the monarch and loyalty to the throne were something they had absorbed with their mother's milk. Sergei was a professional soldier, a major general in the Russian army, the bulwark of the empire. For the last several months, like all the Decembrists in Siberia, he had been "living" with the Crimean War, identifying himself with the soldiers at the front, praying for victory for his troops. Like the rest of the country, Sergei was deeply stirred by the heroism of the defenders of Sebastopol; it brought back that feeling of patriotism which he experienced on the eve of Napoleon's invasion of Russia, the great patriotic war for the defense of the fatherland. How could he remain indifferent to events in the Crimea? He would have given everything to be young enough to enlist in the ranks. But he was an old man who had betrayed the tsar in his youth, and was not wanted now.

In spite of the general feeling of expectancy, no news came of an amnesty. And Maria's health was giving cause for concern. Triggered by general fatigue and worry about her son-in-law's difficulties with the law, her old kidney complaint reappeared and she was in almost continuous pain. There was the satisfaction she derived from the success of the new theater, the popularity and affection she enjoyed in town and the surrounding countryside, and her pleasure at Misha's progress in the civil service, but her anguished thoughts flew constantly to her daughter's side in Moscow. Sadly, Elena's life had not turned out as Maria had hoped, for, much to the family's dismay, Molchanov's past began to catch up with him. A rich merchant from Okhotsk called Zanadvorov revealed that while on official duty in northeastern Siberia, Molchanov had accepted a bribe of half a million rubles from him. It has never been clear what prompted the merchant's charge. Was it a particular grievance, or had he been disappointed in obtaining some hoped-for concession? Why had he waited so long to make his complaint public?

Governor Muraviev-Amursky had rejected the accusations outright. According to a contemporary account, when the merchant appeared to state his case, "the governor leaped upon him and ticked him off, so he had to run off like a dog . . ." But Zanadvorov was a persistent fellow. Having been humiliated by the governor, he was now determined to get the better of him and of his protégé. By bribing two judges and a handful of smaller functionaries, he succeeded in having his case taken out of Muraviev's jurisdiction and tried in the court of western Siberia at Tobolsk. Once there, it dragged on for over a year and became the talk of Siberia. Molchanov claimed that he was innocent: he had borrowed just over a thousand rubles to pay off a gambling debt, and had returned the entire sum before leaving Okhotsk. He admitted that this was improper behavior on the part of an official on a mission from the governor, but he swore that no favors went to Zanadvorov in return. Witnesses came and went; Molchanov was summoned to Tobolsk to testify, but finally the case was adjourned and transferred to Moscow's supreme court. Molchanov was eventually acquitted of taking bribes, but he was severely reprimanded for "irregular behavior." The judgment came too late for him to feel satisfaction; by now he was dying of a brain tumor, which the doctors believed had been aggravated by the agony and stress of the prolonged trial. The case had its murky undertones, and Molchanov did not emerge from it with an unscathed reputation, but the real victim was Elena. She had barely had time to get used to her family and her new existence in Moscow and St. Petersburg when the storm broke. Their son, Seriozha, was still a baby and needed her constant attention; she had to remain in Moscow through a long, hot, and dusty summer at a time when cholera had broken out, to nurse her husband. She felt alone in the big city and missed her mother's wise counsel. She knew through her letters from home that Maria had not been well recently, but believed that if only her mother were allowed to leave Siberia for a time, the Moscow doctors would restore her to health. At the suggestion of the Grand Duchess Maria, a daughter of Nicholas I and a friend of her uncle Prince Repnin, she turned for help to the new empress, who like her husband was known to feel compassion for the exiled Decembrists. In August 1855, the desired permit was granted.

In the meantime, in Irkutsk, the Volkonskys had given up hope for an amnesty and began to contemplate spending the rest of their lives in Siberia. "I don't grieve for myself," Sergei wrote to his son, Misha, who was on an inspection tour with the governor in the Pacific Northeast. "After all, I did bring it all upon myself. But I feel immensely sorry for your mother; she has been despondent since her friend Katyusha Trubetskoy's death." Katyusha, Maria's old friend and companion, the first of the wives to set off on the journey to Siberia, had died of cancer a few weeks before and was buried on the grounds of the Znamenskoe Monastery, near her house. Maria was convinced that it was only a matter of a few years before she, too, would be buried in the same spot.

In the first week of September, as Maria was sitting in her garden bent over a piece of embroidery destined for Katyusha's young daughter, Muraviev-Amursky's French wife, Catherine, was announced. She ran toward Maria and embraced her. "I have brought you good news; your permit for traveling to Moscow has just arrived. We both rejoice for you and Elena." The permission was for a return of a year, after which she was expected to go back to her husband's place of exile. This suited Maria, for she would not have wanted to part permanently with Sergei; he would be well looked after by Masha, their faithful housekeeper, in her absence.

Maria reached Moscow in late September, traveling along the well-worn track she had traversed nearly twenty-eight years before. It was only after she crossed the Ural Mountains and beheld the familiar landscape of fertile fields, rich meadows, and onion-domed churches resplendent in the autumn sunshine that she began to feel mounting excitement. The prospect of returning home, seeing Moscow and St. Petersburg, the members of her family, and all the well-remembered places revived her. At Kazan she stopped at the same hotel where she stayed on the eve of her twenty-first birthday and which she had left in a raging snowstorm. It had greatly expanded, taking over the Nobility Club, which had moved to larger and grander quarters down the road. After staying two days at Novgorod to recover and "get used to the unfamiliar Russia around me," she reached Moscow in the last week of September.

That evening, as Elena returned to her Moscow apartment after visiting her husband in the hospital, she found her mother sitting on her drawing-room sofa, holding her little grandson on her knees.

Throughout the next several weeks, Maria remained in

Elena's apartment, resting after the long journey, consulting doctors, and receiving the visits of countless nieces and nephews and their children. They had all grown up with the legend of their amazing Dekabristi aunt in Siberia, and now they wanted to see her in the flesh. Brother Alexander and his wife came to call. Maria noticed how "kind and very much like our father Alexander had become"; all traces of the former cynic, the model for Pushkin's Demon, had disappeared. He arranged that some much needed money be paid to his sister from their parents' inheritance. Ekaterina's children and grandchildren came to see her; Ekaterina herself was at the family's property on the Gulf of Finland, but she, too, was hurrying back to Moscow to see her sister.

That autumn, Molchanov, Elena's ill-fated husband, died. At his funeral, his old tormentor, Zanadvorov, was seen driving along in a splendid carriage, "beaming." The sight infuriated Alexander Raevsky, who attempted to push him out of his coach. It was a sad postscript to the tragic saga of Dmitri Vasilevich Molchanov, whose innocence forever remains in doubt. But for beautiful Elena and her young son, it was a merciful deliverance. It altered the pattern of their lives, and from then on, happiness came their way; in her marriage to Prince Kochubey two years later, Elena found unclouded joy, everything her mother had dreamed for her.

In the summer of 1856, Governor Muraviev-Amursky was summoned to St. Petersburg to attend Alexander II's coronation. He brought Maria's son, Mikhail Volkonsky, with him. As a member of the staff of the famous Muraviev-Amursky, Mikhail was to take part in all the coronation festivities. It was a strong position from which to introduce himself to the family he so far had known only by letter. They were delighted to meet this handsome man who had such a charming way about him, spoke perfect French, and, as Ekaterina Orlov remarked, "possessed an unusually pleasing speaking voice." Coming straight from Siberia, from the newly conquered territories on the Amur River, he had an aura of mystery and romance which added to his attraction, and he effortlessly took his place in fashionable circles, for both official St. Petersburg and old Moscow accepted him as one of the great governor's bright young men. Everyone wanted to meet him.

The summer of 1856 was a magic summer in Moscow. The Crimea had been forgotten; there was a new feeling of hope in the country; windows were being opened and doors unlocked. Since the accession of the new tsar, one by one Nicholas's iron shackles were falling off. People wondered how they had ever endured the long-drawn-out winter of the previous reign. Their hopes were not disappointed. Early in the new year, the ban on travel abroad was rescinded and foreign passports began to be issued again. Censorship was eased; the writings of Pushkin and Gogol reappeared on the publishers' shelves. Writers took a new lease on life, and students, whose existence had long been unbearable, hailed the new reign with "cheers and songs." The conduct of the Crimean War had revealed the terrifying extent of official corruption, a bureaucratic cancer in the body politic and the inevitable outcome of thirty years of police government. Alexander responded to the general atmosphere of buoyancy, but at first his actions were only palliatives. The core of the needed reform could not be touched until he had tackled the problem of the emancipation of the serfs, the issue for which the Decembrists had fought and still languished in Siberia.

The great day of the coronation was to be marked with unprecedented splendor. Russia had lost much prestige during the Crimean War, and a cloak was to be thrown over the shame and the grief of that period. The new emperor decided to im-

press visitors from abroad with his country's glories. As one of
the foreign visitors put it: "The old city of Moscow was raised to
the pinnacle of its 'rainbow-colored triumph.'" All the palaces
and houses were repainted; flowers were planted everywhere;
within the Kremlin walls, roofs, belfries, domes, and cupolas of
churches were regilded and done over, "until the whole re-
sembled a rainbow-lit fairy city." Rich landowners from remote
provinces, with no private houses of their own in Moscow, had
painted pavilions built for their use during the coronation,
oblivious of cost. St. Petersburg was temporarily deserted, demoted from its preeminence as everyone set off for the fashionable Nicholas Railway Station, opened just a few years before at
the eastern end of the Nevsky Prospect, to travel to the old
capital.

In Moscow, Maria contented herself with watching the joyous crowds from the windows of Elena's apartment on the
Tverskoy Boulevard. She was still officially a "non-person"; she
expected that she would be going back to Siberia in September, to
live out the final act of the Decembrist legend. However, Mikhail,
Elena, and her little boy would remain, to resume their position
in the national life of the country, and they owed this achievement to her, so she was smiling and serene. Her drawing room
was the center of family activities.

The day of the coronation was one of blazing sunshine; the
night was warm, enabling thousands of spectators to spend it in
the open and watch the magnificent procession, which stretched
for more than a mile, entering the Kremlin through the Spassky
Gate. It was led by a squadron of cavalry guards, followed by
the high dignitaries of the nineteen chief cities of the empire.
Then came the open gilded carriages of the court hierarchy,
each man bearing the gold and jeweled insignia of his office.
Behind them, driven by eight richly caparisoned bay horses, in
a gold-and-glass coach, its roof surmounted by a crown, came

the empress, her diamonds dazzling against her purple velvet robes. And finally, as the cheering grew deafening, drowning all the bells of Moscow and the music of countless bands, came the new emperor's coach, the eight grays stepping very slowly. Alexander sat alone, erect, his head bare, his face grave but happy. The people saw in him the living symbol of a radiant future, and as the silver-and-glass coach went by, rows upon rows fell on their knees.

Elena and Mikhail sat in official seats within the precincts of the Kremlin and were able to watch the ceremony at close hand. Afterwards, they went back to join their mother in Elena's apartment. "It was after six o'clock in the afternoon," recalled Mikhail, "when suddenly the doorbell rang. A uniformed policeman appeared with a summons that I was to report instantly to the office of Prince Dolgoruky, chief military officer, in the Kremlin." Still wearing his coronation finery, Mikhail hailed a passing fiacre and drove to the citadel. The old prince was waiting for him, a roll of parchment in his hand. "The emperor commands me to give you this Manifesto of Amnesty," he solemnly addressed Volkonsky. "It is His Majesty's pleasure that your father be the first to be informed—he hopes you will do this in person."

Mikhail left that night for Siberia, following the route that his mother had taken so many years before. He covered the four thousand miles between Moscow and Irkutsk in fifteen days, traveling in a bone-shaking tarantass, hardly stopping to rest; for he was far too happy to sleep. At relay stations beyond the Urals, he read the tsar's manifesto aloud to the public and excitement spread throughout Siberia.

There was a court ball at the Kremlin on the night of the coronation, and the emperor, as was his custom, set off to mix with the crowds. He stopped in front of a dark-haired beauty in a white muslin dress embroidered with velvet pansies. "I am glad your father is coming back," he said, smiling. Elena, tears running down her face, plunged into a deep curtsey.

No one had ever made as fast a journey as Misha. When he reached the Angara, the river was in full spate due to early autumnal storms, but oblivious of danger, he crossed it in a small boat despite very rough winds. In Irkutsk, though nothing was known of the tsar's pardon, there was a feeling of expectancy in the air. From time to time, one or the other of the old men would drive out onto the highway to see if there was a sign of a messenger. Misha arrived at dawn and went straight to his father's house; he rang the bell. "Who is that?" shouted Sergei. "It's me, Misha, I have brought forgiveness." And they embraced.

Within a week, Sergei was ready to leave. He packed his letters and his archives, made travel arrangements for Masha the housekeeper and her son to follow them with some of the furniture and Maria's belongings, said goodbye to his friends in the bazaar, and attended a farewell Mass at Katyusha Trubetskoy's graveside with her husband. Alessandro Poggio and his wife decided to stay behind for the time being. Poggio, the romantic dreamer, was involved in what for him was an unlikely activity: speculation in the Siberian gold fields. He hoped it would make him a rich man.

The Volkonskys were lucky in that they had a young family eagerly awaiting their return, and a country residence to go to. But for many of the other Decembrists, the amnesty came too late. "The grave will be no warmer in western Russia than in Siberia," sighed Bashmakov. To some, it brought merely additional worry, problems, and anxiety, for it meant giving up homes in a country to which they had by now become accustomed, in order to return to a Russia they had nearly forgotten. Thirty years is a long time. Wasn't it too late to organize a new life? How would they be received back home?

And yet, as Basargin recalls, "the temptation was irresistible." After all, it was about Russia they had dreamed all these years, and it was for Russia's sake that they had suffered their exile. Many felt it was their duty to go back, and those who had children rejoiced at the prospect of leading a normal life again. Many of the Decembrists had died in the five years preceding the amnesty; only about thirty lived to hear the glad news. Of those, all but two returned home.

On September 27, 1856, the Volkonskys, father and son, set off for Moscow. This time, in view of Sergei's age and frail health, they traveled in slow stages, stopping on the way at Tobolsk to see the Annenkovs. Ivan had been allowed to join the civil service in Siberia, and had become assessor of the Tobolsk charity board. Now that the manifesto had been proclaimed, he and Pauline were preparing to return to the Annenkov estates in the Nizhny Novgorod Province, where he was to become an active leader of the nobility and Pauline a much-respected dowager, just as the French clairvoyant had predicted years before. At Orenburg in the Urals, a civic reception was held in honor of the son and grandson of the beloved former governor, Prince Grigory Volkonsky, Sergei's father.

They reached Moscow in the third week of October, and on the Sunday after their arrival, the Volkonskys and their two children attended divine service in the Cathedral of St. Basil. The cathedral, "that masterpiece of caprice," as the Marquis de Custine called it, stands in all its "crazy magnificence" at the southern end of what today is Red Square, near the Kremlin. News had spread of the Decembrist Prince Volkonsky's return, and strangers came up to them to greet Sergei and welcome him home. He was happy, but he had forgotten so much that every-thing now surprised him and he had to keep asking questions.

Since Maria's return a year earlier, Alexander Raevsky had been planning to hold a ball to celebrate the Volkonskys' return. It took place on the day after Christmas, on Maria's birthday, at the splendid Nobility Club in Moscow. All the members and all three generations of the two families were there, and so were countless friends and relations. Maria, in a dark red velvet dress, wore a necklace of diamonds and rubies, which had been Em-press Catherine's wedding gift to her mother. Nikolai Raevsky's son led the dancing. Maria's thoughts must inevitably have gone back thirty years to her twenty-first birthday, when in a raging snowstorm she was speeding toward the Ural Mountains.

The warmth and profound respect with which the Decem-brists were received in Russian society, now attuned to the new tsar's liberal reforms, transformed Sergei. Young Belogolovoy, who arrived in Moscow after the coronation, found him "pale as the moon, but lively, hearty, well dressed, even dandified, as I had never seen him in Irkutsk. His long silver hair was carefully combed, his silver beard trimmed and groomed, he was a picture-book old man of biblical beauty." Those who had known him in his younger years remarked that he had been "much embellished by the passage of time"; they remembered him as a "rather mediocre man, nice-looking but neither clever nor stupid, kind but weak." Now, with his tall figure and his long silvery locks, he combined the distinction of an aristocratic patriarch with some-thing soil-bound and typically Russian. "Had Russia become a republic, Sergei's looks would have made him a good president," remarked one of his old cronies at the Nobility Club in Moscow.

The transformation went deep; Sergei, it seemed, was intent on forgetting everything about his life in exile, including his folksy habits, which he left behind in Siberia. He had become open, talkative, and passionately interested in the coming emancipation of the serfs. He felt no bitterness for the past. "My beliefs brought me thirty years of oppression. I am back now; it is time to go forward again," he said to his brother Repnin. Even his health changed for the better.

Maria rejoiced at her husband's contentment—but she herself found it difficult to slip back into the pattern of life of her younger days. Years before, she had thrown the whole of herself into the role of a Decembrist's wife; each day, she faced obstacles which she conquered through her indomitable will and endurance, while carrying the full brunt of the family's responsibility on her shoulders. She could lay down her burden at last, now that she had steered them safely back to home port. But the process of unwinding was slow, made harder by her deteriorating health. Unlike her husband, she did not wish to erase Siberia from her mind; too many of her emotions had been invested in that long span of years. She knew that Siberia had been a personal triumph for her, and occasionally she even felt a tinge of nostalgia when something reminded her of that countryside—the primitive beauty of the banks of the Angara, Lake Baikal glistening among the towering peaks, the flower meadows of Chita. "Nature here still has the dew of creation upon it," Alessandro Poggio used to say about the wild open spaces of Transbaikalia.

Muraviev-Amursky arranged for leave to be granted Mikhail from the civil service so he could enroll at Moscow University in the autumn and later join the Ministry of Foreign Affairs. But, before that, he advised him to travel abroad. Mikhail needed no encouragement. A few weeks later, he was in Paris, making his way to Montmartre to visit the command post from which his grandfather, General Raevsky, had occupied the city at the time of Napoleon's abdication. He then went on to Rome.

Under the terms of the amnesty, the Decembrists were at first not allowed to reside either in St. Petersburg or in Moscow; nor did they officially recover their titles, though their wives and children were permitted to use them. But in the generally relaxed atmosphere of the time, these restrictions were treated lightly by the police. Everybody understood that after years of primitive existence in frontier Siberia, the men could not remain isolated in the country, far from their families and their friends, most of whom spent the greater part of their time in the two capitals. A far more thorny problem was the return of the confiscated property, much of which had by now passed into alien hands, or been annexed by greedy relatives. Sergei refused to take his sister Sophia to court over the annexation of his lands; he contented himself with the ownership of Voronky, the small estate in the Chernigov Province in the Ukraine, which had come to him through one of his aunts. (It later went to Elena.) Boltyshka, Maria's childhood home, now belonged to Alexander and his wife, and Maria spent a long month there shortly after her return to the west, communing with her childhood memories and praying at her father's grave.

In the winter of 1859, Elena married Prince Kochubey and left for Paris on her honeymoon. About that time, Misha, now twenty-eight, became engaged while in Rome to the granddaughter of his eccentric old aunt, Princess Sophia, Sergei's sister. By a strange twist of fate, the bride's grandfather was the all-powerful General Benckendorff, chief of Tsar Nicholas's secret police, who for so long had controlled the Decembrists' lives. The wedding was to be in Geneva. It became the occasion for Maria's first trip abroad. She traveled alone, as Sergei was forced to discontinue his journey in Dresden because of ill health; he remained there for several months, while Maria went on to Italy to stay with Princess Zenaida.

Zenaida's villa, which now houses the British Embassy in Rome, stands on a hill in what was then the outskirts of the city, near the great Neronian spur of the Claudian aqueduct, marked by a number of tombs dating back to the first and second centuries. In those days, the terraces at the end of the garden opened up on a lovely view of the Roman campagna and the Alban hills. The formal gardens were filled with sculptures brought by Princess Zenaida from Russia, including a huge bust of Alexander I on a granite pillar. Those were the last days of Papal Rome, when the ruins of the old Roman Empire were not yet surrounded by railings but blended naturally with the life of the street; the fountains were not enclosed and served to water both man and beast. The cardinals, dressed in scarlet, still drove around in their own carriages, and pilgrims kneeling under the high balcony of St. Peter's basilica came to the Pope for his blessing. Princess Zenaida was nearly seventy; she had only two more years to live. In Rome she was a famous and revered figure; the poor called her La Beata, the Blessed One. Years before, she had joined the Catholic Church, in reaction against the "narrow nationalism and Orthodoxy of the Russian Church," and because she admired Rome's universality and its worldwide missionary work. Her niece, Princess Varvara Repnin (the daughter of Sergei's brother, Prince Repnin), recalled that when Nicholas I heard of her conversion, he ordered that she be "brought back to her senses" and sent a priest to convert her. She reacted with "a *crise de nerfs* and convulsions," which effectively put an end to the tsar's efforts. The emperor allowed her to leave Russia, though her husband, a courtier, had to remain behind. She went abroad with her son and her widowed sister and decided to settle in Rome. As part of the tsar's drastic measures against converts, a portion of her property was confiscated by the state, but the Volkonskys managed to transfer some of the lands to her son, from whom she received an allowance. It was only a fraction of her former riches, but enough to lead a princely existence in Rome and help others. As in Moscow or Paris, her house became a center for writers and intellectuals: Italian, French, Polish, Russian—they all flocked to Princess Zenaida's drawing room. She was a friend of the Italian poets Belli and Jacopo, of the great French preacher Lacordaire, and of Comte Montalembert, who fought for the reintroduction of religious education in France; later came the Polish poet Mickiewicz; Alexander Herzen also visited her at one time. It would have been easy for the princess to remain an admired hostess and a fashionable convert, but she was too sincerely devout, charitable, and active not to respond to the needs of other people. First she became involved in collecting funds to help pilgrims and repair churches in Rome; she then turned her energies to founding schools for destitute girls and generally helping the poor, to whom she gave most of her money. She gave not only alms, but even her clothes. Her sudden death was caused by pneumonia, after she had gone out on a frosty day, had met a poor woman shivering in the street, and had taken off her warm skirt and given it to her. She died on February 5, 1862; her funeral cortege was followed by hundreds of the Roman poor.

Alexander Volkonsky, Princess Zenaida's son, recalled in one of his letters that his mother's meeting with Princess Maria was "very touching." It was as if the years had been rolled back to that evening in Moscow on the eve of Maria's departure for Siberia when she stood by the piano, her hand locked in Push-kin's, and begged for the music "to go on and on." Zenaida had been her most faithful correspondent during the long exile: she wrote every few weeks with world and family news, sent seeds, music, and drawings. The prisoners' flower and vegetable gardens in Chita, and in Petrovsky Zavod, had been started from the seeds sent by Princess Zenaida.

Maria would have liked to remain in Rome for the winter, but she had to hurry back to Dresden, where she was meeting Sergei, who had spent the last month in Paris. He was there on the day that the Act of Emancipation, giving freedom to the serfs, was proclaimed in Russia. Choked with emotion, he had attended the solemn *Te Deum* at the newly built Russian church in the rue Daru, wishing Maria could have been at his side.

When Maria arrived at Dresden, the old capital of the Saxon kings, to meet her husband, she saw, at the same hotel, a figure from her remote childhood—Count Gustav Olizar, friend of her young days in Kiev, and her first suitor. He had married again, had more children, had become a distinguished traveler, scholar, and wonderful raconteur; his time was spent pleasantly between Russia, Poland, France, and Italy, where the children of his first marriage lived. Olizar recalls that he found Maria "deeply marked by her exile, but still very good-looking, with abundant dark hair [Maria never turned gray], wearing a black muslin cap, which framed her now rather serious face. Only occasionally did her old gaiety filter through, but her eyes were still wonderful..."

The Volkonskys went from Dresden to Danzig and traveled the rest of the way by sea to St. Petersburg, where the Kochubeys were now living. Staying with Elena and her husband was Alessandro Poggio, with wife and daughter. They had left Siberia at the end of the year, after disaster had overtaken Poggio's gold-mining investments. Alessandro was penniless and, at Elena's suggestion, was given the job of manager of Sukholovo, a Kochubey property north of Moscow. The property belonged to Prince Kochubey's nephew, who unfortunately was young, impatient, and inexperienced, and the Poggios found him very hard to deal with.

Maria's last years were spent between Voronky and Fall, Misha's property on the Baltic, which reverted to him through his wife's mother, a Benckendorff, the daughter of their father's jailer. Fall, called after a scenic waterfall in the park, is near Reval in today's Estonia. It was beautiful. The large house in a "pleasing Gothic style" was surrounded by a park full of white birches and huge horse-chestnut trees, with lawns sloping down to the sea. There were splendid views of the Baltic from the terraces and from each of the windows. Maria loved it; her grandson, Misha's son, recalls how fond he was of his grandmother, because "she told him wonderful stories and often kept the gardener from raking over his sand castles."

In the spring of 1863, Alessandro Poggio, who by now had decided to live in Italy with his family, came to see Maria at Voronky. They spent a peaceful month reminiscing.

Gradually, all the strands of Maria's life were coming together. She had recently heard from little Liutik and from merchant friends in Siberia that her theater was thriving, that the foundling hospital was well run, and that the children's choirs she had established had become a feature of life in the town. People there remembered her warmly, and the street that ran by their house had been paved and renamed the Volkonsky Ulitsa, in their honor. That pleased her.

Poggio was the last of her friends to see Maria; shortly after his departure, her kidney condition worsened, followed by occasional loss of consciousness. Sergei was at Fall, staying with Misha and his wife; he himself had been ill all that spring and was still very weak. When news came of Maria's condition, he tried to rush back to the Ukraine but was not well enough to travel.

Maria died on August 10, 1863, "just as the sun was rising over the faraway steppe," with her children and grandchildren at her side.

When Misha went through his mother's papers, he found two portraits—one of Pushkin, a watercolor painted at Gurzuf during that halcyon summer in the Crimea when they all translated Byron together; and one of Poggio, drawn by Bestuzhev, showing Alessandro planting his flower borders at Chita.

After his wife's death, Sergei went into an eclipse. He returned to Voronky, to "place my life beside her, who saved it for me." Though confined to a wheelchair, he remained mentally alert, ordering foreign journals and working on his memoirs. He died on November 28, 1865, while writing a sentence: "The Emperor said to me: I . . ." He was seventy-seven.

Elena and Misha had a church built over their parents' graves and placed in it the icons Maria had kept in her room in Siberia. Above them are engraved two lines:

> The Lord decided to enchain us . . .
> The Lord will restore us from misfortunes.

Epilogue

AFTER THEIR PARENTS' DEATH, Elena and Mikhail Volkonsky
continued to look after Alessandro Poggio. Mikhail, now
a distinguished civil servant and married to the Benckendorff
heiress, divided his time between St. Petersburg and Fall, their
lovely property overlooking the Baltic Sea. (In 1914, the first
year of World War I, his son, Sergei, entertained Nicholas
and Alexandra when the imperial yacht called there; in 1916,
the house at Fall was burned down by revolutionary troops.)
Elena continued to live at Voronky with Prince Kochubey, her
second husband.

In spite of changing circumstances and his marriage, Poggio
could not bring himself to break away entirely from the Volkonskys and the circle of Maria's memories. Sergei himself had arranged for a generous loan to be made to the Poggios from his
own and his son's funds. He also put pressure on the children of
Poggio's brother Giuseppe to share with their uncle part of their
parents' inheritance; they reluctantly agreed to a small settlement. In 1864, Elena's husband fell ill with tuberculosis, and at
the family's request, Alessandro accompanied them to Italy,
where they hoped the prince would regain his health. But he died
late that year, and it was Alessandro who escorted his body back
to Russia. He remained at Voronky with Elena for several
months, to comfort her and see her take up her old life again. He
then returned with his wife to Italy, where they lived with relatives near Novara. In Switzerland, where they also spent some

time, Alessandro met Alexander Herzen and formed a close friendship with him.

In 1873, Poggio knew that death was approaching. He had never felt completely at home in his native land; he disagreed with the new brand of liberals and was out of tune with the terrorist ideas of Garibaldi's followers. Russia remained the country closest to his heart, and above all, he wanted to see Elena again. He did indeed act toward her like a father. That summer, he and his wife returned to St. Petersburg, where Elena, now married to her third husband, Rakhmanov, received them with great affection. They went to Voronky together to pray at Maria's grave. Alessandro died there in Elena's arms in early autumn of 1873. He is buried, as he requested, near the Volkonsky grave at Voronky.

Alessandro's wife, Larisa, returned to Siberia to be with her family after her husband's death. Their daughter, Varya, remained in Moscow and, ironically, joined Moscow's anarchist circles. She became a friend of Sophia Perovsky, who was involved in the assassination of Alexander II.

Throughout the second half of the nineteenth century, the Decembrist legend took on new force and glamour. The memoirs of individual Decembrists such as Rozen, Yakushkin, Basargin, Lorer, and others were published, and the survivors, such as Zavalishin, were treated with veneration and awe. Numerous marriages took place between the children of the former exiles. Being a descendant of a Decembrist, it was said, was a distinction almost equal to being a descendant of the Romanovs.

The present-day Soviet government has an ambivalent attitude to the 1825 revolution. They are keen to exaggerate the Decembrists' hostility to Nicholas I, but they forget how different the concept of freedom of those first revolutionaries was from the pitiful sham of what is understood by freedom in today's Russia. "It was easy to love a man in the nineteenth century," says one of the characters in *The First Circle*, Alexander Solzhenitsyn's novel about modern Soviet bureaucracy. "The wives of the Decembrists—do you think they performed some heroic feat? Did personnel sections call *them* in to fill out security questionnaires?"

It may be said that Maria and her companions, despite the horrors they faced at the start, had perhaps a somewhat less implacable path to tread than the countless Soviet victims of latter-day mechanized police-state terror have had. But this does not take away from the magnitude of the Decembrists' achievement, for their pioneering efforts were above all a triumph of love, courage, and humanity over the "system." No Decembrist woman, as she was setting off on her incredible trek across Asia, had any political motivation: her enemy was Tsar Nicholas I's bureaucratic system. Only in her later years did it become for Maria a fight against the inhumanity that this tyranny stood for. As for the rest of the women, they went forth to follow their men, and they saved them.

Selected Bibliography

The literature on the Decembrist uprising is immense; most of it is in Russian. The most complete account in English is in Anatole G. Mazour's *The First Russian Revolution, 1825*, published in 1937 by Stanford University Press. I have read a vast number of works for background material, but in the latter stages of research I concentrated mainly on the story of Maria Volkonsky as it unfolds first (her childhood) in the Raevsky Family Archives, then in her own memoirs, and finally in the reminiscences of other Decembrists and their wives who shared her exile in Siberia. The following works have been particularly helpful, though the list is not exhaustive.

ANNENKOVA, POLINA. *Zapiski Zheny Dekabrista* (Memoirs of a Decembrist Wife). Moscow, 1915.

BARANOVSKAYA, M. *Dekabrist Nikolai Bestuzhev.* Moscow, 1954.

BARRATT, GLYN. *Rebel on the Bridge: A Biography of A. Rozen.* London, 1975.

———. *Voices in Exile.* Montreal, 1974.

BASARGIN, N. V. *Zapiski* (Memoirs). Petrograd, 1917.

BELOGOLOVOY, N. A. *Vospominaniya* (Reminiscences). Moscow, 1897.

BERLIN, ISAIAH. *Russian Thinkers.* New York, 1978.

BLANCH, LESLEY. *Sabres of Paradise.* London, 1960.

CHENTSOV, N. M. *Vosstanie Dekabristov* (Decembrist Uprising). Moscow, 1929.

COCHRANE, J. *A Pedestrian Journey through Russia and Siberian Tartary.* Edinburgh, 1829.

CRANKSHAW, EDWARD. *The Shadow of the Winter Palace.* London, 1976.

CUSTINE, ADOLPHE, MARQUIS DE. *La Russie en 1839* (4 vols.). Paris, 1843.

CZAPLICKA, C. Z. *Aboriginal Siberia.* London, 1914.

DIOFZEGI, M., and J. HOPPAL. *The Shamans of Siberia.* Budapest, 1979 (translated from the Hungarian).

DISBROWE, CHARLOTTE. *Original Letters from Russia, 1825 to 1828.* London, 1878.

ERMAN, G. A. *Reise um die Erde* (2 vols.). Berlin, 1838.

GERSHENZON, M. *Istoriya Molodoi Rossii* (Story of Russian Youth). Moscow, 1908.

HERZEN, ALEXANDER. *My Past and Thoughts* (4 vols.), trans. by Constance Garnett. London, 1968.

HINGLEY, RONALD. *The Russian Mind.* London, 1977.

KENNAN, GEORGE. *Siberia and the Exile System* (2 vols.). London, 1891.

———. *Tent Life in Siberia.* New York, 1870.

KROPOTKIN, PRINCE PETER. *Memoirs of a Revolutionist* (2 vols.). London, 1899.

KUCHAEV, L. N. *Biography of Stanislav Romanovich Leparsky.* Moscow, 1897.

LEDNICKI, WACLAW. *Russia, Poland and the West.* London, 1954.

LORER, N. I. *Zapiski Dekabrista* (Memoirs of a Decembrist), edited by M. N. Pokrovsky. Moscow.

MACLEAN, FITZROY. *Holy Russia.* London, 1978.

MAMONOV, DMITRI. *Dekabristi v Sibirii* (The Decembrists in Siberia). Moscow, 1895.

MASSIE, SUSAN. *Land of the Firebird.* New York, 1980.

MAXIMOV, S. V. *Sibir i Katorga* (Siberia and Forced Labor). St. Petersburg, 1871.

MAZOUR, ANATOLE G. *The First Russian Revolution.* Stamford, Conn., 1937.

MICKIEWICZ, ADAM. *Pamietniki* (Memoirs). Paris, 1842.

NABOKOV, VLADIMIR. *Commentary to Eugene Onegin.* London, 1975.

NICHOLAS I. *Zapiski* (Memoirs), as quoted in *Krasny Arkhiv*, Vol. VI.

OBOLENSKY, E. P. *Vospominaniya* (Reminiscences).

OLIZAR,COUNT GUSTAV. *Pamietniki* (Memoirs) (2 vols.). Lvov, 1892.

———. *My Youth* (in Polish). Vilno, 1840.

PALMER, ALAN. *Alexander I.* London, 1974.

PINKERTON, ROBERT. *Russia.* London, 1833.

POGGIO, A. V. *Zapiski Dekabrista* (Memoirs of a Decembrist). Moscow, 1896.

POKROVSKY, V. T. *Zheny Dekabristov* (Decembrist Wives). Moscow, 1906.

PONIATOWSKI, MICHEL. *Histoire de la Russie, de l'Amérique et de l'Alaska.* Paris, 1954.

Selected Bibliography

POPOVA, O. I. *Istoriya Zheny Volkonskogo* (Story of the Wife of S. G. Volkonsky) (excerpts from documents). Leningrad, 1934.

PRITCHETT, V. S. *The Gentle Barbarian*. London, 1977.

ROZEN, BARON ANDREI. *Zapiski Dekabrista* (Memoirs of a Decembrist). St. Petersburg, 1897.

SHCHEGOLEV, P. E. *Istoricheskie etyudy* (Article on the legal rights of the Decembrist wives). St. Petersburg, 1913.

———. *M. N. Volkonskaia*. Moscow, 1928.

SCHTEINGEL, V. I. *Memoirs* (in Russian). Moscow, 1904.

Slavonic and East European Review, Vol. 39. University of London, 1960.

SOKOLOV, B. M. *Knyaginya Volkonskaya v Zhizni i poezii Pushkina* (Maria Raevska, Princess Volkonsky, in the Life and Poetry of Alexander Pushkin). Moscow, 1922.

SZYRMA, LECH. *Revelations of Siberia by a Banished Lady* (in Polish). London, 1853.

TROYAT, HENRI. *Pouchkine*. Paris, 1946.

———. *Alexandre I-er*. Paris, 1980.

TRUBETSKOY, SERGEI P. *Zapiski* (Memoirs). St. Petersburg, 1907.

TRUNEV, P. *Collection of Documents on the Decembrists in the Nerchinsk Mines* (in Russian). St. Petersburg, 1897.

VENTURI, FRANCO. *Il moto decabrista e i fratelli Poggio*. Milan, 1956.

VOLKONSKAIA, M. N. *Zapiski knyagini* (Memoirs), in manuscript. St. Petersburg, 1902.

VOLKONSKY, PRINCE ALEXANDER. *The Ukraine Question*. Rome, 1920.

VOLKONSKY, PRINCE MICHAEL. *Die Dekabristen*. Berlin, 1946.

VOLKONSKY, PRINCE SERGEI G. *Zapiski Dekabrista* (Memoirs of a Decembrist). St. Petersburg, 1902.

VOLKONSKY, PRINCE SERGEI M. *My Reminiscences up to 1825* (2 vols., translated into English). London, 1925.

VRANGEL, A. *The Raevsky Family* (in Russian). Paris, 1952.

YAKUSHKIN, I. D. *Zapiski* (Memoirs). Moscow, 1925.

ZETLIN, MIKHAIL. *The Decembrists*. New York, 1958.

ZYLBERSTEIN, N. C. *Nikolai Bestuzhev*. Moscow, 1977.

Index

Index

Index

Index